CW00542043

CAPTAIN
JACK HELM

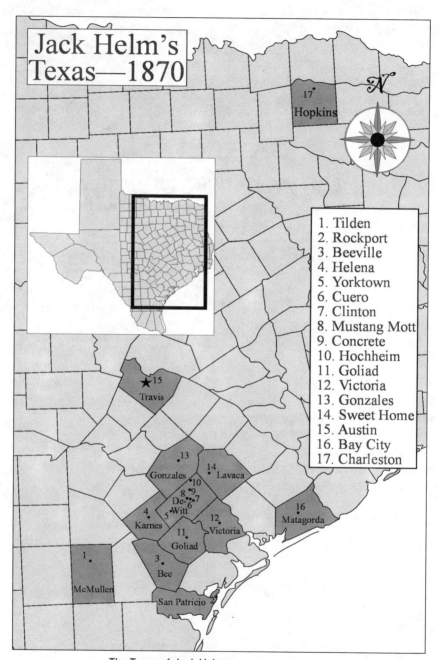

Jack Helm's Texas—1870

17. Hopkins

1. Tilden
2. Rockport
3. Beeville
4. Helena
5. Yorktown
6. Cuero
7. Clinton
8. Mustang Mott
9. Concrete
10. Hochheim
11. Goliad
12. Victoria
13. Gonzales
14. Sweet Home
15. Austin
16. Bay City
17. Charleston

15. Travis
13. Gonzales
14. Lavaca
10. 9. 8. 7. De Witt 6.
4. Karnes 5.
12. Victoria
11. Goliad
1. McMullen
3. Bee
San Patricio 2.
16. Matagorda

The Texas of Jack Helm. MAP BY CHARLES D. GREAR.

CAPTAIN
JACK HELM

A Victim of Texas
Reconstruction Violence

Number 18 in the A.C. Greene Series

BY CHUCK PARSONS

FOREWORD BY KENNETH W. HOWELL

University of North Texas Press
Denton, Texas

©2018 Chuck Parsons
Foreword ©2018 Kenneth W. Howell

All rights reserved.
Printed in the United States of America.

10 9 8 7 6 5 4 3 2 1

Permissions:
University of North Texas Press
1155 Union Circle #311336
Denton, TX 76203-5017

The paper used in this book meets the minimum requirements of the American National Standard for Permanence of Paper for Printed Library Materials, z39.48.1984. Binding materials have been chosen for durability.

Library of Congress Cataloging-in-Publication Data

Names: Parsons, Chuck, author. | Howell, Kenneth Wayne, 1967- writer of foreword.
Title: Captain Jack Helm : a victim of Texas Reconstruction violence / by Chuck Parsons ; foreword by Kenneth W. Howell.
Other titles: A.C. Greene series ; no. 18.
Description: Denton, Texas : University of North Texas Press, [2018] | Series: Number 18 in the A.C. Greene series | Includes bibliographical references and index.
Identifiers: LCCN 2017049115| ISBN 9781574417180 (cloth : alk. paper) | ISBN 9781574417265 (ebook)
Subjects: LCSH: Helm, Jack, 1837–1873. | Sheriffs—Texas—Biography. | Police, State—Texas—Biography. | Outlaws—Texas—Biography. | Reconstruction (U.S. history, 1865-1877)—Texas. | Frontier and pioneer life—Texas. | Violence—Texas—History—19th century. | Sutton-Taylor Feud. | Hardin, John Wesley, 1853–1895.
Classification: LCC F391 .P263 2018 | DDC 363.28/2092 [B]—dc23
LC record available at https://lccn.loc.gov/2017049115

Captain Jack Helm: A Victim of Texas Reconstruction Violence is Number 18 in the A.C. Greene Series

Cover painting: Original art work courtesy Bob Boze Bell, *Jack Helm Keeps on Riding* created especially for this work in 2016.

The electronic edition of this book was made possible by the support of the Vick Family Foundation.

*This work is dedicated to my wife Pat D. (Baker) Parsons;
she has helped me mightily along every trail.*

CONTENTS

LIST OF MAPS AND ILLUSTRATIONS

＋·＋·＋

FOREWORD

•——•——•

The Murky Middle Ground of Reconstruction

by Kenneth W. Howell

BETWEEN 1861 AND 1877 THE UNITED STATES endured one of the most tragic periods. The country experienced a prolonged and bloody civil war that claimed the lives of more than 620,000 soldiers, approximately two percent of the total population. (If the same ratio of Americans lost their lives today, the death toll would be a staggering six million people!) This figure does not include those who perished in the South during Reconstruction, the turbulent era following the Civil War. During the post-war years, no southern state escaped the violence of this sanguinary age, including the Lone Star State.

Chiefly immune from Union invasions during the war, Texans witnessed tremendous violence between 1865 and 1877. Following the war, ex-Confederates and conservative Democrats, intent on keeping antebellum society intact, launched ferocious guerrilla campaigns against their former slaves, white Unionists, northern "carpetbaggers," Freedmen's Bureau agents, and occupying federal troops. Unrepentant southerners, these Texans were determined to prevent black Texans from gaining civil and political rights. At the same time, a small number of desperadoes used the "Lost Cause" as a ruse to justify their pillaging, raping, and murdering of the freed people and their white allies. Texas was a bloody and dangerous place during the Reconstruction era—it was undeniably the darkest hour in the state's history.

White Texans faced difficult choices as the death toll in the state increased. A significant number of individuals felt compelled to support the outrages committed by ex-Confederates and conservative Democrats, while others were ready to put the war behind them. While both groups generally believed in the idea of white supremacy, those in the former camp were more willing to support the criminal activities of assassins and miscreants in order to restore social control over the freed people. This group of Texans was just as guilty as the men who murdered, raped, and stole from the most vulnerable in society, whose only crime had been to exercise their newfound freedom and civil rights. While there were those who attempted to maintain law and order in the state, most whites found themselves somewhere in the middle.

Lawmen of this era were reflective of the society that they served. Some officers were corrupt, engaging in crimes against blacks and their white allies. Others did their best to bring murderers, rapists, and thieves to justice. Most, however, performed their duties within a murky middle ground, where they attempted to maintain order but often provided some citizens greater protection than they did others. In this environment, a man's personal character and life experiences dictated the type of lawman he would become.

Jack Helm's story is a prime example of those law officers who operated on the fringes of the law. During the Civil War, he fought briefly for the Confederacy. Following the war, Helm assisted Captain C.S. Bell in tracking down members of the "Taylor Gang" during what scholars refer to as the Sutton-Taylor Feud. At one point, he briefly joined another body of law officers operating in a region that included Bee, San Patricio, Wilson, DeWitt, and Goliad Counties. Known by contemporaries as "regulators," the group was in reality a vigilante force that apprehended numerous "outlaws," most of whom were murdered after their capture. Helm rejoined

Bell in rounding up members of the Taylor Gang, and was involved in an incident that resulted in the death of Hays Taylor and the wounding of Doboy Taylor. By many counts, the only difference in men like Helm and those he pursued was the badge on his chest. In July 1870, Helm became one of four captains that Governor E. J. Davis appointed to lead the newly formed State Police. A little more than a month later, Helm was at the center of another controversial issue. Helm's men were involved in a shootout with Henry and Will Kelly, members of the Taylor Gang, while trying to arrest them for disturbing the peace in Lavaca County. Following this episode, Governor Davis, who wanted to avoid public outrage against the State Police, dismissed the notorious captain. Helm's actions against the Taylors would come back to haunt him. In 1873, John Wesley Hardin, a hired gun for the Taylor Gang, and Jim Taylor assassinated him in Albuquerque, Gonzales County.

Helm's story is important in understanding violence in Reconstruction Texas. As an officer of the law, he served the cause of "justice" by using tactics just as infamous as those practiced by the men he pursued. He became embroiled in the Taylor-Sutton Feud, murdering members of the Taylor Gang, whom he believed to be a blight on society. Despite his importance, however, Jack Helm has received little scholarly attention. Fortunately, Chuck Parsons's biography rescues this controversial Texas lawman from the dust bin of history, and effectively explains how he traversed the murky middle ground of this tumultuous period of history.

KENNETH W. HOWELL
Director, Central Texas Historical Association,
Blinn College, Bryan, Texas

PREFACE

THE NAME OF JACK HELM is familiar to many readers and writers of Wild West literature. During his lifetime, during the Civil War and Reconstruction, he became notorious, having been an anti-unionist preceding his desertion from the Confederate army, then changed his allegiance to serve under General J.J. Reynolds during the heyday of the Fifth Military District. In 1870 he was commissioned a captain in the Texas State Police in which he gained additional notoriety prior to his dismissal from that force. Once ousted from Governor E.J. Davis's police force he continued his violent ways as the leader of a group known as the Regulators, considered by some as nothing more than a vigilante mob. During this time he dealt with alleged horse and cattle thieves and murderers, sometimes delivering them to the county jail, sometimes killing them and leaving their bodies where they fell, using the worn excuse that the prisoners had "attempted to escape." Jack Helm may have lived longer if he had not become one of the leaders of the Sutton force, a group that was feuding with the Taylor clan in a regional conflict today known as the Sutton-Taylor Feud. As a leader of the Sutton force, a number of men wanted him killed, taking revenge with his death for perceived wrongs. He may have lived longer if John Wesley Hardin had not allied himself with the Taylor faction; with Hardin aggressively hunting Taylor enemies, Helm became a primary target. J.J. Helm, as he signed his name, did not survive the July 1873 attack, and by most he was forgotten, considered just another victim of the post-Civil War violence. Indeed, to most historians, if he had not been killed by John Wesley Hardin and his companion James Creed Taylor, he would be forgotten by history.

In the near century and half since the days of John Marshal Jackson Helm no biography has appeared. Historians continue to treat him as a peripheral character. The first serious study of the conflict between the Sutton and the Taylor forces appeared in 1880, while some of the feuding men were still battling for their freedom in the court system. That work was a small history of sixty pages published by the New York firm of J.J. Little, authored by Texas journalist Victor Marion Rose. The effort provided little biographical information on Helm. From 1880 until nearing the twentieth century, little attention was given to such frontieresque individuals. The first time attention was given to Helm was ironically from the pen of the man who is often credited with killing him. Sentenced to a term of twenty-five years in the state prison for an 1874 killing, Hardin changed behind the walls of Huntsville; finally pardoned in 1894 he intended to become a model citizen and live down his youthful killings. In the early 1890s he began writing his life story, providing history with an explanation as to why he had become the man-killer he became. In his autobiography he devoted several pages to his meetings with Jack Helm and why the final gunfight took place as it did. All of what Hardin wrote is certainly not accurate (although some of it is) and must be used with caution. Hardin nearly always presented himself as a near victim of ruthless men wanting to kill him or deprive him of his liberty; in his mind he was a freedom fighter. Many who have an idea of who Jack Helm was carry a negative picture of the man, having accepted the writing of Victor M. Rose and John W. Hardin as accurate.

In 1935 Doubleday Publishers brought out Thomas Ripley's study of western gunfighters entitled *They Died with Their Boots On*. It is a study focusing principally on John Wesley Hardin, William Preston Longley, a Hardin contemporary, and Ben Thompson, another contemporary, as well as various lesser known individuals. One of the lesser known individuals is Jack Helm. Ripley wrote a few preliminary lines about the essential characters of his work. Of Helm he wrote with colorful and dramatic prose: "His star glistened in the sunlight, but in the dark it went out. Cold fingers gripping a useless pistol, crimson on his buckskin vest." Ripley, who should have known Helm had no pistol in his hand at the time of his death, wrote his saga while there were people still alive who had known the characters he wrote about, but unfortunately he created conversation and drama which did not contribute to the historical accuracy of his work.

In 1937 Jack Hays Day, a member of the Taylor family, wrote his version of the feud in which several of his relatives had lost their lives. He had been a teenager during the feud and knew personally many of the participants and could have written an accurate account, but for reasons best known to himself provided history with only a biased account. Of Helm, who he consistently identified as *Helms*, he wrote only of his death, indicating Jim Taylor and John Wesley Hardin searched for Helm and located him "at a blacksmith shop in the country." There is no mention of Hardin shotgunning Helm, only that Jim Taylor did the killing. "Like the rest of the [Sutton] gang" Day wrote, "Helms couldn't face a gun. Used to taking to his heels, there was no avenue open this time for cowardly flight. No one interfered with Jim and Wes, who calmly remounted their horses and rode back from whence they had come."[1]

George D. Hendricks attempted to provide history with a "fairly detailed description" of many bad men of the west, including Helm, acknowledging that he had found no photograph of many of the men he wrote about, but did provide a physical description of Helm. Hendricks wrote that he was "heavily bearded, handsome" and of his demeanor he was "determined and unswerving." Physically he was "deep-chested [wore] black clothes, high boots, big spurs, fine figure, [was a] participant in Sutton-Taylor feud in Texas."[2]

The popular and prolific historian Dr. Charles Leland "Doc" Sonnichsen began his research into the feuds of Texas in 1944, and of course one of the principal conflicts was the Sutton-Taylor Feud. The result of his research was *I'll Die Before I'll Run: The Story of the Great Feuds of Texas*, first published in 1951. Sonnichsen was able to not only examine early newspapers and court records but also located people who actually survived the feuds and who were willing to talk about them. In his lengthy chapter on the Sutton-Taylor conflict, which he called "the worst of the Texas feuds," he interviewed such men as Lewis Delony, Judge Sam Lackey, Ed P. Cox and Jack Hays Day—men who lived through the feud and knew of it personally. Dr. Sonnichsen devoted about three pages to the Helm-Hardin meetings, although he was most vague as to when Helm met his death, writing "in May or June of 1873." For certain, Sonnichsen concluded, at some point in his research, "Helm is hard to trace."

Sonnichsen wrote how he was able to begin his research. In the "Sources and Notes" he explained: "The Texas State Historical Association obtained a grant-in-aid from the Rockefeller Foundation for me in the summer of 1944 which enabled me to dig deep into libraries, newspaper files, and the recollections of men and women all over Texas." His first feud book was published in 1951 and he had sufficient material for a follow-up volume, *Ten Texas Feuds*, which appeared in 1957.

Of course through the years many articles have appeared based on Hardin and the Sutton-Taylor Feud, and Jack Helm receives some attention in many. Helm became one of the first four captains of the Texas State Police, the creation of Governor E.J. Davis, which was a worthy attempt to reduce the amount of lawlessness in Texas following the Civil War and the period of Reconstruction. The first serious treatment of the force did not appear until 1969 with an article in the *Southwestern Historical Quarterly*, "The Texas State Police During Reconstruction: A Reexamination" by Ann Patton Baenziger. She stressed that the police force was not as bad as some critics had painted it, but many actions of Jack Helm were illegal.[3] Pressure upon the governor to be rid of Helm resulted in his dismissal by the end of the first year of the force's existence. The Baenziger work was a precursor to a totally objective book-length study of the force—*The Governor's Hounds: The Texas State Police, 1870–1873* by Barry A. Crouch and Donaly E. Brice in which Jack Helm receives some attention.[4]

Since the works of Ripley, Day, Sonnichsen, Baenziger, Crouch, and Brice there have been several serious studies on John Wesley Hardin and the Sutton-Taylor Feud in which he and Helm figured so prominently. Noteworthy are Richard C. Marohn's *The Last Gunfighter: John Wesley Hardin*[5]; Leon Metz's *John Wesley Hardin: Dark Angel of Texas*[6]; David Pickering and Judy Falls's *Brush Men and Vigilantes: Civil War Dissent in Texas*[7]; James M. Smallwood's *The Feud that Wasn't: The Taylor Ring, Bill Sutton, John Wesley Hardin and Violence in Texas*[8]; Chuck Parsons's *The Sutton-Taylor Feud: The Deadliest Blood Feud in Texas*[9] and most recently Parsons's and Norman Wayne Brown's Hardin biography: *A Lawless Breed: John Wesley Hardin, Texas Reconstruction and Violence in the Wild West*.[10]

For years I was fascinated with John Wesley Hardin and his relatives, his enemies, and other associates. After a number of articles focusing on Hardin, and two books dealing with his capture and then a biography of his brother-in-law J.R. "Brown" Bowen, my efforts finally resulted in a full-length biography of the noted Texas man-killer, co-authored with Norman Wayne Brown. During those years I found Jack Helm as interesting as well, and finally determined to research his life and career. Happily, I discovered that researching Jack Helm's life and career was quite as rewarding as that of Hardin, although much more difficult. Hardin had a family who preserved his letters as well as many photographs; Helm had two families, but died relatively young, did not write an autobiography, and apparently no one preserved personal letters or even a single photograph. Fortunately documents pertaining to his official life, letters written as a Regulator as well as a State Police captain, newspaper articles, and other contemporary material allowed me to flesh out his life. With this amount of published material devoted to Helm's contemporaries and his violent era I felt it was time for a full-length biography of the man who became so notorious in South Texas yet for so many years remained mysterious—the man Doc Sonnichsen described as being "hard to trace." Hopefully this effort will bring Helm from that difficult and misty area of history into greater clarity.

ACKNOWLEDGMENTS

ALL MY READERS FULLY RECOGNIZE that such a work on Jack Helm could not be done without the assistance of many others who realized the need for such a biography. The following are those who willingly helped, whether in seeking out some obscure document or walking with me in some cemetery looking for the grave of a forgotten individual who played a small part in this story. I have long since forgotten the names of some, such as the experience I had with Karon Mac Smith and her old black handyman who drove us to the grave of Jack Helm for my first visit to the McCracken cemetery. They both have long since passed on, but they are not forgotten. I may have overlooked some, but for those whose names I unintentionally overlooked my sincere apologies.

Ronnie Atnip, Bonham, TX; Sheron Barnes, now retired from the Special Collections, Victoria College & University of Houston-Victoria, Victoria, TX; Bob Boze Bell of *True West* magazine, Cave Creek, AZ; Debbie Blalock, Bullard, TX; Donaly E. Brice, Research Specialist—Texas State Archives, Retired, Lockhart, TX; Larry R. Busby, Sheriff Live Oak County, George West, TX; Cliff R. Caldwell, Independent Historian, Kerrville, TX; Frances Cherry, Assistant Clerk—Wilson County Court, Floresville, TX; Marc Coker, Independent Historian; Caddo Mills, TX; Ron DeLord, Founder, CLEAT (Combined Law Enforcement Association of Texas), Georgetown, TX; Mickey Dennison, Assistant Director, Yorktown Public Library, Yorktown, TX; Dalton Elam, Martindale, TX; Peggy Engledow, Caldwell County Genealogical

& Historical Society, Luling, TX: Judy Falls, Cooper, TX; Pam Fanelli; Gary Fitterer, Kirkland, WA; Tabeth Gardner, DeWitt County Clerk and her staff, Cuero, TX; Leah Glaze, Victoria, TX; Sandra Glenn, Sulphur Springs, TX; Halley Grogan, Photo Archivist, Texas State Library & Archives, Austin, TX; Peggy Hailey, Director-Runge Public Library, Runge, TX; Patsy Hand, Victoria, TX; Cheryl Lynn and Scott Highley, San Antonio, TX; Elizabeth Hilkin, Tarlton Law Library, Austin, TX; Kurt House, San Antonio, TX; Kenneth W. Howell, Director, Central Texas Historical Association, Blinn College, Brenham/Bryan, TX; Laurie E. Jasinski, Texas State Historical Association, New Braunfels, TX; Kathryn Kenefick, Library Assistant, Briscoe Center for American History, Austin, TX; Doug Kubicek, Chair Lavaca County Historical Commission, Hallettsville, TX; John H. Luckey, Whitehouse, TX; Ken McCracken, Independent Historian, Colleyville, TX; Rick Miller, Bell County Attorney, Retired, Harker Heights, TX; Carl Moneyhon, Little Rock, AR; James A. Mundie, Independent Historian, Kenner, LA; David Murrah, Aransas County Historical Society, Rockport, TX; Rebecca Norton, Executive Director, Frontier Times Museum, Bandera, TX; Louise O'Connor, Victoria, TX; Bill O'Neal, Texas State Historian, Carthage, TX; Shelley Parks, Goliad Center for Texas History, Goliad, TX; Ona Lea Pierce, Blessing, TX; Roger Raney, Lavaca County Historical Commission, Yoakum, TX; J. Slater Reese, Western History Collections, Norman, OK; Ann Rose, Luling, TX; Kate Ruckman, San Antonio, TX; Steve Schiwetz, Corpus Christi, TX; Zenalda Silva, District Clerk, Bee County, Beeville, TX; Paul N. Spellman, Wharton County Junior College, Richmond, TX; Nancy Stell, Sanibel Island, FL; Charles Tipton, Edna, TX; Andrea Weddle, Special Collections & Archives, Texas A&M- Commerce, TX; Janie Collier White, President

Aransas County Historical Society, Rockport, TX; Henry and Linda Wolff, Victoria, TX.

A very special thanks also is due my publisher, Ron Chrisman, Director of the University of North Texas Press and his editor Karen DeVinney who has worked with me on previous books.

1

A Nation Torn Apart

"One of the foulest murders that ever stained the soil of Texas."
—Creed Taylor

AN HISTORIAN WITH A PESSIMISTIC outlook on life might be tempted to say that the only reason to remember Jack Helm is because—in popular memory—he was killed by the notorious gunfighter John Wesley Hardin sometime in the 1870s. To many that simple fact of life might be the only worthwhile reason to remember him, but that unfairly diminishes the man. He was much more than one of the many victims of the notorious man-killer; he was a Confederate soldier during the Civil War, but then changed allegiance to serve the victorious occupying Union army, answering to General Joseph Jones Reynolds during Reconstruction. He then became a notorious figure as a "Regulator," a county sheriff and vigilante— these reasons more than any other are why he deserves our recognition. He may not have earned the admiration of many, but he does deserve our respect. After all, those who become lawmen do deserve some degree of honor just because of the dangerous position they hold in society. Their name on a wall listing fallen lawmen should suffice as a memorial, although at the time of his death Helm was a disgraced State Police captain, but still the sheriff of DeWitt County, Texas. In recent years, long after his violent death, two modest ground-level headstones mark his grave in a lonely cemetery in rural Wilson County.[1] His name, although misspelled

1

as *Helms*, does appear on the wall of The Lost Lawman Memorial in Austin, Texas.[2] He is not totally forgotten, although essentially Jack Helm is mostly remembered as just one of the many victims of John Wesley Hardin.

Helm acted as a vigilante during the Civil War as well as in the subsequent years during Reconstruction. As just one example of his vigilante activities, on one particular Saturday, February 15, 1862, he participated in the quasi-legal execution of five men sympathetic to the Union cause; there is evidence he was the hangman, rather than merely an observer, although the source is not the most solid evidence history can unearth.

It is horrendous to be placed on a six- or eight-inch board with hands and feet tied, with a noose around the neck, knowing that within moments that narrow wooden support will be kicked away, leaving you suspended. Will the fall break your neck? Or, even worse, will it not, leaving you to slowly strangle? Your hands are tied; your legs will kick as there is nothing left to do but pray to God for a merciful and quick death. What was happening did not occur to just one unfortunate man, but to five.[3] What was their crime? This quintet paid the ultimate price for showing sympathy to the Union cause during the second year of the war in a seceded state—Texas. The wives and children of these five men witnessed their abrupt end of life on this earth. One of the men, Henry T. Howard, was a preacher, and his final words echoed appropriately an innocent man's final prayer from centuries before, "Lord forgive them; they know not what they do!" Then the executioner—Jack Helm—sprang the drop, or as evidence shows, kicked the board out from under them. That act "launched the souls of these brave, innocent men into eternity and this act closed the scene on one of the foulest murders that ever stained the soil of Texas."[4] That quotation is from a memoir written by Creed Taylor years later, a man who had not only seen much violence but participated in violent action in Lone Star State history. He added this note regarding the action, which may be only coincidental to the hanging: "It is a fact that one of the trees, a thrifty young pecan, never put forth its leaves, again, but died."

Hanging a quintet certainly is not done by one individual but the action of a group, and Jack Helm did not act alone. How did they become prisoners? The five had earlier taken refuge in one of the vast areas that then were common in northeast Texas, Jernigan's Thicket, and as the expression was in those days, had "taken to the brush." To get them out of the thicket would be difficult

A remnant of Oxford's Bridge which is now located on the lawn of the Cooper Public Library, Delta County. The placard reads: "This bridge timber was taken from the South Sulphur River about one and one-half miles south of Charleston, Texas, in October of 2007. Led by Eddie Trapp, a group of people from Delta, Hopkins, and Lamar Counties participated in the excavation. The bridge, known by several names (one being the Smith Bridge), was used as a crossing between Hopkins and what is now Delta County. This twenty-seven foot long bridge was built before the Civil War."
AUTHOR'S PHOTO.

A modern view of where Oxford's bridge was located south of Cooper, Delta County.
AUTHOR'S PHOTO.

and could be costly. Finally, with their food supply dwindling, John Marshal Jackson Helm, known to all simply as Jack, inveigled his way to them and convinced them that if they would come in and surrender they would receive a fair trial and probably be acquitted. As Helm had deserted from the Confederate army earlier, he now was acting to have that blight removed from his record.[5] Finally, whether it was from Helm acting alone or with others, the five men, three Howards and two Hembys, surrendered and left their security for a meal and the promise of a fair trial. The "trial" was set for Friday, February 14. Again, we'll go to Texas pioneer Creed Taylor[6] who experienced more than his fair share of conflict during Reconstruction, as he describes their fate:

> It was well known that they were Union men, which they did not deny, and this served as a pretext for their destruction. Charges were trumped up against them, one or two were arrested while

the others fled and found concealment in the Jearnagin [sic] Thicket. Efforts for their capture there having failed, resort to treachery [was] obtained. Word was sent to them if they would come home and surrender that they should have a fair and honorable trial and as the charges against them were not serious in their nature there could be no doubt of an honorable acquittal. These men accepted their offer came in and gave up.[7]

As this was their crime, these five men would pay the price for sympathizing with the Union cause: in this instance a hanging offense. The question of secession had been foremost in everyone's mind for some time and some men gave speeches in support of it; others bravely spoke out against it. In Lamar County, Ebenezer Lafayette Dohoney and Micajah Lewis Armstrong spoke out against secession, and among the listeners was Henry T. Howard who took notes on the ideas expressed. Howard later prepared his own speech, which he gave back in his home county of Hopkins (present day Delta County). Howard's speech, according to historians David Pickering and Judy Falls, included "arguments followed closely on those of Dohoney and Armstrong." In essence Howard expressed his belief that the Confederacy could not survive a war against the Union due to the Union's superior numbers, a fact which then would draw soldiers from other countries which did not accept slavery.[8] Howard's talk proved that free speech was not to be allowed. He and his closest followers were driven from their homes.

It was not Howard's first brush with dangerous talk. Earlier he had been arrested and placed on trial for his beliefs, tried before the most influential man in Lamar County—Hendley Stone Bennett. Bennett, if not the richest man in the area, was among the wealthiest. The census of 1860 shows his real estate valued at $50,000 and his personal worth at $85,000. This fifty-year-old Tennessee-born farmer had a wife and children who could have helped on his plantation, but they probably contributed little to the working of the soil: he owned a total of eighty-six slaves.[9] "Judge" Bennett determined Howard's "crime" was not a hanging offense, although Howard was a Union man and "a damned Abolitionist."[10]

In Hopkins County things were different when a vigilante group ordered men to leave their homes for their political views on the secessionist question. His influence crossed county lines, and H.S. Bennett was possibly the leader or at least the driving force behind this group. Among those who were deemed guilty of treason and sentenced to death was Howard, his two brothers, and two men named Hemby. Dohoney, whose account of the doings in Hopkins and Lamar Counties during this period does not identify the leader of the vigilantes that coaxed them out of hiding, states that the mob's driving force was "a prominent citizen and rabid secessionist." The mob was composed of men from Hopkins and Lamar County, Bennett's home county.[11]

The secessionists were not content to let them survive, and having been found guilty as charged they were sentenced to death. The execution occurred at Oxford's Bridge, some three miles south of Charleston, the seat of Hopkins County.[12] The court accused these men of favoring the Union cause. It further denied them the right to speak in their defense and threatened the witnesses who wished to speak in their defense. In addition, the men making up the kangaroo court stated that the five posed a danger to the community. The "trial" ended on Friday, February 14, 1862, the verdict a foregone conclusion. The five who died together the next day were James E. Hemby, Jonathan Hemby, Henry T. Howard, Thomas Howard, and James K. Howard.[13]

The execution was carried out on schedule. The five were hanged in view of their families. Who were the executioners? Among the court's officers were Charles H. Southerland, George W. Helm and his son Jack Helm, David Simeon George, Thomas Rufus McGuire, Rice Warren, James McGlasson, and J.W. Stansbury.[14] From what we know of Jack Helm's later conduct it is entirely possible that he was the one who kicked the plank out from under the five as they stood on the "gallows." Creed Taylor, who later became a bitter enemy of Helm, again described the scene:

> A few steps South of the bridge, a large pole was erected between two large trees and this served as a gallows. Under this a rude platform was erected with a drop attachment. When the fatal hour arrived these innocent men were placed upon this platform and the noose put about their necks by executioner Jack Helms [sic]. When they mounted the scaffold, pinioned, their faces were turned northward and in the direction not five hundred yards away of the humble homes of the two Hembys.[15]

Creed Taylor of course was not there as a witness to this vigilante action, but certainly learned of it from associates of Helm when he later became notorious in south Texas.

Five members of the group involved in the execution were arrested in August 1865 by soldiers under command of T.J. Mackey and placed in the Lamar County jail. Their charge: "mobbing and hanging" the Howards and Hembys at Charleston. The Paris Press identified them as George W. Cox, David Simeon George, J.W. Helms, Robert McFarland, and Charles H. Southerland. The "J.W. Helms" was an incorrect identification of George W. Helm, father of Jack Helm.[16] A number of individuals who were actively involved in the trial—including Jack Helm himself —became alarmed that they too would be arrested and charged with the execution. The editor of the Paris Press, speaking for the military authorities, assured his readers that once all the facts of the case were established only those who instigated the hanging would be punished while those who were "led or dragged into the affair" would not be punished. Young Jack Helm — yet in his early twenties—was one of those latter individuals who were still concerned about what would happen to those who actually placed the ropes around the necks of the five men. The editor's assurances may or may not have calmed Jack's fears.[17]

George W. Helm and his son Jack were both there at Oxford's Bridge, participants in what—in reality—was a lynching. The fate of father and son, even though both were now murderers, took different paths. George Washington Helm was born February 14, 1809, in Virginia, the son of Jacob Helm.[18] George W.

This original stone marks the burial place of George W. Helm with a recently placed ground level marker. Helm's wife is also buried here but her grave is not marked. Shown here at the grave of Helm are Pat Parsons, Lee Herring, and Marc Coker.
AUTHOR'S PHOTO.

Helm lived down the incident at Oxford's Bridge and became a stalwart pillar of his community, living long enough to be included in a "vanity book" telling of his illustrious career. That life ended on October 15, 1904, in Delta County, Texas. He is buried in the rural Union Grove Cemetery near the Charleston community.[19]

George Washington Helm, the father of the notorious Jack Helm, had continued as a farmer as his father had been back in Virginia.[20] About this time the G.W. Helm family moved to western Missouri, settling near Kansas City in Jackson County. On September 10, 1829, George W. married Ruth Mayo Burnett; born about 1811 she was eighteen years of age, the daughter of Jeremiah and Martha Burnett of Patrick County. Where the two met is uncertain.[21] In April 1837 George W. was among thirty-two men who purchased town lots in Harrisonville, Cass County, Missouri. Those individuals had the option of purchasing front or back lots—the former going for $20 and the latter for $10. The county at that time was named Van Buren, but citizens renamed it Cass County in 1849.[22] Helm's choice of a home was just south of Kansas City, and it is reasonable to suspect that the next move to Texas was due to Helm's perception—like many other frontier figures—that the area was becoming too crowded.

By 1841 the Helm family had moved to Lamar County, Texas, the northern border of which is the Red River separating Texas from what was then Indian Territory but now the state of Oklahoma. They were among the first settlers in Lamar County, George Helm receiving a class 4 certificate, which awarded him 640 acres of land. The record shows his date of emigration as October 1841.[23] George W. and Ruth Burnett Helm gave eight children to the world, with Jack being the second born. Although born in

Missouri, probably in 1837, son Jack did his growing up in Texas. There was nothing special about his childhood, with the occasional death of a newborn.[24] But as we shall see in this book, he diverged from the path his father took in life and ended up shot dead by two vengeance-seeking feudists in 1873.

Ruth Mayo Burnett Helm, Jack's mother, died sometime in 1853 but the exact date remains unknown. She was laid to rest in Union Grove Cemetery where her husband would be later buried, but her grave is not marked with an informative stone. After his first wife passed, George W. Helm married a second time, on May 23, 1858, to Charlotte Madden Chapman, the widow of Isaac Chapman. Jack now had half-siblings but by the time of his father's second marriage he was an adult and would have hardly known these other half-brothers and half-sisters.[25]

Not unusual in those days were extended families living in the same household, and such was the case of the Helm families. George Helm was head of household number 946 in the 1860 Hopkins County census: a crowded household with the thirteen adults and children.[26] At household number 947, possibly just "next door" or maybe a few miles distant, the census taker visited the household of "John J. Helms" as the enumerator spelled his name, incorrectly as was his father's. Jack Helm is shown to be twenty-three years-of-age, Missouri-born, laboring on the farm with his real estate valued at $200 and personal estate valued at $250. His wife, Minerva McCown, whom he had married December 18, 1857, is shown as eighteen-year-old "Manerva" born in Texas; their two-year-old son George W. was also Texas born. This first child born to Jack and Minerva Helm was named George Washington after his grandfather but history knows him as "Pony" Helm for an unknown reason. Pony Helm later married Sarah E. Shepherd on January 7, 1875. Daughter Armittie

Virginia, their second child, was born on September 2, 1860; she died May 23, 1937.

After visiting the Jack and Minerva Helm household, the enumerator Syl Walker next visited household number 948, that of Alonzo L. and Sarah A. Leech. He was a farm laborer, twenty-six years old and a native of Tennessee, living with his wife Sarah who was Jack Helm's eighteen-year-old sister. These eighteen individuals made up three neighboring households in Hopkins County in 1860.[27]

Farming and stock-raising provided the family's essential needs. In 1860 George W. Helm held but few slaves; the slave census shows he owned an eighteen-year-old male and two females, sixteen and fourteen years of age. No names were given these three individuals, although from the ages shown one might suspect they were siblings who worked the land as well as helping as household servants.[28] Head of household George W. Helm may have left the farm work to the slaves and older children, as he was also involved in politics. Jack's father earned respect in neighboring Lamar County, as several times he was elected to the position of Justice of the Peace. Concerns for adequate rain for the crops and care for the large household were not the only matters to worry about, as Indian raiding parties were an occasional problem for settlers in that period. George W. Helm also became active in the work of the Methodist Church. In October 1847 Pastor John Graham certified seven citizens of Paris, the county seat, as trustees of the Methodist Episcopal Church, one of whom was George W. Helm.[29] Certainly trustee Helm's wife and children were at least occasional if not regular attendees to church services. Whether son Jack had any experience fighting marauders, or regular attendance in the Methodist Church, is uncertain. But when the war came in 1861 he did volunteer to fight for the Confederacy. In spite of the Christian work of George W. Helm, animosity with neighbors could not be avoided due to the erupting conflict over the issues of states' rights and slavery. The local conflict, tearing the county apart as well as the nation, would very soon become a part of the violent Helm legacy.

Jack Helm's record as a soldier is anything but impressive. On August 8, 1861, John H. Anthony, Enrolling Officer for the militia from Precinct No. 3, forwarded to Brigadier General Henry Shelton a list of eighty-seven privates with the names of their eight officers: Capt. John Garrett, two lieutenants, four sergeants, and one corporal. In addition to the name of private John J. Helm (misspelled as Helms) are other names of interest: Alonzo L. Leech, husband of Jack's sister Sarah Ann Helm; James C. Elmore who married Jack Helm's sister Sarah Ann after she became a widow, and Charles H. Southerland, who would participate in the hanging of the five men at Oxford's Bridge early in the war. Enrolling Officer Anthony stated that he was having trouble in precinct No. 3, although he did not specify the nature of the trouble.[30] The Helm, Elmore, and Leech families were all residents of precinct No. 3.

On October 14, 1861, J.J. Helm was mustered into Capt. Lorenzo D. King's Company of Mounted Rifles as part of William Bradford Sims's Regiment of Texas Volunteers at Camp Reeves, Grayson County, Texas. Colonel Sims was an Arkansas-born soldier, who before the war worked as a merchant in Clarksville, Red River County, Texas. He survived the war and lived out his final days in Jefferson, Texas.[31] Whether Jack was a fervent Confederate or was simply tired of life on the farm is unknown, but the young man, listed as twenty-two years of age on the muster roll, signed up for a period of twelve months. Alabama-born Captain King had lived in Hopkins County since 1856 and was known by those men who had signed up to join the Confederate army. Those soldiers elected King to be their captain, a common practice of the military in that period. When King applied for a pension years later, two witnesses to his application, J.A. Foxhall and J.M. Wester, swore before County Judge F.W. Patterson that they had known King "to be a faithful and true officer and soldier and devoted [to] his men from enlistment to close of war." King's application for pension was approved. Perhaps Jack Helm voted for King to be his captain as well. King served throughout the war until his surrender at Shreveport, Louisiana, in 1865.[32]

The mustering officer made no comment regarding Helm's character, but valued his horse at $120 and the equipment issued him at $25; a later evaluation of his mount placed it at only $100. After marching north Helm mustered in at Fort Gibson, Indian Territory, for the October-December 1861 period, intending to serve for a period of ten months. The remaining document shows he was again mustered in for March and April 1862. According to one source Helm had been "in numerous battles and he had the makings of a good soldier,"[33] but the battles are not identified. The 9th Texas Cavalry saw action at the Battle of Round Mountain on November 19, Indian Territory, in present-day Payne County, Oklahoma. When hostilities erupted many tribes in the Indian Territory were torn between whether to support the Union or the Confederacy. Col. Douglas H. Cooper was commander of the Indian Department whose mission was to procure an interview with Creek Chief Hopoeithleyohola (or Opothleyahola) for the purpose of convincing him to support the Confederacy, not the Union. He failed in his mission; realizing this Cooper determined he would force him to pledge allegiance to the Confederacy or else subdue him. Part of

his attacking force included Colonel Sims and his Company G
which included not only Helm but also Leech and Elmore. The
result of the attack on Hopoeithleyohola's force was a complete
victory for the Confederates. This was Jack Helm's first experience in battle; additionally, it was the first battle of the Civil
War in Indian Territory. The 9th Texas Cavalry also contributed
to the victory at Chusto-Talasah, (also known as Bird Creek
or High Shoal), in present-day Tulsa County, Oklahoma, on
December 9, 1861. But at Pea Ridge, in Benton County, Arkansas, on March 6-8, 1862, the battle was a defeat. Unfortunately,
no specific details of Helm's action as a soldier have surfaced in
any of these engagements. He had been last paid on February
28, 1862, but there is also this remark: "Deserted April 14 at
Des Ark Arkansas." This was over a month after the Confederate defeat at Pea Ridge, or Elkhorn Tavern as the engagement
was called by the Union. No official reason for his desertion was
provided, although Creed Taylor stated it was because Helm's
regiment was dismounted and he refused to continue as an
infantryman.[34] As it is known that Helm was at the Oxford's
Bridge hanging in February he may have deserted once before
his recognized desertion of April 14. Had he left his unit, come
home, and then returned to remain until April 14? Des Ark,
a major community in Prairie County, Arkansas, was some 300
miles northeast from his home county and travel back and forth
between Des Ark and his home was certainly possible to arrange.

Jack Helm had married Minerva Catherine McCown on
December 18, 1857, a few years before the war started. The couple began their matrimonial journey together in Fannin County,
although exactly where the wedding took place is uncertain.
Records show their first child, a son they named George Washington in honor of Jack's father, was born November 18, 1859. Then

on September 2, 1860, a daughter was born whom they named Armittie Virginia but generally called "Mitty."[35] Family sources reveal the marriage was not what either had hoped for, as either during the Civil War or soon after it ended Jack and Minerva Helm separated. Following the breakup of their home, little George W. was reared by his grandfather George W. while daughter Armittie was reared by Virginia "Jenny" Helm Stell, Jack's sister. Although few details of the children's lives are verified, they were at least reared by close family members.[36]

Minerva C. McCown was born in 1842, a young lass by today's standards when she married Helm, but in those days a fifteen-year-old bride was not uncommon. Once the war started and Jack went off to fight Yankees, Minerva and the children resided at the home of Jack's sister—Sarah Ann, sometimes called Sallie, now Mrs. Alonzo L. Leech. Leech also joined the army, and on October 14, 1861, the men of Company G elected him 3rd Lieutenant. The non-detailed report indicates he died of disease in May of 1862 but where or of what disease is not indicated. Whatever the cause of Alonzo L. Leech's death, Jack's sister Sarah Ann Leech was left a widow.[37] Supposedly Sarah Ann had communicated to her brother Jack that Minerva was having an affair with neighbor James C. Elmore. Another version is that Minerva was having an affair with Jack's brother-in-law, Alonzo L. Leech. Either way, as local lore has it, Minerva was not a faithful wife to Jack. It is possible but not definite that he left the army to return home to deal with his wife's alleged adulterous relationship with her lover, whoever he was. We do know that Jack deserted and returned home and Minerva McCown Helm then disappears from history.[38] Various historians provide some information, the most credible being the statement of Delta County historian George Douglas Albright. From

Albright's research he determined that "John Jack Helm deserted from the Confederate service, after he learned of his wife's infidelity, with Alonzo Leech. His, John Jack's sister was the wife of Alonzo Leech. . . . John Jack killed someone and had to go to south Texas. I feel like it was Alonzo Leech. I do not know what happened to Minerva McCown Helm, the adulterous wife. Minerva was living with Sallie Helm Leech; she later married an Elmore."[39] One might suspect that the disease Leech supposedly died of was "lead poisoning" but that remains speculation.[40] Certainly Jack Helm would have dealt harshly with the man who allegedly cuckolded him.

Sarah Ann Helm, born August 9, 1842, had married Alonzo L. Leech on May 1, 1859, he a twenty-six-year-old farmer born in Tennessee. She was not yet eighteen. Sarah Ann Helm Leech then married James C. Elmore on October 12, 1863, in Hopkins County. Sarah Ann Elmore lost her second husband in Taylor County, Texas, on September 2, 1927. She lived until June 22, 1934, dying in the home of her daughter from "old age, which was hastened by shock due to falling from chair" according to John A. Bubblis, M.D. who filled out the official death certificate. She had been living on her late husband's pension since 1927.[41]

Minerva's fate remains a mystery. Did the Helm marriage end in a legal divorce—rare at that time—or did Jack merely kick his adulterous wife out of the house, or did he kill her? Whatever happened to their mother, the children were "farmed off" to relatives. The life of a soldier was behind Jack; the battles he had fought in had taught him much about life and death and survival. Although his life as a Rebel soldier was over he would continue as a fighting man: he would become a Regulator, a sheriff, a captain in the soon to be organized Texas State Police. He would forget Minerva and find another woman to become his wife and have a second family; he would also become notorious in South Texas. The life he entered into after his period as a soldier in the army of the Confederate States of America would become as dangerous as being on the battlefields.

Conditions after the war became very chaotic between the newly freed blacks and supporters of the now defunct Confederacy. Some blacks felt that the Freedmen's Bureau, organized to help the former slaves cope in the changed society and to provide relief to the thousands of refugees who had been displaced by the war, would provide them with pensions and subsidies so that they would "be repaid for redress for their slavery."[42] In Charleston one freedman felt himself "somewhat elevated" and actually became "very arrogant" toward Helm—so much that "a clash was bound to occur." Local legend has it that the unidentified freedman one day was sitting on Helm's corral fence and started whistling "Dixie" in his presence. The action "infuriated" Helm so much that he drew his pistol and shot the whistling freedman to death.[43] Curiously, historian Chris Emmett in his biography of cattleman Abel Head "Shanghai" Pierce also relates that story of a freedman sitting on a fence whistling and who was then shot to death by Helm. In this version the man whistled "Yankee Doodle" in Helm's presence. This infuriated Helm so much that he drew his pistol and shot him "square between the eyes" and for no discernable reason the corpse remained where it had fallen. The "bleached skeleton" proved to be "a grim reminder to musically inclined Negroes."[44] Emmett suggests that the incident may have occurred in 1870 but if it happened at all it was certainly sometime before that year, as by the late 1860s, at least by 1867, Helm was firmly in the good graces of the occupying Federal forces and was already working for them, headquartered in Austin. As such he would be required to *protect* the former slave, not *murder* him for such an innocent act of whistling. Until some contemporary account of this killing is located the incident must remain as merely local legend. Whatever the reasons, Helm found it expedient to leave the Hopkins County area. The area south of Austin appealed to him and this former Rebel could find employment there working with the occupying Federal troops.

2

Troubles on the DeWitt-Lavaca County Line

"Now pursuing some thieves to the mountains."
—Jack Helm, June 30, 1869

JACK HELM DID LEAVE NORTHEAST TEXAS for a variety of reasons, ultimately working and living in the Austin area and further south. As described in the previous chapter, several possible reasons explain his locating in an area far from Hopkins County: he may have been fearful of prosecution by the authorities for the Hemby-Howard lynching; or the killing of a freedman (if that happened) may have caused him to leave the area. Or he simply wanted to remove himself from the area where there were so many reminders of his failed marriage. Whatever the cause of his departing northeast Texas, perhaps all of the above, he was by the late 1860s in the DeWitt-Lavaca Counties area, the center of much resistance to the Reconstruction policies of the occupying government forces.

Helm would become a notorious figure in Central and South Texas, but before settling there he already had a fearsome reputation. His "unsavory" name was familiar to some at least, one such figure being the titular head of the large Taylor clan. Creed Taylor, who was to experience tragedy at the hands of Helm, described him as "this scourge of mankind" but admitted he had not the means to ascertain where he came from. He then recalled that people who knew Helm prior to the war considered his "associates" as "generally of low character and it was a common saying among the people there [Hopkins County] that when hearing of a neighbor's losing a horse, 'Jack Helms [sic] can find him.'" The meaning was clear: Helm and his friends stole the best horses, concealed them in the "trackless wilderness of the Sulphur bottoms" and after a time notified the owner of their location and "for a stipulated price *find* their stock."[1]

Taylor related the first time he ever saw Jack Helm, remembering him as being about five feet eight inches tall (about the average man's height in those days), rather heavy set, but "well made" with black hair and eyes and dark complexion. His appearance was not "disagreeable" but "his conversation was too much about himself, and what he had done to be fascinating. His vanity was unbounded, his egotism was immense, while his education was very limited." So Creed Taylor recalled Helm in his memoir.[2] We have to take his word for how he remembered him, as it is suspect just how often Creed Taylor did see Jack Helm. Did Taylor actually recall Helm, years after his death, as described? He certainly was aware of who he was so he may have contributed to the description from first hand observation. A writer of a later generation, Thomas Ripley, who may have actually interviewed people who had known Helm or people who had been associated with him for his book, provided this word-picture of the man, describing him as "Deep-chested, heavily bearded, and not unhandsome in his black clothes, high boots, and great spurs, Helms [sic] cut a fine figure as he rode the trails in pursuit of justice within the boundaries of his county." Ripley further noted that although people may have accused him of "hard prejudices and depredations in his reckless ruling of a tough country . . . it can be said he was honest in his belief that he was doing his duty as he saw it."[3] A vitriolic reporter in Austin described Helm as "a merciless villain," an opinion which the families of his victims certainly would agree with. No known photograph of Helm exists; curiously in all the various articles and books dealing with noted gunfighters such as John Wesley Hardin, Ben Thompson, and Bill Longley[4] no one has presented an image purporting to be of Jack Helm. Thus we are left with only Taylor's and Ripley's physical description of him, which could easily fit many men.

Victor Marion Rose, influential editor of the *Victoria Advocate* and an early historian of the Sutton-Taylor Feud, provides another explanation as to how Jack Helm became notorious in the DeWitt County area of South Texas. A man Rose describes as Helm's future brother-in-law, unidentified but certainly James A. Crawford Jr., moved to the community of Sweet Home in Lavaca County, which neighbors DeWitt County. Supposedly about that same time Jack Helm "showed up in that region as a strong Unionist who had ever been 'truly loyal' to the Federal power." In addition he was "an implacable foe to every man who had in any shape, form or manner, aided or abetted the cause of the late Confederacy."[5] It is entirely possible that James A. Crawford did bring Helm to the Lavaca-DeWitt Counties area in the mid- to late-1860s although documentary proof is lacking. Helm early became aware that being a strong law and order man could be of great benefit. In addition, he was not adverse to consider the possibility of becoming a family man again. He did notice a young female member of the Crawford family, Margaret Virginia, and began courting her, all the while expressing his concern about the amount of lawlessness in the area. Helm's courting produced the desired result as he married Margaret Virginia at the DeWitt County courthouse, then in Clinton in January of 1869.[6] Courtship did not interfere with his pursuit of desperate men and he willingly shared with the governor's office his plans. He was actively working to impress the area citizens with his enthusiasm for ridding the country of thieves and other desperadoes. He was also very much aware of the workings of the Fifth Military District , and certain stockmen became convinced that Helm was the man to deal hardest with thieves. Concerned citizens prepared a petition to get Helm the power to do what the local sheriff and deputies seemingly could not or would not do. Among the documents dealing with this issue is a petition signed by eight citizens directed to Maj. Gen. Charles Griffin, commanding the Department of Texas. It is undated, but from what we know about Griffin it must have been composed in the summer of 1867. Griffin had been named to his Federal position in January of 1867 and worked mainly in South Texas. In September of that year he was working in Galveston but became ill with the deadly yellow fever epidemic, which cost him his life.[7]

This document is not complete, and the eight names thereto may be only a small portion of the original signatures. The first man to stand forth and sign was that of stock raiser Madison G. Jacobs, a fifty-three-year-old veteran of the war; then N.L. Norton; then Augustine Douglas, a Pennsylvania-born farmer and stockman; Charles Coleman remains but a name; Jordan Morris was a relatively young man, compared to the others, as he was but thirty-two years old when he signed the petition. This Georgia-born farmer had a wife and three children. John Thomas Jefferson Culpepper was from Alabama, forty years of age and farming in Lavaca County. The two remaining names are illegible.[8] "We the undersigned citizens of De Witt & Lavaca counties" the petition began, "Satisfied from the most positive evidence that organized bands of thieves & desperadoes exist in our midst as in various other sections of the State rendering almost every species of movable property insecure & proportionably [sic] valueless" certainly had General Griffin's attention, although he may have become inured to letters describing the high rate of lawlessness in Texas. The thieves and desperadoes "set the Laws at defiance & endanger the lives of our citizens without regard to race or political antecedent." Moreover it was clear to these petitioners that the civil authorities were totally unable to deal with the matter, were unable to give "Legal protection or consequent Safety to our people." The concerned citizens then offered the solution: the petitioners "therefore request & petition that you authorize & empower Mr J J Helm the deputy Sheriff of Lavacca [sic] county to arrest & bring to justice such offenders against the Laws as he may be able to find [;] & further if it be compatible with your view of Justice, that you furnish him Such police force as may be necessary to carry the proposed affect into execution."

If General Griffin gave Helm the power and authority to do what the petitioners wanted, then their property would be safe. It appears he would be allowed to deal with thieves and desperadoes, or at least those he considered members of that class, as he saw fit. The Jack Helm version of law and order was to come to the lawless area. These men were farmers and stock raisers according to the census record; they were concerned with the security of their property as well as the safety of their families and knew that thievery would damage their livelihood and by extension the health of their families.

On July 15, 1867, Jack Helm had someone (the letter is in someone's handwriting other than Helm's) write to Brig. Gen. James Oakes, perhaps from a desk in the capitol building, what his immediate plans were.[9] "I am the legally appointed and qualified Deputy Sheriff in and for La Vaca [sic] County Texas" the scribe began. Helm wanted to make clear to General Oakes that what he was doing was legitimate, and only then did he explain his recent actions. "Recently, in the discharge of my official duty, it became necessary for me to pursue some horse thieves from La Vaca Co[unty] through the interior of this State to Red River [County]." This is quite an undertaking—especially for a lone traveler, without the added effort of pursuing a number of horse thieves—as leaving from Austin to any point on the Red River would be between 350 and 400 miles. Doubtful the thieves would travel in a straight line, thus adding many additional miles. Helm's dictation continued: "While in said pursuit I discovered there is a well organized band of robbers and desperadoes extending throughout the interior of the State." He continued, explaining that the band communicated with each other in order "to assist one another in the perpetrations of their villainies, and for mentioned protection against the constituted authorities." Helm intended to convey the notion that the thieves were in small groups and thus communicated with each other to relay important information. Helm further explained to General Oakes what he had learned which would be of interest to those of the Fifth Military District headquarters. There were eleven "armed men assembled in the upper part of Bell County" and fourteen "on the waters of the Bosque in McLennan County" and in Johnson County—nearly 100 miles north from Belton, the Bell County seat—some twenty-two or twenty-three desperadoes. Helm failed to identify any of these men by name or reveal how he was able to determine these specific numbers. He did stress to General Oakes that the band was "of all political parties, and its objects are in no wise political." Helm now stressed his own intentions: "I have been an[d] am now activated solely by a desire to discharge my duty as an officer and to see Justice done." Jack Helm could not envision how General Oakes would respond to this communication, but continued, sharing his concern: "I am satisfied that under the circumstances, the civil authorities are not able to suppress the organization, or afford protection to the citizens, and that the assistance of the military is absolutely necessary."[10] Helm did expect a reply as he gave his address as Sweet Home, Lavaca County.

How General Oakes responded to this report, if he did prepare a written response, is not known. The amount of time Helm expended on this pursuit from his home country to somewhere along the Red River was significant. Even if it did not result in action from military headquarters it made a very positive impression on the citizens of Lavaca and DeWitt Counties. He was eventually elected sheriff of DeWitt County on December 3, 1869; General J.J. Reynolds made this election official with his Special Order No. 65 on March 23, 1870.[11] As before when the eight or more men had submitted the petition in the summer of 1867, stock raisers were concerned over the amount of cattle and horse stealing in the area. Cattle were illegally rounded up not to feed hungry families but to be killed and their hides sold; many stockmen perceived the rustling as rampant. In Lavaca County, a fifty-year-old New Yorker, Wesley Benjamin Ogden, then judge of the 10th Judicial District,[12] circulated a petition which was delivered to Gov. Elisha M. Pease. Among Ogden's petitioners were Samuel C. Lackey, District Attorney of the 10th Judicial District and W.H. Coleman, Lavaca County sheriff, along with forty-five others. These men requested Governor Pease "to confer upon J.J. Helm the authority to pursue and arrest a gang of Horse theives [sic] and Robers [sic] that now infest our county and the right to call upon any and all officers and citizens to assist him in so doing in whatever County they may be found." This in effect gave Helm the power to raise a posse, similar to the legal right of an elected sheriff to deputize additional manpower. The petitioners requested that Jack Helm be given the authority to act virtually as judge, jury, and executioner.

Curiously the document is undated, but addressing the petition to Governor Pease places the timing between August 8, 1867, and September 30, 1869, his appointed term as governor, and before Helm was elected sheriff. Perhaps Helm had been acting without Governor Pease's knowledge at this point, and county officials felt he should have the head of state's blessing for his actions, hence the petition.

Ogden, whose name appears first on this document, provided a description of Helm which is quite different from the image presented by Creed Taylor, John Warren Hunter (author of a quasi-biography of Creed Taylor), or Thomas Ripley. If nothing else, it is certain that Ogden did know Helm personally and could give an accurate description of him. The image of Helm that Ogden

John Warren Hunter (1846–1915), who prepared a biography of Creed Taylor based on interviews and selections from the *Victoria Advocate*. In addition to beginning various newspapers in the Texas Hill Country he founded *Hunter's Magazine* which became the popular *Frontier Times*, preserving much of the history of 19th century Texas.
Courtesy Billy Huckaby and Wildhorse Media Group.

Texas Revolutionary hero Creed Taylor (1820–1906) as he appeared in his later years.
COURTESY THE ROBERT G. MCCUBBIN COLLECTION.

provides presents a look into Helm's character rather than just his physical attributes, seeing him as "an energetic industrious young man and competent to discharge the trust that may be confided to him." Helm was "prudent and cautious, and with such authority we think will be of great service in releiving [*sic*] the County of this infamous crowd that are now prowling over the western County." Among the signers were J.A. Crawford and J.L. Crawford, brothers of Margaret Virginia Crawford, the future Mrs. Jack Helm.

The lawlessness of the Lavaca and DeWitt Counties area was considered equally rampant in neighboring Goliad County, and

Wesley Benjamin Ogden as he appeared in the 1880s. Ogden was instrumental in getting Jack Helm to the Lavaca and DeWitt Counties area to work against lawlessness.
PUBLISHED WITH PERMISSION OF THE TARLTON LAW LIBRARY, JAMAIL CENTER FOR LEGAL RESEARCH, UNIVERSITY OF TEXAS SCHOOL OF LAW.

Helm would soon be accused of creating terror there with his manner of dealing with alleged desperadoes. Already in mid-1867 at least one "vigilance committee" was at work, soon to be known as the Regulators, although with varying leaders and fluctuating members. During the night of August 14, 1867, a party of armed men entered Goliad County. Military authorities were able to identify at least thirteen of them by name but there were more. The mob took four prisoners from the Federal authorities: James Wilkerson, Martin Dickerson, and two others identified only as a black man and a boy. It was believed by Goliad officials that the quartet was to be delivered into neighboring Victoria County. Scarcely had the group left the Goliad community limits than Wilkerson was shot to death. The fate of the others remained uncertain at the time. The question remains as to what brought about Wilkerson's abrupt fate: had he in fact attempted to escape and his captors shot him to death to prevent his escape, or did they simply murder him and then claimed he attempted to escape? [13] Few considered the question to be of real importance but it would become a matter of concern at the highest office within a very few years.

Capt. Pythagoras E. Holcomb, commander of the military post in Goliad, managed to arrest only three of the vigilance committee: A.G. Brown, Jordan Perkins, and Henry Thompson, although no details have been preserved as to how he accomplished this feat.[14] This raid remains significant as it foreshadows what Helm and his Regulators would become notorious for doing within a short time: the Regulators determined a group or a single individual was guilty of horse or cattle stealing or some other offense which was repugnant to the group. They would be "arrested" and either delivered to some county authority or too frequently shot to death or lynched, with the excuse or reason being given that they had attempted to escape. This happened often enough and became common knowledge so that to easily explain what happened to an individual, the term "Helmized" became part of the regional vernacular.[15]

Of particular interest in this party who invaded Goliad County is the identification of several, some remaining only a name while others became associates of Helm or themselves became a victim of mob action, although no one was ever charged with the murders. The name of Ragland is on the list, but only the surname. He was Henry Ragland and he became a principal figure siding with the Sutton faction in the developing feud with the Taylor clan. The name of Neal Brown is of interest as well as he became a victim of Wiley W. Pridgen on September 20, 1867, scarcely a month after the Goliad County raid. The two men argued over the result of a horse race with the argument ending with Pridgen killing Brown.[16] Obviously the fact that these two were together in August did not prevent their becoming enemies soon after. Men working together in a common cause could easily develop animosities due to changing circumstances. Wiley Washington Pridgen himself later became a victim during the feud, although no one was ever officially charged with his murder. Jack Helm's name does not appear in this list of vigilantes but he certainly learned of the incident, and may have been directly influenced by it.

In June 1868 Jack Helm was in Caldwell County, that dangerous area surrounded by Bastrop, Fayette, Gonzales, Guadalupe, Hays, and Travis Counties, whose settlement in the 1830s was disrupted by the Runaway Scrape after the fall of the Alamo. Another significant incident was the Battle of Plum Creek in 1840 between a large number of Comanche warriors and Texas settlers. When the Civil War was imminent, Caldwell County voted for secession and several hundred men went to the various battlefields in the east. During Reconstruction several incidents of racial violence occurred in county seat Lockhart and the nearby village of Prairie Lea, causing Federal troops to be stationed in those two communities.[17] At least one incident of the Sutton-Taylor Feud occurred only a few miles south of Lockhart—the murder of a prisoner after being arrested in neighboring Bastrop County. It remains a mystery as to why Jack Helm was then in Caldwell County—exactly where unknown—but he may have been there due to a flare-up of some incident connected to one of the "troubles" which brought so much notoriety to Texas as a violent state.

Even with spending much time hunting alleged cattle and horse thieves as well as other desperadoes, Helm found time to court a young lady of DeWitt County. On December 28, 1868,

Helm obtained a marriage license. Six days later, on January 3, 1869, in Clinton, then the county seat, Minister of the Gospel A.H. Walker united John Marshal Jackson Helm and Miss Margaret Virginia Crawford in holy matrimony.[18] Although the license does not provide the details we would like, at least James A. Crawford, the bride's brother and a signer of the earlier petition, was shown to be a witness. Probably the bride's other siblings were there to witness their marriage as well. There was the potential for a large gathering; James Alexander Crawford Sr. had died October 17, 1861, but his wife Rachel Sawyers Crawford must have been there, and she had another decade of life.[19] The Crawfords gave ten children to the world, but with no guest book there is no way of knowing how many relatives and friends of the family were actually present as witnesses to the marriage. Not surprisingly, virtually nothing is

The marriage license of Jack Helm and his second wife Margaret Virginia Crawford, now preserved in the DeWitt County Historical Records. Author's Collection.

known about the lady who became Mrs. J.J. Helm, Jack's second wife. The 1860 census shows her to be twenty-one, indicating she was born about 1839. A family tree preserved in genealogist Karon Mac Smith's papers shows Margaret Virginia died on March 18, 1877, but there is no indication as to where she died or what caused her death, nor is the source of Miss Smith's information provided.[20] Were any of the wedding guests aware of the groom's former wife and children, or his desertion from the Confederate service, or his involvement in the lynching of five Union sympathizers, or anything really of his background? Probably not. Perhaps the couple spent an enjoyable honeymoon celebrating their marriage vows; if so on their return Helm soon put farming secondary as he now took the lead in the fight against suspected thieves and murderers.

Among his earliest concerns was what to do in regards to the murder of Andrew Ruff, committed allegedly by George Johnson. O.P. Coppedge, Justice of the Peace, farmer and medical doctor, wrote out the notice to the sheriff or "any Constable of Dewitt County" informing him that the examination held on the body of Andrew Ruff indicated his death was caused by a pistol ball fired by George Johnson. He was to be arrested and "him Safely keep" until he could be brought before him or any Justice of the Peace of the county. Whoever did arrest Johnson was to "make due return" of the proceedings, i.e., report the details on how he was captured.[21] Jack Helm was aware of Johnson, and communicated to Governor Pease that he was "a man of the worst character" who had committed the murder "in the most unprovoked manner and done with out provocation." He added that the murdered man was "one of our best citizens." Helm explained that he was not at home when the murder was committed "on the highway near my house" and strangely requested advice from the governor as to how best to proceed in the matter.[22] Seemingly Helm would not have had any great difficulty in tracking George Johnson, but whether he would "him safely keep" may have been a different matter. George W. Jacobs was then county sheriff, and perhaps Helm was acting as his deputy. His appointment as sheriff would not take place until April of the following year.

Some considered Helm acted with his personal set of rules regarding law enforcement. At times he was on his own and handled himself with confidence and self-assuredness. Even though he usually had a group of fellow man-hunters at his back, ready to follow his orders, at times he had to deal with a dangerous situation alone. On Monday, April 12, 1869, an unidentified man stole a horse in Hochheim, commonly known as "Dutchtown" due to the large number of German-speaking families there. The thief may not have realized whose horse it was, but the animal belonged to Jack Helm. The Guadalupe River was only a few minutes west of Hochheim and quickly the thief and horse were in the water intending to cross over. Helm had followed him and now administered quick "justice," shooting the man, who immediately disappeared under the water. That was not the end of it however, as there were several men on the opposite side of the river who fired several shots at Helm, but without effect. They quickly decided that there were horses elsewhere that could be stolen at no cost. If Helm recognized any of the thieves, he failed to identify them. He apparently captured his horse but no one recovered the dead would-be horse thief. This certainly proved Helm was no coward and would stand up to defend his property as well as his life and certainly his honor.[23]

George W. Jacobs, now sheriff of DeWitt County with four months' experience, met with Helm at Clinton in late April. District Court had been in session and from that session Jacobs was able to summarize the results, providing names of several individuals who were convicted and their punishment: William Lambert was convicted of theft of $110 in silver coin and sentenced to five years in the penitentiary; George Lunchien was convicted of sheep theft and fined $100 and ten days in the county jail; Henderson Brown was convicted of illegally branding cattle and was fined twenty-five dollars. Almost regretfully, Jacobs added, "No other criminal cases tried." But Jacobs had remained active since district court closed: he had made arrests, and noted there were five capiases for Jesse Pullen.[24] But there was a problem, as "I find the citizens here are almost all his friends [Pullen's] and Keep him posted in Regard to my movements." Pullen was charged in DeWitt County with assault upon a Justice of the Peace and assault with intent to kill and murder of two persons in Bastrop County. Pullen further had informed Jacobs that if he attempted to arrest him "that one of us would die." For this reason, Jacobs believed he could not arrest him. A more important name perhaps was that of James Madison "Matt" Peace of Goliad County, who was charged with theft of beef cattle. Helm was aware of these concerns of Sheriff Jacobs who also provided a physical description of Peace: "about five feet high Black hair and Eyes weighs about 110 lbs." One other name that carried a large reward was that of Hays Taylor, a son of Creed Taylor; Jacobs must have been aware of the deadly affray at Fort Mason in which a major and a sergeant of the U.S. army had been killed, by Hays and his brother Doboy. He now noted Taylor was wanted as well for a murder in Calhoun County.[25]

Jack Helm roamed over the area south of Austin while pursuing thieves. In June 1869 he was in Caldwell County, perhaps in Prairie Lea, where on the thirtieth he penned a letter to Gov. E.M. Pease regarding warrants for various individuals whom he hunted. He explained why he could not keep up with the paperwork, as his time "was constantly imployed [sic] in pursuit of thieves." Since the last time he had met with the governor he had arrested "Some of the worst parties in the state and I find a party of some fifty on the west side of the Nueces river." Not knowing specifically where this "party of some fifty" hunted men were one must estimate that he would be following them for about 150 miles, the approximate distance from Caldwell County to the nearest point on the Nueces River. If he intended to approach this "party" he certainly would have to have additional men to help him, not only in attacking them but in returning them to civil authorities. He explained that he would not "attact" [sic] them without first consulting with the governor. Equally important Helm wanted the governor to obtain the approval of "the general," no doubt General Joseph Jones Reynolds. To be sure and to gain that approval of what he was doing he explained he was "working for the Good of the people" which meant "claring [sic] the country of thieves and murder[er]s not having any political points in view whatever." Helm explained that he could not go and see the governor in person as he was "now pursuing some thieves to the mountains" where he expected to recover "considerable stolen livestock." In lieu of mailing the letter he had it delivered to the governor by an unidentified individual, ending the communication with "Your friend and humble servt Jack Helm." [26]

If Helm was following some thieves headed for the mountains, we must wonder if he intended to follow them as far as what is known generally today as the Hill Country, the closest geographical feature from Caldwell County that could be construed as mountainous. And if he was in pursuit of thieves with stolen stock then he was certainly not alone but we know nothing else of this venture. Victor M. Rose stated that Helm "took the field" about June 1, 1868, but it is apparent that he was active during the year

Victor Marion Rose, editor and publisher of the *Victoria Advocate*. His newspaper provided significant information on the post-war violence in south Texas. COURTESY LEAH GLAZE.

previous. Whether in the year 1867, 1868, or 1869, Helm became the head of a volunteer force numbering as many as fifty men. At times he had a United States sergeant in full uniform accompanying him; the posse, or murderous mob, depending on your point of view, was "armed and equipped as the rules of the service direct."[27]

DeWitt County sheriff James F. Blair resigned his office in November 1868. During this time of Reconstruction General J.J. Reynolds had the authority to appoint his replacement, and on January 19, 1869, he had appointed George Washington Jacobs[28] to be the new sheriff of DeWitt, based on the recommendation of Governor E.M. Pease. He would serve until March 23, 1870, when he was removed from office and replaced by Helm. Helm certainly had the reputation of a man capable of being sheriff, whereas why Jacobs was the chosen one is unknown. Whatever efforts Helm had made to be named sheriff had not proven to be effective—yet.[29] Helm may have felt some resentment in not being chosen county sheriff, but the two remained at least outwardly civil. In March of the following year Jacobs would be a member of a militia group captained by Helm to operate against alleged thieves and murderers.

The summer of 1869 became, in Helm's mind at least and to many others, a period of purging desperadoes, thieves, and murderers from South Texas, a noble intention indeed. The men under Helm became known as the Regulators and by early 1870 Helm was considered a man to be reckoned with. He was named captain of a group of citizens who would work in the vicinity of

Fifth Military District General Joseph Jones Reynolds, from an image made during the Civil War. Courtesy the Don Chaput Collection.

the Guadalupe River. The existing enrollment document shows the names of twenty-nine men, some of whom earned a degree of notoriety during the following years of Reconstruction and the Sutton-Taylor Feud.[30] His orders were clear that upon receiving reliable intelligence that horse or cattle thieves or individuals or bands of men were in the area defying the civil authorities, any number of the enrolled men could turn out in pursuit. The captain was to promptly notify the Post Commander of their action and while out the captain would be held "strictly accountable for the sobriety and orderly conduct of his men."[31] In theory none of the men would be drinking and their conduct would not be detrimental to the military. The muster roll of men under Helm's command provides specific names, whereas the term "vicinity" allows a broad interpretation as the Guadalupe River today flows between DeWitt County seat Cuero and one-time county seat Clinton. It rises in western Kerr County—in the "mountains" as Helm would consider the countryside—and then flows some 230 miles before converging with the San Antonio River and then emptying into San Antonio Bay and the Gulf of Mexico. Helm did not have to remain in DeWitt County in the pursuit of suspected horse or cattle thieves.

3

The Choate Ranch Raid

"Jack Helm on the War Path!"
—*Goliad Guard*, **August 2, 1869**

THE REGULATORS' WORK BEGAN in earnest in June 1869 in Goliad County where Sheriff Andrew Jackson Jacobs had requested help from the state due to the amount of lawlessness in his county. A.J. Jacobs, brother to DeWitt County Sheriff G.W. Jacobs, had been appointed to that office on July 15, 1868, by Special Order No. 156 from military headquarters. Sheriff A.J. Jacobs, on March 27, 1869, wrote to federal authorities at Helena for assistance in helping him enforce the law as troubles seemingly were overwhelming. At the last term of district court on March 5, 1869, the grand jury found fifty-two indictments, many of which were for felonies. Then on the night of March 11 a group of unidentified men burglarized the district clerk's office. Many of the indictments as well as other official papers were taken out and burned. The next night, riders came to liberate two prisoners, but the two refused to leave their cell, fearing they were to be killed. Jacobs suspected the prisoners knew the riders as among those who had burglarized the courthouse and feared for their lives. In addition, Jacobs claimed to see on the streets of Goliad every day indicted men but no one would assist him in making arrests. He wanted military assistance as no local men would help him, and he had no deputies or even a constable.[1] Jacobs had legitimate concerns, but apparently no response was ever received in Goliad. Jacobs had no wish to play the hero's role in acting alone as he had a family to support. He and his wife, the former Mary Jane Wilcox, a forty-year-old Mississippi native, now had five children. Mrs. Jacobs was a sister to George W. Jacobs's wife, but he had his own problems in DeWitt County and simply could not come to the aid of his brother, even though the distance between the two county seats was only thirty miles. The letter A.J. Jacobs sent never brought about a response, and the concerns he had were not baseless. It would have been useless anyway, for on the fifth of June a pair of brothers, James Madison "Matt" and Christopher "Chris" Peace, the sons of Henry and Rachel Peace, shot the sheriff to death.[2] The fifty-year-old Jacobs had been appointed sheriff less than a year earlier. Jacobs had been "waylaid and killed . . . within half a mile of his residence." The only reported reason was that Jacobs had "showed partiality in making arrests."[3] Jacobs left his forty-year-old wife, a teen-aged son, and four younger daughters to mourn the loss.[4]

The killing of Sheriff Jacobs and the immediate aftermath remains somewhat mysterious. The killing took place on June 5, but curiously no inquest was immediately held. Reportedly the burial also took place on June 5, but then an inquest was ordered and the body had to be disinterred. Dr. E.R. Lane determined that Jacobs had been shot seven times by both pistol and shotgun, and that the shooting had been done by the Peace brothers.[5] Who led the investigation is uncertain, but 2nd Lieut. William Thompson, commander of the military post at Helena, Karnes County, determined what had happened and reported it to his superiors in Austin. He had found that James S. Stapp of rural Goliad, a relative of the Peace brothers, had invited Jacobs to his house. Jacobs then made inquiry there about the brothers as they had threatened to kill him. Stapp claimed he had not seen them lately, which was an obvious lie, as the brothers shortly before Jacobs's arrival had left Stapp's residence. The Peace brothers waylaid the sheriff soon after he left the house, proving that Stapp had "set up" the sheriff. On June 12 certain citizens had determined what was to be done. Those concerned citizens, some seven or eight possibly including Helm and some of his Regulators, were in disguise when they arrested Stapp and both Peace brothers. Although Stapp was not directly involved in the assassination of Jacobs, he believed he could arrange bail for the brothers and willingly accompanied the posse. Their stated mission was to deliver the three prisoners to county seat Goliad. The group never arrived, as within four miles of Stapp's residence the posse ruthlessly shot and killed prisoner Stapp. No one was ever charged with the killing, but the usual excuse, or reason, for such shootings was that prisoners had attempted to escape. Shooting them down of course was the only means to prevent their getting away. No reason has been given as to why the posse men were in disguise in this instance, which ought to have given not only Stapp but the Peace brothers as well great cause for concern. Was Jack Helm in this group? In no other action of delivering prisoners had he been in any type of disguise. He may have been but quickly realized there was no need for a disguise for his line of work. When the designated "posse" and the prisoners failed to arrive at the jail when expected, a search party went to locate them. They found the corpse of Stapp but no indication of what had happened to the Peace brothers.[6]

Senator Bolivar Jackson Pridgen, serving in the Twelfth Legislature, was very concerned about lawlessness in his district, in particular the tendency of prisoners to be shot while "attempting to escape." He wrote that it was not only Stapp who had been killed but also a freedman who was with him. None of the contemporary newspapers mentioned this, either because they did not know of it

Senator Bolivar J. Pridgen consistently and relentlessly condemned the lawless acts of Jack Helm. COURTESY WESTERN HISTORY COLLECTIONS, UNIVERSITY OF OKLAHOMA, IMAGE #384.

or because they failed to see any relevance in reporting the death of the black man. But Pridgen, not giving dates to the incident, wrote with a degree of sarcasm that the Regulators had gone to Stapp's residence, "arrested him and a negro [sic], took them off into the woods, and 'brought them to justice.' They too had been guilty of the impropriety of attempting to escape." Further, according to Pridgen, it was some days later before Stapp's "putrified body was found on the prairie" while the corpse of the lynched man was "dangling between heaven and earth." Someone had taken the time to take a strip of paper and scrawl in lead pencil "one voter less" on it and attach it to the poor man's shirt-sleeve.[7] Lieutenant Thompson, of the military post, learned little else, determining only that Stapp, the son of prominent pioneer Texan Milton W. Stapp,[8] had been shot to death. Had Stapp and the Peace brothers made an attempt to escape and in the ensuing effort to prevent the escape—by shooting the prisoners—only Stapp was killed? The lieutenant determined that his body was "perforated with balls" suggesting each of the posse members had fired a round into him. Thompson further reported, based on evidence of DeWitt County Sheriff George W. Jacobs,[9] that Matt Peace was "severely wounded in the melee and has since died."[10] Sheriff Jacobs's information was not correct although Matt Peace may have been wounded; later Helm was in pursuit of both brothers, so obviously they both were alive. Lieutenant Thompson received information that at least one of the brothers had gone to Galveston and then on to Trinity County in east Texas, but he never caught up with the object of his pursuit. Lieutenant Thompson did not go alone but took with him Joseph Tumlinson, William W. Wells, and Joseph P. "Doc" White, three men who gained prominence in the troubles with the Taylor party. The lieutenant had made a sincere attempt to capture the Peace brothers, but he believed that one of their relatives, a Mr. McCormick, who was Chief of Police of Galveston, had betrayed him, notifying the brothers of his and his posse's actions. "Having been defeated in securing these desperadoes, I left Galveston on the 11th inst. Arriving here [Helena] on the 14th." Thompson further assured his superior, Capt. George Gibson Huntt, that it would be possible to continue the pursuit of Christopher Peace, who was "at the present time, near Sour Lake, 25 miles from Liberty, Liberty County."[11] There is no evidence that this was done.

The editor of the *Goliad Guard* stressed that the "lawless acts"—killing the sheriff and then Stapp—"exhibit a truly lamentable state of affairs, and should be and are deprecated by every good man in the country."[12] Nearly a decade before, the census taker had enumerated James Stapp as a farmer with real estate valued at $250 and personal estate valued at $150. By 1869 he was still farming but also studying law under his father's direction. If his reason to accompany the Peace brothers was to provide bail for them, he no doubt knew what was necessary for that to be done.[13] Of the four men or possibly five involved in this Goliad County tragedy—the killing of Jacobs by the two Peace brothers and then the killing of Stapp and possibly the freedman—little care was given their bodies. The remains of the victims were buried in a Goliad County cemetery but none has a marker on the grave. Even though no marker is known for Sheriff Jacobs, he is not forgotten as his name is on the Texas Peace Officer's Memorial, located on the state capitol grounds in Austin. In addition his name is on the wall of the Lost Lawman Memorial located at 1601 South Interstate 35 in Austin.[14] Following Jacobs's assassination General Reynolds appointed Sergeant N.W. Jenkins of Company H, Fourth Cavalry, as Goliad County sheriff.[15]

The Peace brothers had made their escape from the disguised posse. They may have been aware of what the posse intended to do whereas Stapp—perhaps in all innocence—was not, and therefore could not make his escape. James Stapp's widow, who had seen the posse members, claimed she could not identify any of the men who had arrested her husband; perhaps she could have but chose not to through fear of reprisal. Helm admitted that the Peace brothers had "effected an escape" but failed to provide any details as to how this was done or exactly how he learned of their escape—unless he was among the posse. He claimed that Stapp had been killed in attempting to escape, and further claimed that the brothers went to the ranch of John Choate in San Patricio County, distant some fifty miles southeast, stating to Choate that they were being pursued by a "vigilance committee" and desired protection.[16] As Jack

Helm later was dismissed from the State Police for committing illegal acts—such as murdering prisoners in his custody and afterward claiming they were killed in their effort to escape—one can only wonder if he was indeed one of the disguised men and his efforts to kill all three men failed.

In July Helm and his men continued their vigilante work in Goliad County. On the thirteenth James W. Lunsford was killed. Lunsford, the son of Hiram and Amelia Lunsford, seventy-one- and sixty-six-years-old respectively, was a forty-five-year-old farmer from North Carolina with a wife and child.[17] He allegedly had killed a man named Sessions,[18] had then been placed in the county jail in Clinton from which he escaped not long before the Regulators began ridding the country of alleged desperadoes. These were not secret killings committed in the dark hour of midnight, but in the brightness of open daylight. Little publicity was given to this killing, and it is unknown why Lunsford was killed. Even Senator Pridgen, who seemed to be able to catalog all of Jack Helm's misdeeds, had little to say of this killing. He wrote of it saying the Regulators had taken Lunsford from his wagon, carried him a short ways distant and then "Helmized him, left him, and excused the murder by saying that they killed him through mistake for his brother Dave."[19] Following the murder of their son the Lunsfords moved away from DeWitt County, but Hiram soon lost Amelia Lunsford. In 1880 widower Hiram Lunsford was a boarder in a household in Bosque County, having lost both his son and his wife.[20]

Occasionally citizens who believed in the work of Jack Helm expressed their satisfaction to the press. A newspaper contributor in Mission Valley, a small community north of Victoria, reported in August 1869 that "seven murderers, horse and cattle thieves have been disposed of by the regulators" and identified them as James Stapp, "Cain" Pease, certainly meaning Christopher Peace,

James Bell,[21] Charles Moore, Rutland [sic, Russell] Jones, Tobe (or Tobias) Poole and Jim "Zunsford," obviously Lunsford.[22] Interesting that Christopher Peace was reported dead at that time, for as late as December 1870 State Police Private Cornelius V. Busby reported that *both* Peace brothers were spending "most of their time" at East Bernard, Wharton County, and were using the alias of Chris and Matt Cox.[23] Helm, clearly believing both were alive, claimed he followed the brothers to the Choate Ranch, giving him the reason to raid that place.

The thought of these victims being found guilty in a court of law apparently did not cross the Mission Valley correspondent's mind. The deaths of several of the listed men did not go unnoticed by Senator B.J. Pridgen however. In his later condemnation of Jack Helm, the senator wrote of how the Regulators went to James Bell's house and after arresting him (the offense not identified) "took him off in the woods" where they killed him "and left him to the mercy of scavengers generally and reported that 'he attempted to escape.'" Charles Moore's death was on the same day, according to Pridgen, and they treated Moore no differently than Bell, apparently meaning they took him into the woods before killing him, and then made the same report that he had attempted to escape. At Russell Jones's house they "tore him from the embrace of his beloved wife and children, and when a little way from the house, gallantly dispatched him in the presence of his crying little ones, who had doubtless followed along in anxious expectation of what would be done." Jones also had "attempted to escape." It was a Friday, July 16, 1869, about 5:00 in the morning, when they dealt their wrath on Russell Jones and Tobias Poole "at their houses."[24] Pridgen was most comfortable in his office, and it was from there that he waged his journalistic war on Jack Helm.

If the Regulators had wanted publicity for their activities they could now be satisfied, as reports of their actions appeared in the *Victoria Advocate* and later in the *Lavaca Commercial* as well as the *Galveston Daily News*. The *Commercial* editorialized that it had learned "from other sources" that the Regulators had killed these men because of their "depredation on the stock of the country." It concluded with an important message, a warning: "Horse stealing and cow-skinning are getting to be dangerous employments in Texas."[25]

In Goliad County today there are no statues or memorials dedicated to Jack Helm, but the state did deem his work worthy of being recognized in the form of a state historical marker, now one of several markers on the lawn of the courthouse. The legend reads, in part:

> Gen. J.J. Reynolds, commander of the Federal forces in Texas, appointed Jack Helm special marshal to the Goliad area in June 1868. A former deputy sheriff of DeWitt County, Helm captained a vigilant band of 50 men, mostly local ranchers, known as the Regulators. Based at Middleton (now Weesatche), these volunteers pursued criminals with vigor and often with cruelty. They ordered known and suspected lawbreakers to leave the state within 10 days. Those who defied the warning were shot without benefit of trial. In 1870 Helm was appointed by Gov. E.J. Davis to the newly formed state police force but was soon discharged for his ruthlessness.[26]

Horse stealing and cow-skinning were getting to be dangerous occupations indeed. Rumors circulated that the Regulators, or Vigilance Committees, from DeWitt and Gonzales Counties had lynched five or six men "supposed to be horse thieves" during the week of July 11-17. A Gonzales correspondent, identified only as "R." [Regulator?] wrote that the rumors or "doings" of the Regulators had formed "the main subject of conversation" wherever he went. Correspondent R. stated that people generally disapproved of such "summary proceedings," which furnished "too much scope to the exercise of personal vengeance." There were rumors circulating that an anti-mob group was to be formed to fight the Regulators. "I should not be surprised at such a turn of matters," he added, "in which case trouble may be expected."[27] In addition, although R. did not state it, two groups of violence-prone men, ready to eradicate each other on the imagined foundation of establishing respect for law and order, would involve members of various families so the war against lawlessness would evolve into a feud which could last for years.

Helm's reputation was growing, but the event that brought greater recognition—and unwanted negative publicity to him in Austin—was the murderous affair at the Choate Ranch in San Patricio County on August 3, 1869, several counties farther south from his home county of DeWitt. "Jack Helm on the War Path!" in bold print is how the *Goliad Guard* headlined its report, following this eye-catching headline with details on the so-called battle between the Regulators and those within the Choate house. Initial reports placed the dead at five men, but in reality only two men died that day: John Choate and his cousin Crockett Choate. In addition, one of Helm's men named Kuykendall was also shot but survived for one day. Two other Regulators were wounded. The Regulators blasted away with shotguns and pistols, severely wounded Francis O. Skidmore, a young man who was visiting the Choate family that day, but he survived. Besides the dead and wounded, the John Choate ranch was "broken up" and the Regulators helped themselves to whatever horses were there to replace their own, or simply to add to their own stables. Indeed the Choate family did pay heavily with the deaths of two of their members,

Francis Osborn "Frank" Skidmore who as a young man, although severely wounded, survived the attack on the Choate Ranch by Helm's Regulators. COURTESY STEVE SCHIWETZ.

not to mention the horses removed from their *caballada*. Helm of course had his particular version of events, denying some accusations but justifying his every move as legitimate.[28]

Helm claimed that the Peace brothers, after having narrowly escaped death at the hands of the Regulators in Goliad County, then went to the ranch of John Choate in San Patricio County for protection. Helm also claimed—although without revealing how he learned this information—the Peace brothers went to inform Choate that the vigilantes were in pursuit. Again, according to Helm, John Choate then went to the ranch of Joseph "Captain Joe" Tumlinson near Yorktown in DeWitt County and informed him that the Peace brothers were at his (Choate's) ranch and that he had loaned them $150, which they would need in their escape to Galveston.

Crockett Choate, who along with his cousin John Choate, was killed during Helm's raid in San Patricio County. COURTESY CHARLES TIPTON.

Presumably once there they would board a steamer and be free of the continued pursuit by the Regulators. Choate then insisted that Tumlinson join him at his ranch, emphasizing that the house was "well fortified" and he could "whip Jack Helm anywhere." Even if this were true, Tumlinson rejected the idea as he believed Jack Helm to be a good man, that he was acting with legal authority and that he (Tumlinson) "intended to co-operate with him." Tumlinson further stated that he considered the Peace brothers to be "murderers and thieves" and that he had hunted them before and would hunt them again. Helm's version suggests that Tumlinson was part of the disguised mob which had killed James S. Stapp.

Helm's report contained remarkable statements, which we must either accept or reject as we have only his word that what he wrote was the honest truth. His lengthy explanation of his actions continued:

> Becoming convinced that Joe Tumlinson was not his man, Choate proceeded to the *rancho* of Creed Taylor, about fifty miles distant, where he remained about three days, when he came to the neighborhood of Yorktown, in company with four or five desperadoes, Hayes [sic] Taylor among the number. Choate now sent word to Tumlinson if he did not join him he would be killed, and that the Yankees had offered twelve hundred dollars reward for him, for the supposed killing of Stapp.

Tumlinson replied that if he had done anything wrong he was willing to surrender to the proper authorities of his county, but would have nothing to do with Choate or any of his gang. Choate replied that Tumlinson would have to "risk the consequences of his folly."[29] Helm then described how Choate had gone to the house of Jim Bell, took the clothing "and other effects" of Chris and Matt Peace and delivered all to his house in San Patricio County.

Texas Pioneer "Captain Joe" Tumlinson, a leader of the DeWitt County Regulators. Along with Jack Helm he waged war on the Taylor party. COURTESY JACK CAFFALL

Apparently Helm had additional knowledge provided him—perhaps from Charles S. Bell, the former Union scout and spy—as he now listed men who were taking shelter at the Choate house. He named the Peaces, Fulcrod,[30] the Broolans, the Doughtys, the Gormans, and the Perrys "and about forty-two others, all known desperadoes, and many having indictments against them for thieving."[31] Helm further described the house, which he could not have done until after the raid there, describing it as "fortified" and "in condition for a regular siege, having look-holes cut on all sides, and secret passages connecting from room to room." Anticipating a siege, Choate, according to Helm's report, had a keg of powder, 500 shotgun cartridges, 200 Spencer rifle cartridges, "preparations for receiving" 500 gallons of water, "provisions, and all that was necessary for conducting a siege fifty days by fifty men."[32]

Helm's statement remains suspect. Journalist Victor M. Rose chose not to express an opinion on this lengthy report from Helm; instead, he wrote: "We shall make no comment on this report, as it is thought most advisable, in telling the 'over-true tale,' to let the actors, as far as it is practicable, speak for themselves."[33] The idea of the Choate ranch fortified with that amount of weaponry seems more like the work of a Nueces Strip rancher preparing for an onslaught from border bandits, such as Captain Richard King did for his ranch, whose defense actually included cannon. One does suspect that Helm's lengthy report was intended to justify his raid against a family who needed to defend itself against marauders such as Jack Helm and his Regulators, not the *banditti* from across the Rio Grande.

Quite likely what Helm did know of the Choate *rancho* was from a freedman who lived on the acreage but not within the main house. Martin Choate was a fifty-year-old black farm laborer from Louisiana with a wife and four children, who before Emancipation was a slave of the Choate family's.[34] If Helm learned of the interior of the house it was probably from talking with Martin Choate. According to a later report by Senator Pridgen, when the Helm party arrived they captured the man who was familiar with the contents of the main house and who was in it at the time. With this knowledge Helm then formed his Regulators in line and asked if there were any Masons among them. There were, and rather than expect them to confront the Choates, whom Helm believed were also Masons, he ordered those men to go and guard the horses. Then Helm picked a "detail of his most trusty and tried marshals and aids [*sic*], to charge the house at daylight in the morning. At the appointed hour they charged the house, yelling and firing like so many savages." This is what Senator Pridgen learned and reported in one of his numerous letters to the *Weekly Austin Republican* newspaper.[35]

Captain Helm claimed to have 125 "of the best citizens of the county" with him when he made the raid. As the first rays of dawn appeared he—believing, or so he claimed, he would be fighting one hundred desperadoes—"proceeded to carry the house by storm." The reality of the Regulators' raid on the Choate ranch was far from what Jack Helm claimed. There was but a handful of people in the Choate house, including family members and visitors, not even close to 100 desperadoes. However many freedmen were there on the property who would take no part in a battle between the ranch owners and Regulators is unknown. If Helm's 125 men had stormed the house the alleged 100 desperadoes within would have carried on a bloody battle lasting several hours. If that number of individuals had met intending to do battle Helm's report of the day's doings would have been drastically different from what appeared in the *Victoria Advocate* and other journals. Instead of the siege Helm had believed the Choates had prepared for, he lost only one man killed—wounded but who died later—and at least one other man wounded. At best the exchange of gunfire would be rightly called a skirmish, hardly a battle. Helm claimed that John Choate "perfidiously" attempted to shoot him after surrendering, and then was killed himself. The fight was over then. Helm claimed to have then made "all preparations for interring the three dead, which was done."[36] What Helm meant was that the two dead were buried "shallow" in their initial graves so that relatives who cared to exhume them and reinter them elsewhere could do the work easily. This was done with the bodies of the Choate cousins, as they are today buried in well-marked graves in the Rockport Cemetery in neighboring Aransas County.

Later Helm learned there were rumors that he and his Regulators had pillaged the Choate ranch, taking what they wanted. "And right here" Helm blustered in his letter of justification, "let me nail to the counter those lies that allege that my men disturbed any of Mrs. Choate's property or the property of anyone else. They did no such thing."[37] This is the result of the Choate ranch raid, the events leading up to it, and to Helm's way of thinking how it ended. The Regulators then moved on toward Beeville in Bee County and then to Oakville in Live Oak County.[38]

Helm's version of events was that his pursuit of the Peace brothers had led him to the Choate ranch and the ensuing battle, leaving John and Crockett Choate dead and at least two men wounded. What Helm never saw is the account of one of the individuals who was in the ranch house when the raid occurred. He was Francis "Frank" Osborn Skidmore, who was severely wounded, but lived to tell about it.

Francis O. Skidmore was a young man apparently on his own in that August of 1869 but he had with him a brother, Charles, five years younger. Francis O. was born in Virginia on November 16, 1849, the son of Samuel C. and Elizabeth Anna Keyser Skidmore. After first moving to Texas in 1857 the family settled on Aransas Creek.[39] In 1877 Frank Skidmore recorded his recollections of that tragic day at the Choate residence. Victor M. Rose included the Skidmore memoir of the day's events in his book *The Texas Vendetta*, to balance Helm's account. Rose, who may have actually solicited Skidmore's report for his history, wished to be fair in his treatment of the controversial incident, stressing that he wanted both sides to be represented. Skidmore's account was in the form of a letter dated August 29, 1877, at Aransas, Bee County. The community of Aransas in Bee County no longer exists, but ironically the town of Skidmore, named after the family, does, in south central Bee County with a population of about 1,000.

Skidmore had frequently stopped at the Choate ranch, he being an "intimate friend" of the Choate family. On the night of August

2 he stopped and he and his younger brother, Charles, were invited to spend the night, which hospitality of course they had expected. Mrs. Choate spoke of three boys within the house but she did not identify who the third one was. Prior to retiring for the evening he and John Choate "conversed much" about the rumors regarding the "high-handed measures" of Jack Helm and his Regulators. The Peace brothers had previously been there, but Choate had sent them on as he did not wish to be accused of harboring fugitives, wanting to avoid any trouble. Choate further made it clear he would fight off any mob which came, but if need be he would surrender to any authorized officer, be he a Federal or State of Texas officer.

Skidmore was aware of who was in the house: Crockett and John Choate, cousins; Skidmore and his younger brother who was fourteen and another youth of the same age; and of course Mrs. Choate. Some freedmen were about the ranch but they had separate quarters, and they took no part in the ensuing firefight. About daybreak Skidmore's sleep—and no doubt the sleep of everyone in the house—ended when the Regulators yelled "Charge!"—taking the house by storm as Helm had expressed the battle cry. Immediately several Regulators stormed into the house.

With such a rude awakening no one should accuse Crockett Choate of first defending himself by shooting one of the Regulators—a man named Kuykendall—and with this show of defiance the Regulators began to seek cover. Kuykendall was severely wounded and was now out of the fight.[40] There were a number of out-buildings, trees, and yard fences behind which the Regulators found some protection. Then Mrs. Choate appeared and addressed Helm. She assured him that her husband would surrender if he—Helm—had the proper authority to make an arrest. Helm responded by saying his authority came from military headquarters—the highest authority in the state. She then informed Helm that there were three boys in the house who had merely stopped for the night, and "they were innocent, and for God's sake not to kill them." Helm told her to have the three boys come out, that they would not be molested. Then Skidmore related what happened next: "When I heard that, I went out on the piazza, and spoke to those who confronted me, and I told them that I would surrender, and without a word of warning they commenced firing on me."[41] Skidmore claimed to have been shot seventeen times, certainly most of which came from a shotgun blast rather than seventeen rifle or six-shooter balls. He then lost consciousness; when he recovered he found himself near a tree in the yard and crawled to it and sat up against it. Even then he was shot at several times. From that position he saw John Choate "receive his first wound."

John Choate had come out of the house when Helm announced he had the proper authority to make the arrest. He left the house, both hands above his head, with Mrs. Choate "a little in advance." Choate said he would surrender but then someone shot, hitting him in the knee. This was his first wound. Mrs. Choate then helped him back into the house. The next time Skidmore saw John Choate the man was dead.

Cousin Crockett Choate made no effort to surrender, apparently realizing what the Regulators' intentions were. When John Choate said he would surrender Crockett ran from the house with his six-shooter in hand. He rushed past Skidmore with "all the crowd following him." Skidmore now took the opportunity to start crawling toward a neighboring Mexican's ranch about a half a mile distant from the Choate residence. Not satisfied with their bloody work, the Regulators pursued the crawling Skidmore and carried him back to the Choate house. There he saw the bodies of John and Crockett Choate. Mrs. Choate was in a state of shock over the tragedy which had just taken place in front of her. She and the young boys could not know what would happen next. Skidmore related what did happen:

> They conducted themselves in an extremely rough and boister-
> ous manner while at the house, appropriating whatever they
> desired, as if they had killed a robber chieftain and had a right
> to appropriate his effects. They left me nothing, not even my
> clothing and pocket change. They stole my saddle, six-shooter,
> and other things of less[er] note.

To show that they were not totally devoid of compassion the Regulators did allow a doctor to come and assist Skidmore in his wounded state. They may have determined he would die anyway with that number of wounds. Dr. E. M. Downs was called and certainly prevented Skidmore from bleeding to death. Helm talked "in a braggadocio style to Dr. Downs, my attending physician."[42] Skidmore, who may have drifted in and out of consciousness, was able to identify only one other in the attacking party: Capt. Joseph Tumlinson. He did not see John Choate fire a weapon, but did see him appeal to Tumlinson as a Mason to save him. This appeal was ignored. As far as Skidmore was concerned he may have wondered at his good fortune; he was miraculously alive, although severely wounded, and as well the other two young boys traveling with him were apparently unscathed. He could not continue however; his wounds were so severe that he was confined to his bed for six weeks, "unable to help myself at all."[43] It is unknown if he remained at the Choate ranch during his recovery period or if Dr. Downs moved him to a convenient home closer to his own residence where he could more easily observe Skidmore's improvement.

Once recovered sufficiently from his numerous wounds Skidmore did not merely forgive and forget. He wanted vengeance, or perhaps justice, and brought suit against Helm and his Regulators in the amount of $100,000 damages for "an attempt to murder." The jury deliberated of course but allowed only the sum of $5,000 in damages. Later, the *Galveston Daily News* editor commented in its review of the incident, that Mr. Skidmore, then an eighteen-year-old boy, "was branding cattle in connection with other stock men, and while at a ranche in San Patricio, Jack Helm and party drove up to them, fired on him, shot him down and kept on firing into him until they had eighteen balls in him. Some of the balls went clean through him, leaving twenty-seven wounds." The editor remarked that he had entirely recovered, and that "he can ride the prairie as well as any man in the country. This is undoubtedly a remarkable recovery."[44]

Catherine A. "Kate" Dickey Choate, the much younger wife of John Choate, was now in early August 1869 a widow. She was the daughter of W.C. and Harriett Dickey, and had been born in Arkansas in 1842.[45] In June 1870 she was residing with her parents in Refugio, perhaps in town, as her father was then working as a brick mason; her mother was "without occupation" but certainly keeping house as most wives did in the 1870s when they had no other occupation. Kate Choate was then twenty-six years of age. She and John C. [Crockett?] Choate had been married on May 15, 1865. On August 21, 1870, she cast aside her widow's weeds and married a man named Warren Wallace who ultimately gave her five children.[46]

The two Choates were initially buried shallow on the ranch, John under a mesquite tree and Crockett nearby. Sometime later the Refugio Lodge of Free and Accepted Masons elected to "assist" in the "funeral obsequies" of the Choates.[47] On October 15 members of the Refugio Lodge undertook the task of removing the bodies from their initial burial place and reinterring them at the

Rockport Cemetery.[48] Their graves today are easily found as they have large above-ground tombs with their names and appropriate inscription engraved on the lids. Helm, in order to give a sense of propriety to the whole affair, stated he made arrangements for the burial of the Choates.[49] He probably also arranged to have the wounded Kuykendall moved to his home in Goliad County.

The deaths of the Choates may have given Helm, Tumlinson, and the Regulators some satisfaction but they could not rest. More importantly there were fugitives with a price on their heads which now attracted Helm; no rewards had been offered for the Choates, either alive or dead, which suggests they were not such desperadoes as Jack Helm and his Regulators believed.

4

Action in Matagorda County

"If you Can give me a squad of 10 men and a territory of about 10 Counties I will soon show the Citizens law and order fully restored."
—**Sheriff Jack Helm, to Governor E.J. Davis, June 14, 1870**

FOLLOWING THE CHOATE RANCH RAID, the Regulators returned to their homes to check on their ranches and stock and give their horses a needed rest. The raid had taken place on August 3, 1869; nine days later Helm was ready to move again against suspected desperadoes. Helm began this new venture on August 12 at Joe Tumlinson's ranch, only a few miles west of Yorktown, where he was joined by a Sergeant Shea and a Private Tom with about fifty

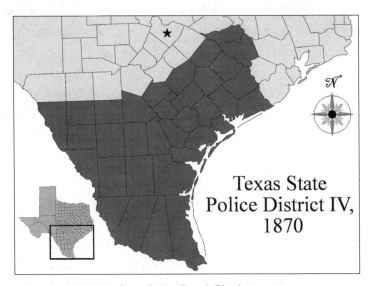

Captain J.J. Helm's State Police Fourth District. Map by Charles D. Grear.

citizens. This large group left the ranch at dark and proceeded to the Presidio in Goliad County. Some twenty miles from Yorktown Charles S. Bell, well-known Union army scout with a group of men, joined the Helm group. Bell traveled with Helm for two days and expressed "great Satisfaction" and complimented his men "very highly." After conferring with Bell, Helm left the group and headed for Austin, although for what purpose is not known. Some of those men left with Bell. Helm remained in camp and now was joined by some thirty more citizens. This large group, numbering between fifty and seventy citizens, left camp at dark and traveled through the night where they again made camp, now on the Coleto Creek in Victoria County. More citizens now joined the group; Helm and his small army proceeded to the forks of the Guadalupe and San Antonio Rivers where Helm "expected a fight having been notified of some desperate men being there fortified but they had left," which must have disappointed him and those many citizens greatly. All was not a wasted effort however, as Helm did arrest several men whom he delivered to authorities. Although Helm did not identify them by name he did say they were "men of bad principal [sic] and very dangerous men to be at large . . . I have very grave charges to make against them." He would make out the proper paper work when he reached Helena where he would turn them over to the military. He concluded his letter indicating he was then in search of the Taylors—brothers Hays and "Doboy"—wanted for the murder of Major John A. Thompson at Mason.[1]

Helm may have been aware of another charge against Hays Taylor, which apparently had not been considered brutal enough for the state to offer a reward. Taylor and companion Joseph Clarke were suspects in the killing of Private Samuel Hargus of Company "K," 7th U.S. (Black) troops, on the road to Indianola.

The single Texas State historical marker that carries the name of Jack Helm is situated on the grounds of the Goliad County Courthouse. Erected in 1978 the legend reads in part: "Gen. J.J. Reynolds, commander of the Federal Forces, appointed Jack Helm Special Marshal to the Goliad area in 1868. A former deputy sheriff of DeWitt County, Helm captained a vigilante band of 50 men, mostly local ranchers, known as the Regulators."

AUTHOR'S PHOTO

The killing and theft of his horses was believed to have happened on August 31, 1866.[2] Assuredly Hays Taylor was a wanted man, but the rewards had been posted for his capture due to the killing of Major Thompson and another soldier.

Helm's search for the Taylors may have been done because it was legally and morally right, although we have little indication Helm did things for altruistic reasons. In truth, Jack Helm and his Regulators now began looking for fugitives from justice with large rewards offered. Three such fugitives were John Hays Taylor, his brother Phillip Goodbread "Doboy" Taylor, both sons of Creed Taylor, and Randolph "Ran" Spencer. They were supposedly within

Helm's "jurisdiction" and each one carried a reward of $500 for his delivery, dead or alive, to the proper authorities.[3]

Helm and his men had gone into Goliad County searching for this trio, who had killed two men of the military in Mason back in 1867. The official report indicated Major Thompson was "murdered by the three desperadoes named while attempting to quell an altercation between them and a party of soldiers. The desperadoes escaped."[4] It was understood that Helm had "been commissioned by Gen. Reynolds to apprehend certain parties" who had so far successfully "eluded all military efforts and stratagems to capture them." Helm had met with DeWitt County Sheriff George W. Jacobs on the third of July to make plans to capture the fugitives. Nothing was accomplished in locating the Taylor-Spencer trio in spite of their careful planning. Although they had fled the country, Helm had somehow learned that they were willing to be tried by a civil tribunal but not by the military—they fearing a military trial would result in a death sentence. Having failed in their mission to capture either of the Taylors or Spencer, Helm—"instead of wasting his time with them"—continued to work in Goliad County.[5]

Helm wanted to give the impression he was not concerned with the Taylor-Spencer trio, thus giving C.S. Bell free rein to apprehend them. This remained partly true as the pair at times worked together but it was Bell who succeeded in catching up with the Taylors. On Wednesday, August 18, 1869, he and his posse numbering twenty-five citizens of the Yorktown area along with two military men, a Sergeant Curtis and one unidentified man of the 4th Cavalry, began the hunt, hoping to either capture or kill them. Another fugitive was with them, Henry Westfall, or so Bell believed. By the evening of August 21 he and his command were encamped in a dense thicket near Campbell's ranch above Helena. During the daylight hours of Sunday, August 22, he scouted the countryside near Creed Taylor's ranch, twelve miles further north. Bell worked alone in this scout, trusting no one else, as "past experience having taught me that secrets cannot be kept by Texas people."[6] During that night Bell moved his group closer to thickets in Taylor's pasture, a mere half-mile from his house. He then managed to surround the house without being detected. Once all were in place Bell called out to Creed Taylor to come out and talk. He indicated that he believed the boys, Hays and Doboy, were in the house, but Creed denied that they were. Bell accepted that they were not there but suspected they would be coming home soon. He was right in that regard, and at sunrise they approached. Bell summarized what happened next: "Soon after sunrise—while a heavy fog hung over the earth—and my men completely concealed lay in the weeds—was heard the tramp of advancing horsemen. I gave orders to my men to not fire till my rifle first broke silence."[7] The horsemen were Hays and Doboy Taylor and a third rider, identified as Henry Westfall, all heavily armed with shotguns and revolvers. Strangely the trio somehow suspected danger and attempted to fire, but Bell fired first. "I shot Dobe Taylor through the shoulder and his arm dangled at his side" Bell related. His shot, breaking the morning silence, brought a barrage of gunfire from the others, "from every quarter, a withering fire" as Bell expressed it. The trio then fled, "pierced with numerous wounds." With Bell and his men in pursuit, Hays Taylor fell from his horse about 200 yards from the house, dead with numerous bullet wounds. Further on the posse found a dead horse, and then two more wounded horses, but neither Doboy Taylor nor Henry Westfall were found.

Not giving up hope, Bell continued on and by noon had captured the wounded Westfall, the other Taylor having escaped. Bell could not help but feel a degree of admiration for Westfall, "wounded in three places—although his wounds must prove mortal, he had ran, *on foot*, over a mile. Such tenacity of life is remarkable." With Hays Taylor dead and his brother Doboy on the run Bell was exuberant. Doboy was seen two miles from "the scene of action with a broken shoulder, and *spitting blood*." Bell was confident he could capture the wounded Taylor later in the day. There were certainly others with Hays and Doboy who barely missed the August 23 gunfight that resulted in the death of Hays Taylor. The *Austin Republican* reported that an unstated number "of the Taylor gang, who escaped after its fight with Capt. Bell . . . passed through Austin Wednesday night of last week at midnight [the 25th], all well mounted and armed. They were traveling eastward."[8]

Bell ordered the group to move the dead Taylor into the house of his father and place it in a passageway. He then had the grieving father delivered as a prisoner to Helena, describing him as "the worst living man in this country," certainly an unbelievable statement with no basis in fact. Further, Bell stated that Creed Taylor's life had been "one of robbery and murder." Bell recommended Taylor be held "for further action" apparently determining the fact that he could have charged the man with aiding and abetting fugitives not sufficient. Bell concluded his lengthy report stating that he had one casualty in the battle, that Charles Maddox had been slightly wounded, having been shot in the leg by Hays Taylor. Bell thought then that "there would be a space of peace throughout the region, now that the Taylors have been crushed."[9]

In case Captain Morse may have wondered what Jack Helm was doing at this time Bell added, as a postscript, "Helm has been operating to the northward for several days past—I do not know what he is doing but that he has about a hundred men and is hunting horse and cattle thieves. He wished to turn over his entire command to me on the 18th but I declined to accept—desiring to capture the Taylors." Bell wrote this informative report to Captain Morse on Monday August 23. On the same day he prepared a brief report to General J.J. Reynolds asking him to do him a favor, the favor having to do with the reward. He first pointed out: "I killed Hays Taylor yesterday morning and wounded Doboy so badly that I hope to take him today." He then explained he had sent Creed Taylor to Helena but would deliver him to Austin "under grave charges a week or so hence." He never itemized those grave charges in a written report.

Bell was asking Reynolds to inform Governor Pease that for his killing Hays Taylor he was claiming the state reward, and that he would deliver the proper papers within a few days, upon his arrival in Austin. Again not forgetting Jack Helm, Bell pointed out to Reynolds that Helm was "to the northward" and he (Bell) would submit a report of his operations on his arrival in Austin. Bell was obviously aware that Helm was already derelict in informing his superiors of his action.[10] Bell also intended to receive the entire reward for the Taylors.

Creed Taylor, in mourning for his son and jailed in Helena apparently without any charges yet filed against him, may have dreamed of revenge against Charles S. Bell and all who worked with him. He later stated that "Hays Taylor was buried on the Eclato [sic] near my old home in Wilson County." If his grave was ever marked its location has since been lost. Bell, as Taylor expressed it, got the blood money "for the killing of my son but it burned his hands so bad that he left Texas immediately to escape the righteous vengeance of the Taylors." Creed Taylor claimed Bell had received the $1,000 reward, but Helm, "claimed to have originated the enterprise and expected a division of the spoils." It is not known if Helm actually received any of the reward offered for the capture of the Taylors or Spencer. It is doubtful, but Creed Taylor was in error when he spoke of Bell receiving the $1,000 reward. Actually the reward offered for each of the trio was only $500, per Governor E.M. Pease's reward notice of October 1868. The $500 reward was to be paid even if the man was killed, which was the case with Hays Taylor.[11]

Creed Taylor suspected that Bell wisely left Texas, ultimately continuing his career in the eastern states.[12] Taylor believed Helm, once back from his doings "northward," went to Goliad County "under the pretext to catch cow thieves, which was merely an excuse, since the sheriff of that county and his deputies could have arrested the parties so charged any day in the week." Taylor was aware of the deaths of Jones, Poole, and Purcell and the severe wounding of George Blackburn, "shot and left for dead"[13] and was aware that their deaths at the hands of Helm and the Regulators were unnecessary.

C.S. Bell was not through with his efforts at ridding the country of the other Taylor and others whom he considered outlaws. On August 26, only days after the successful hunt for Hays Taylor, he was at military headquarters in Austin and urged authorities at Bastrop and LaGrange to arrest Doboy Taylor, James Cook, and George Callison. He noted that Taylor was "wounded in the right arm near the shoulder" while Callison had a scar on the neck, the "result of a gunshot wound received long since."[14] Bell believed the trio were heading for some point in north Texas and would have to cross the Colorado River on their way.[15] After leaving Austin, Bell continued the pursuit, tracing them to Coryell County, "where they evidently divided and took to the brush, and escaped."[16] He never did catch up with Doboy Taylor but did later capture Randolph Spencer who was with the Taylor brothers when they killed Major Thompson in Mason.

A correspondent, identified only as "Subscriber," identified Helm's work—no doubt with tongue in cheek—writing that five or six men had "suddenly taken off" but he knew not what caused their death or "what particular ailment they had." Those who had come to a "sudden end" were rumored to have "borne rather unenviable characters." Subscriber could only hope that "henceforth and forever" everyone would respect the law.[17] Certainly there had been a number of men who had "suddenly taken off" and the Goliad County mortality schedule reveals their names. Edwards S. Roberts, census enumerator for the county and thus also obligated to prepare the county mortality schedule, added his comment in the remarks column of the form: "shot by vigilantes." Most were stock raisers. A.K. Jones, forty-eight years old, was shot in July; Reuben Purcell, twenty-seven, was shot in August; two blacks—Frank Banks, twenty-six, and Louis Moore, twenty-two, had been shot in January, suggesting the Regulators—or at least a group acting in that capacity—had been active prior to the summer action of Helm. John "Kurkendal" of the Choate Ranch raid, as Roberts spelled the name, was thirty-four years old and was "shot by vigilantes" causing one to suspect that he had lost his life due to "friendly fire"; James C. Bell and Charles Morse had been shot down in June. Of course the sheriff was also listed, identified as Jackson Jacobs, fifty years old, married, and who had lost his life due to being "Murdered."[18]

Little is known of this Regulator whose wounds may have been accidentally inflicted by his companions. In 1860 John M. Kuykendall resided in Goliad County, Texas born, twenty-four years of age, with a wife and daughter. Some reports stated Kuykendall was killed at the Choate Ranch in San Patricio County, but his name does not appear on that county's mortality schedule. The name John "Kurkendal" does appear in the Goliad County Mortality Schedule, indicating that although he died in Goliad County he was the man wounded in San Patricio County.

Roberts gave his age as thirty-four which would be correct for the man being twenty-four in 1860.[19] Apparently the wounded Kuykendall was placed in a convenient wagon—probably belonging to the Choates—and then transported to his home in Goliad where he soon died. The seats of the two counties were only a good day's ride apart.

Over the next few weeks Helm became conscious of reports criticizing what we would today term his leadership style. He had killed too many men in his campaign against lawbreakers; many had been arrested but never delivered to the proper authorities. The complaints that he merely murdered prisoners—"Helmized" them—and then claimed they had tried to escape, which in Helm's mind justified their being killed, so common in 1869, would follow him throughout his career. The complaints were not ignored. Helm, or someone in military headquarters who acted to provide a positive interpretation to negative actions, prepared for publication what would be called "spin" in terms of modern journalism. This apologia, then termed a "card," first appeared in the *Victoria Advocate* and was then reprinted in numerous newspapers across the country, including the influential *Galveston Daily News*, one of the state's most popular journals. The Galveston publication headlined its report: "Leader of the Regulators." Was Helm himself aware of such criticism and was bothered by it, or was it his superiors in Austin who found his actions troubling and decided to do something about it? Most likely a clerk at the office of the Fifth Military District prepared the announcement, rather than Helm himself sitting down at a desk to compose it, although Helm certainly had the mental acuity to prepare such a defense of his actions. It appeared in the *Victoria Advocate* of August 19, 1869, and the *Galveston Daily News* of August 24 and the *Dallas Times Herald* of the same date. *Flake's Daily Bulletin* of Galveston of August 26 addressed the card "To the Citizens of Western Texas," and there were certainly other newspapers, giving Helm state-wide notoriety. Helm was referred to in the third person singular as the leader of the Regulators, suggesting it was written by someone else, with no additional or explanatory comment provided. Newspaper editors knew full well such a statement from Jack Helm would be of great interest to their readers.

The report is printed in full, as it reveals what the Regulators believed was their duty. First there is blame placed on the media, a tactic not uncommon even in the twenty-first century by those who resent what actions might be reported in a negative manner. Helm believed his purposes had been wrongly presented to the public. The first paragraph is the attempt to justify his actions.

> As an erroneous impression has, through the misrepresentations of certain journals of the State, gotten abroad, respecting Jack Helm and those co-operating with him to arrest and bring to justice thieves and desperadoes who have been holding high carnival for years in our midst, I take this opportunity of saying to the people that Jack Helm is acting under the highest authority in the State, (orders from Military Headquarters.) He seeks to molest no one. To the honest, law abiding citizens he offers protection. For those thieves who have been depredating upon the stock interests of the country with impunity, he has orders to arrest and bring them to justice. That this will be done, and effectually done, there is no doubt.

Here the writer pauses and blames further the legal system for allowing such lawlessness to prevail. He now attempts to bring in everyone who respects the law to follow his way of thinking, whether stock raiser or not.

Fellow citizens, this is the last resort.[20] Grand juries have failed to accuse, and the law has been impotent to convict in multitudes of cases. As citizens of the country, we are interested in the suppression of crime, whether we are stock raisers or not. That you will respond with alacrity to assist me, I ask no further guarantee for the future than your conduct in the past.

And finally, he assures the public that he and his men are lawful, that no one can rightfully complain of his actions. And above all, he is acting not for monetary gain but for altruistic reasons; knowing the righteousness of his work will be sufficient reward for all his efforts.

My men are kept under control, and no citizen can complain of the least injury at our hands. I labor for the supremacy of the law, without compensation or reward; and when the robbers are brought to justice, the majesty of the law vindicated—when honesty and industry can receive the fruits of their labors, I will be repaid for all, in the knowledge that I have done my duty.

Hoping, fellow citizens, that you will now understand me, I subscribe myself your obedient servant, JACK HELM. [21]

The unknowing newcomer, the stranger to the area who was totally unaware of the events that had recently occurred in several counties around DeWitt, Goliad, and San Patricio, might accept totally the content of the apologia as presented above the name of Jack Helm. This statement from Helm was not limited to Texas as due to various newspapers having "exchanges" it received national attention. In Louisville, Kentucky, the influential *Courier-Journal* noted: "Jack Helm's party in Texas seem[s] to hold full sway, and the military and civil authorities alike powerless to check his lawless career." Commented Alfred Horatio Belo, the editor of the

Galveston Daily News: "Jack Helm's party are acting under orders from the military authorities—at least he has so published it in a 'card'."[22] Apparently editor Belo had doubts about under whose authority Helm was working.

R.T. Davis, the editor of the *Goliad Guard*, had a high opinion of the man Helm, contrary to those who considered Helm the leader of a "party," which overpowered military and civil authorities. Mr. Davis claimed that "Helm's party" was "composed of the best citizens of the county" and that Helm was "only endeavoring, by authority of the law, to bring to justice those outlaws and thieves whose audacity has become such that the whole country between the Guadalupe and Nueces has been, in a manner [of speaking], given up to them for two years past."[23]

Only days following this justification of Helm's actions, Charles A. Wikoff, Captain of the 11th Infantry then stationed in Columbus, the county seat of Colorado County, sent to Capt. Charles E. Morse copies of documents between Lavaca County Judge A.K. Foster and Helm, "the Leader of a Band of Regulators." Captain Wikoff requested that he be given the same authority "under which Said Helm is acting."[24] Apparently word of whatever successes Helm was having in running down alleged thieves and desperadoes was common knowledge; others now wanted to do the same with the same authority given to Helm. Morse's response has not been preserved, but Helm's name was becoming well known in the region.

The year 1869 was an election year, and as November approached many county officials determined there was a need for dealing with potential troubles at the polling places. Frequently ruffians would attempt to forcibly prevent certain parties, mainly freedmen, from voting to determine the outcome of an election. One such concerned citizen was Mathew Kreisle, the thirty-nine-year-old Wurtemburg-born judge of Goliad County. General J.J. Reynolds had appointed Kreisle to the position as judge; thus it was evident that he had been loyal to the Union cause.[25] His concern now was that unless troops were sent to his community to remain during registration and voting, "there will be trouble." He was convinced that already "the rebel party" was "resorting to low and dirty Schemes to Elect their men." This certainly caused General Reynolds to consider sending troops to Goliad County, but what may have been the final reason was Kreisle's following statement: "[F]urthermore many of the lawless and abandoned characters, who fled to avoid Helm, have returned—Gave Bond for their appearance at the District Court." Kreisle obviously had little faith in the county sheriff or deputies, believing the number of "lawless and abandoned characters" would outnumber those sworn to uphold the law. He feared those who had fled before Helm would return and they would be there during registration and the election "to Commit further Outrages, intimidate freedmen, mexicans [sic], and Other ignorant harmless persons."[26] Whether General Reynolds responded to Kreisle's request is not known.

A mystery surrounds the death of two men, both considered by the authorities as members of the "Taylor gang": Martin Luther Taylor, son of Rufus and Elizabeth Lowe Taylor and nephew of Creed Taylor, and his father-in-law William B. "Dave" Morris. There was no mystery as to when they were killed, November 23, 1869, "killed while attempting to escape" but by whom?[27] Not only does their slaying remain controversial, but also the manner of their "taking off." That both were killed the same day at the same time and place is beyond question, but was it Helm and his Regulators? Or was it Capt. Joe Tumlinson who apparently now had his own regulators? Or was it some other group who took the two prisoners from C.S. Bell and killed them, or a combination of the above?

Jack Hays Day, a Taylor relative and sympathizer, wrote that following the Choate ranch raid in August there was "no quenching the Sutton gang's thirst for Taylor blood." He wrote that Martin Taylor had settled on a ranch between Tilden and Oakville in McMullen County. Captain Tumlinson, whom he describes as "an old member of the [Sutton] gang" led a posse to where W.B. Morris lived, a quarter of a mile from Taylor's.[28] First arresting Morris— "Tying him on his horse"—they then proceeded to Taylor's and arrested him also. Taylor, knowing what was about to transpire, begged Helm not to kill him there as his wife was in bed with a young baby and the action would "frighten her to death." The Regulators then carried Taylor and Morris "into the woods and shot [them] down like dogs."[29] Day wrote that a "hired negro" had seen and overheard what had transpired and "stricken with terror" informed neighbors who then found the bodies.[30] This is what Jack Hays Day remembered, writing about what he had heard had happened some sixty years after the fact, in 1936. Another version which has as much credence is that Mrs. Taylor, after the posse had left with her husband and father, "rode horseback at full speed to the nearest ranch headquarters to get aid" but arrived too late and only found the bodies, "riddled with bullets."[31]

Historian James Smallwood follows Day in part, that Joe Tumlinson, while C.S. Bell was "on the chase" for Doboy Taylor, learned where Martin Taylor and Morris were and managed to arrest them both. Tumlinson had six men with him; Taylor "resisted violently" and while the posse was dealing with him Morris attempted to escape. "During the gunfight members of the posse killed both men." The word "gunfight" implies both sides had weapons. As prisoners they were certainly disarmed immediately; they no longer had their weapons. Taylor and Morris were simply murdered, under arrest and while prisoners.[32]

Perhaps most significantly is the statement of historians Karen Holliday Tanner and John D. Tanner Jr. who wrote of the early days of McMullen County. The Tanners wrote that Jack Helm "led a party of the Sutton faction to the McMullen County ranch of William B. Morris on San Miguel creek. . . . Morris and . . . Taylor were taken at gunpoint with the alleged intention of placing Taylor in the Oakville jail. . . . Near Callaham, in Live Oak County, Taylor and Morris were murdered and buried where they fell."[33]

Where was Jack Helm? If C.S. Bell was "on the chase" and Tumlinson was leading a small group of Regulators in McMullen County, where indeed was Helm? There is evidence that he was part of the group with Tumlinson. At the trial of Bill Taylor for his part in the killing of Sutton and Slaughter in Indianola in March of 1874, a reporter attempted to provide a brief history of the Sutton-Taylor Feud, although he had to accept basically whatever he was told from his interviewees. In spite of the somewhat confused chronology, he indicated that Martin Taylor "was killed by a party with whom Jack Helm was," although no mention was made of Tumlinson. This report does place Helm at the death of Taylor and Morris.[34] In C.S. Bell's lengthy report to Capt. Charles E. Morse written from Laredo, Texas, on November 28, 1869, Bell described how he had been searching for various desperadoes believed to be hiding out between San Antonio and the Rio Grande, actually a huge amount of territory. He identified several he hoped to locate: Jim Wright, Bill Thompson (brother of the more noted Ben Thompson), "Buck" Roland, Jim Hamilton, Jim Henderson, as well as Doboy Taylor and the Peace brothers. He somehow learned that Doboy Taylor was in the vicinity of Oakville in Live Oak County. His "supposition strengthened" when he learned that Doboy Taylor's cousin Martin Taylor was in the area where he was then located. Bell determined to find Martin Taylor and Morris and "examine" them. Bell did not mention anyone with him except Henry Ragland who acted as his interpreter and Jim Cox who acted as his guide. They both had been with Bell "on long and dangerous expeditions in the past and I felt sure of success." According to Bell, Martin Taylor was considered "by his neighbors as a very *dangerous* man." He had been indicted in DeWitt County two years previously for assault with intent to murder. Further, Martin Taylor, along with Hays and Doboy Taylor, had stolen a large number of cattle from the area earlier that year. Others who had been involved in the theft included Ed Glover and one Jack Wright, or so C.S. Bell believed and stated. During Bell's sojourn he stopped at the house of a man identified only as Hill. Amazingly, while there, with Cox and Ragland, Taylor and Morris rode up to within twenty yards of the house. Bell, Ragland, and Cox "rushed out with cocked pieces, and demanded an immediate surrender." With his two prisoners Bell now intended to deliver the pair to Pleasanton in Atascosa County where he could turn them over to military authorities. The charges he would prefer against them included "being members of the Taylor clan," cattle stealing and in Martin Taylor's case, an assault to murder. Bell, with Ragland and Cox, with only the two prisoners in ropes or shackles, should have no difficulty in delivering them to Pleasanton, some fifty miles north. Bell's plans were foiled however, and he did not deliver anyone to the authorities. He explained what happened, which somehow does not ring totally true at all.

My plans were, however, frustrated by a most lamentable occurrence. We had proceeded . . . and were on the Oakville and Frio road, about twenty miles west of Oakville, when suddenly we met a dozen or more armed men. The moon being partially obscured by clouds, I could not distinguish their features, but instinctively I divined their object. I placed myself in front of my prisoners, who seemed also to apprehend the worst, for they instantly turned to run. Preferring that they should escape, rather than be killed by a mob, I endeavored to check the progress of the latter; but they dashed past me with savage oaths, and commenced rapidly firing their weapons. In return for my opposition *I was struck over the head*, and nearly knocked off my horse. I then desisted, feeling that resistance was useless. I was then ordered by a man, who seemed to be the leader, to leave and say nothing, that good people appreciated my actions, but safety demanded the death of such men as I had captured.

This is how C.S. Bell described the incident to his superior, but losing Taylor and Morris was not all. As he rode on with Cox and Ragland he "heard several shots out on the prairie, which would indicate that one of the prisoners had thus far escaped. One had fallen at the first fire." The trio of luckless man-hunters then continued, apparently with little regard to the fate of their two now dead prisoners, not going back to examine their wounds or report their deaths to the county authorities. In truth both Taylor and Morris had "fallen" as both were shot to death, no different from how Helm had numerous times left bodies of his victims for wild animals.

Bell stated he regretted that his prisoners were killed, but concluded: "that while I deeply regret that the prisoners . . . should have been taken from me in so unjustifiable and lawless a manner, I cannot excuse myself of any dereliction of duty, for I ran some personal risk in opposing the mob, [receiving] a severe blow upon the head at the hands of one of them goes to show." He had a final comment: "I can only surmise that the people who lived in the vicinity of the unfortunate men, exasperated . . . rose, as by one consent, and destroyed them. I cannot, however, resist any impulse to condemn their cowardice in thus avenging themselves upon unarmed and helpless prisoners, who, whatever their crimes, were under the protection of an officer of the government responsible for their safety."

Unfortunately we cannot now determine with certainty the identity of the half dozen men who killed the two prisoners. Bell does state that he was unable to recognize any of them, due to the clouds obscuring the moon, but somehow this does not ring true. Helm and Tumlinson were often together in their actions of ridding alleged thieves and murderers, and quite likely they were among the mob. Bell may have cooperated fully with them, yet justifying his action to Captain Morse that he was simply overpowered resisting the mob. In sum, two more desperate men, in the eyes of the authorities, had been killed.[35] What did happen, although it remains impossible to prove, was that Taylor and Morris were Helmized, and now, in theory at least, the citizens of the San Miguel could feel safer. Had Helm now produced another "card" justifying why and how Taylor and Morris were killed, the double homicide would no longer be a mystery. The only newspaper report of the incident yet discovered remains this brief item in the *Daily Herald* of San Antonio, headlined: "Killing on the San Miguel."

> Two men, Taylor and Morris, were killed on the San Miguel a few days ago by an unknown mob of men. The two were charged by their neighbors with various crimes, such as stealing cattle, hogs, &c., and there being no redress by the laws of the State, mob law was resorted to.[36]

Interesting that there being "no redress" mob law was accepted; the charges of their neighbors were accepted as well to determine their guilt.

Definitely the November elections could be the site of trouble in numerous Texas counties. Ruffians could prevent Republicans from voting; could deny freedmen voting privileges; could simply take over the polls and make the idea of a secret ballot a laughing stock. In case there were questions as to the legitimacy of Helm and his actions there was an election in DeWitt County in November 30, 1869. Enough voters believed in Helm to retain

{[4.]

OATH OF OFFICE.

I, _Jack Helm_ , do solemnly swear (or affirm) that I will faithfully and impartially discharge and perform all duties incumbent on me as _Sheriff of De Witt County_ according to the best of my skill and ability; and that I will support the Constitution and laws of the United States and of this State. And I do further swear (or affirm) that since the acceptance of this Constitution by the Congress of the United States, I, being a citizen of this State, have not fought a duel with deadly weapons, or committed an assault upon any person with deadly weapons, or sent or accepted a challenge to fight a duel with deadly weapons, or acted as second in fighting a duel, or knowingly aided or assisted any one thus offending, either within this State or out of it; and that my disability to hold office under the 14th Amendment to the Constitution of the United States has been removed by Act of Congress; and further, that I am a qualified elector in this State.

Jack Helm

SWORN and subscribed to before me this _27th_ day of _April_ , 1870.

Willis Fawcett
Clerk of DWC.

While a captain in the State Police, Jack Helm also served as sheriff of DeWitt County. His oath of office is now preserved in the Texas State Archives. AUTHOR'S COLLECTION.

him in office. The electors also voted for William Griffen, Clerk of District Court; Oliver K. Tuton, Justice of Precinct No. 1; James D. Edgar, Justice of Precinct No. 2; Little Berry Wright, Justice of Precinct No. 3; Ferdinand Ploeger, Justice of Precinct No. 4 and William Byers, Justice of Precinct No. 5.[37] Several of these men would play a part in the growing conflict between the Taylor family and followers of William M. Sutton.

By the end of 1869 Helm must have been aware of the plans to develop state forces to deal with the lawlessness across Texas. A militia group was to deal with problems on the frontier, such as Indian raiding parties, and a police force would deal with internal problems, such as feuding families and outlaws. Men who had experienced the war could be candidates; there was a need for men with leadership skills and who had supported the Union.

Helm was still the sheriff of DeWitt County, not yet a captain in the police force, where he would be awarded his captaincy. On June 14, 1870, he wrote to His Excellency Governor E.J. Davis, who had been in office only since January 8 of that year, and responded to his letter asking him to report any "items of interest" that might come to his observation. This of course was in response to the call for each Texas sheriff to report a list of murderers at large so the governor's office would know as well as each sheriff. Helm reported that on June 4 there was "a very outrageous murder committed" in DeWitt County, one of "the best freedmen" had been killed. The cause of the killing was not known nor the identity of the murderer known, but Helm thought he would be able to work up clues in the case. He had just sent in a report of all the murders committed in DeWitt County to the chairman of the Committee of the State Militia. But more importantly Jack Helm wished to communicate a "certain matter" which he felt was of "a great delicacy" in doing so, but he felt it his duty. The matter was in reference to Charles S. Bell, the well-known Union scout. Helm claimed that "Several of the Best Citizens of Texas" were "constantly writing" to him inquiring about Bell, and stated that he was "passing through the country under different names and Collecting money under false pretense representing himself as an agent for certain publishing establishments." According to Helm's report Bell had not kept any of the promises he had made to these individuals, and the friends who had provided money had not received any payment. Helm's accusation was not clear, but he made it clear enough that even though he had worked with Bell, how long not stated, he did not wish to work with him any more "until he claires [sic] him self of Such Charges." Helm claimed he did not wish to "bring any reproach on my self and other good men." Bell's conduct, according to Helm, was "doing a great injury to the Cause." One must surmise what Helm exactly meant by the term "the Cause"; not clarifying if it meant his version of law and order or something else.[38]

That concern with Bell was but one important item in Helm's letter to the executive. But there was more and perhaps what he concluded his letter with resulted in his being chosen to become a captain in the State Police. Helm wrote of there being "several men" killed near Victoria, in neighboring Victoria County. He had seen the sheriff of neighboring Calhoun County regarding a murder at coastal Indianola, and apparently in Helm's understanding nothing was being done to apprehend the murderers. He did have an idea, however, which he wished to share: "I am just waiting for orders to raise a squad of about 10 men for the purpose of upsetting some of their Calculations. I think if we had something of the kind to help the civil officers that we would soon have peace but I tell you the Civil alone is not Sufficient a bout one man in fifty will help and that is a bout the way of the state at large and I know as well as any one could know for I have worked almost all over the State and we must have law at all events."

Law at all events?

Helm was not through with this effort to advise the governor on how to improve the lawless situation: if he would give him "a squad of ten men and a territory of about 10 counties" to work in, he assured the state's top executive, "I will Soon show the Citizens law and order fully restored." If nothing else, Jack Helm had confidence in his abilities. In that moment of hubris in what he could do he signed his letter as "Your most humble Servant Jack Helm Sheriff of DeWitt [C]ounty."[39] Was this Helm's manner of indicating he was the man qualified for the position of police captain?

Helm obviously had worked with Charles S. Bell, but apparently prior to the pair joining forces Bell had conducted himself in a manner that cast suspicion upon him. Davis responded to Helm's accusations by inquiring as to who had given these reports to him. On June 26, 1870, Helm reported, saying the men included James Cox of DeWitt County, and James Crawford, also of DeWitt County. Cox, according to Helm's description of him was "a good man and has always been a friend to Bell." Crawford, his brother-in-law, was also a good man. Helm did not know how they had obtained their information. He also said he had received a letter signed "Citizens of Dallas" inquiring of Bell's character. He had received other reports as well but was concluding that they were "raised by bad men." He was "very anxious" for Bell to clear his name of such serious charges and had, with Bell, "encountered difficulty and hardships" that had caused them to be "almost like brothers." Jack Helm was now ready to say at any time and to anyone that he believed C.S. Bell to be "a gentleman and strictly honest."[40]

Helm and Bell may at one time have had a high regard for each other but in spite of Helm's praise of his "almost like brothers" partner that warm feeling would soon cool. C.S. Bell, according to the rumor, had been killed in DeWitt County following a gunfight. The news from Clinton was reported to the press in the form of a letter to the editor of the *Galveston Daily News*, written by someone identifying himself only as "Clinton," written on June 7. Headlined "Killing of C.S. Bell" in bold the report stated that the "quiet little village" of Clinton had been "plunged" into the "greatest excitement" with the news. Bell, identified as a "United States Scout," had been attacked by five men in the Guadalupe River bottom some two miles below Clinton. The body had not yet been found, but a black man who had seen the gunfight delivered the news to Sheriff Helm. The sheriff gathered a posse; the group followed the witness to the scene of the alleged crime.

What was found was a "bloody trail" and indications that "a heavy body had been dragged" and in following the trail it led to the banks of the Guadalupe "where the body had evidently been thrown in." The group returned to the original spot where three other trails were found. The horse tracks and blood drops were followed until the trails were all lost. This group did find a silver-handled Navy revolver with "C.S. Bell, Scout" engraved, with five cartridges having been "freshly discharged." This proved to be the only evidence that the missing corpse may have been the scout. The black man who had led the posse to the scene claimed to have witnessed the fight, but had seen it from a distance. He claimed one man was shot off his horse and then five men rode off, leading the fallen man's horse. As they passed near the witness he observed three of them "wounded and bleeding." When the witness approached the wounded man he looked up and then saw two more men coming, which frightened him. Fearful of what might happen to him he ran into the river bottom and hid. He managed to get to Clinton to give the alarm.[41]

Unfortunately, the posse never found anything other than the revolver, and had that really been Bell's possession, or was the entire incident a fabrication? The gunfight supposedly had taken place on June 6. People almost immediately began to doubt that Bell was even involved, although someone may have been killed and his body never found. C.S. Bell himself certainly was not the victim as he soon appeared on the streets of Austin, very much alive. Apparently no one interviewed Bell as to the recent happening as no explanation was forthcoming about what had happened on the Guadalupe River near Clinton. Col. John L. Haynes did decide to contribute a letter to the *State Gazette*, published in the issue of June 20, relating some disturbing news. Colonel Haynes was a respected citizen of Texas even though he had—during the recent war—commanded the Second Texas Cavalry, a Union command from Confederate Texas. He had been an officer in Governor E.J. Davis's First Texas Cavalry, then promoted to colonel of the Second Texas Cavalry in 1863. In addition he had earlier served in the Mexican War.[42] Haynes declared that Bell had stated to him that he and Jack Helm had killed *thirty-one men*, instead of the reported nineteen, in their eradication of suspected horse and cattle thieves. The *Galveston Daily News* and the *San Antonio Herald* both headlined the news "Horrible Murders" but no follow up was printed to add additional information regarding this strange incident. Certainly Sheriff Helm and C.S. Bell were developing a reputation for violence.[43] This incident provided a reason to further criticize the leadership of Governor Davis for working with such men as C.S. Bell and Jack Helm. "Is it any wonder that the barbed arrows of a guilty conscience follow him?" queried the

Herald editor. He continued: "What does this say for a people that have submitted to such treatment as this and without the show of open resistance?" But this was not enough as the *Herald* editor continued: "But there is a higher court before which Jack Helm and C.S. Bell must be judged, and Edmund the I. will not appoint the Judge who sits on that occasion, and from the sentence there will be no appeal." With such editorials as this the name of E.J. Davis was becoming that of a tyrant.[44]

With the new decade beginning, it was time for the 1870 Federal census. Assistant marshal Willis Fawcett enumerated the citizens of DeWitt County, at least those available at the time of his visit to the house. At Jack Helm's place he learned the head of household was not only the sheriff but was farming as well. It was probably Mrs. Helm—Margaret Virginia, née Crawford—who told Fawcett that her husband was a native of Texas (not Missouri as the previous census recorded), and was thirty years of age, suggesting a birth year of about 1840. She was a year younger than her husband, was keeping house, and was a native of Tennessee. While the sheriff of DeWitt County was out enforcing the law and pursuing horse and cattle thieves he had an Ireland-born laborer identified as William Williams to till the soil and tend to the livestock.[45] The paper trail created by Jack Helm suggests the farming was left mainly to laborer Williams, as Helm was now active in putting down what in his mind amounted to lawlessness over a large territory. In addition to the request from Lavaca County for him to assist in destroying gangs of thieves, newly elected Governor E.J. Davis and Adjutant General James Davidson were now finalizing plans for the organization that became the Texas State Police. Following the war's end the amount of violence, white upon black, black upon white, as well as white upon white and occasionally black upon black, was considered a staggering amount, not to

mention the occasional raiding party of Indians intent on stealing livestock and taking captives or scalps. Under the leadership
of Governor Davis the legislature provided funding for both a state
police force as well as a state militia. Governor Davis appointed
Adj. Gen. James H. Davidson as Chief of the Texas State Police;
he was responsible for promulgating the rules and regulations of
the force.[46]

The eastern portion of the state was divided into four districts,
districts identified as I, II, and III to be overseen by a captain. Each
captain was to have under him two lieutenants, five sergeants,
and fifty-six privates. The fourth district, to which Helm would be
assigned, located in the lower Texas counties, was to be overseen by
one captain, one lieutenant, and five privates. Two other portions
of the state were the El Paso district and the Presidio sub-district,
which was overseen by one lieutenant and five privates. Four
men were selected to be the first captains: Edward M. Alexander
of Clarkesville in Red River County; John J. Helm of Concrete
in DeWitt County; Leander H. McNelly of Burton in Washington County; and Mordecai P. Hunnicutt[47] of Waco in McLennan
County. Each man took an oath to uphold the laws of the state
and the constitution.

Helm must have read and signed an oath but if so it has not
survived. Below is the oath that each captain swore to. It reads as
follows, the words in brackets showing the blank line in the form:

> I, [J.J. Helm] do solemnly swear, or affirm, that I will faithfully and
> impartially discharge and perform all duties incumbent on me as
> [Captain], according to the best of my skill and ability, and that I
> will support the Constitution and laws of the United States and of
> this State. And I do further swear, or affirm, that since the accep-
> tance of this Constitution by the Congress of the United States,

I, being a citizen of this State, have not fought a duel with deadly weapons, or committed an assault upon any person with deadly weapons, or acted as second in fighting a duel, or knowingly aided or assisted anyone thus offending, either within this State or out of it; that I am not disqualified from holding office under the Fourteenth Amendment of the Constitution of the United States; (or, as the case may be, my disability to hold office under the Fourteenth Amendment to the Constitution of the United States has been removed by an act of Congress) and, further, that I am a qualified elector in this State.[48]

Just what selection techniques Davis and Davidson utilized in choosing the men who made up the force is uncertain, including how they selected the captains. The backgrounds of Helm, Alexander, Hunnicutt, and McNelly varied greatly. Helm had been a Confederate but then after desertion made himself into a fervent Unionist, while McNelly remained a Confederate throughout the war and had risen to the rank of captain within the Rebel army. Influential men convinced the governor that McNelly, although a Confederate, would be a wise choice for captaincy. The backgrounds of Hunnicutt and Alexander are relatively unknown. Davidson selected Helm because of the enthusiasm the citizens of Lavaca County had for him. By the time the Texas State Police force was formed Helm already had a reputation of dealing harshly with desperadoes but as yet no documentation has been found which would indicate that Helm had actively petitioned Davidson for a position as police captain.

The adjutant general reportedly had "much difficulty" in securing the services of "reliable, energetic and efficient men" and because of this was "compelled" to be "guided by the recommendations of parties of well-known loyalty and good standing."

He selected men who had "courage and nerve," qualities which were "absolutely essential in a police officer"; Davidson assured his superior since "many of the criminals in the State are persons of known desperate character" he (Davidson) always satisfied himself that the men he recommended possessed those qualities. These were admirable intentions. Davidson stated that since many crimes originated in gambling halls it would be in the best interest of the state to get rid of gambling establishments; this he believed would have the "hearty co-operation of all good citizens in the State." Further, carrying a deadly weapon was to be "in all places and under all circumstances" prohibited; and carrying such a deadly weapon should be made a "penitentiary offense." The exception of course would be in those counties on the extreme edge of the frontier.[49]

By the time Helm was appointed captain of the State Police he and Bell had a sizeable reputation. Willis Fawcett, clerk of the DeWitt County Court, belatedly prepared the paperwork indicating Helm was officially the DeWitt County sheriff on April 27, 1870. It was not received in Austin until May 11, 1870. Helm, as sheriff, was legitimately considered the leader of the Regulators, men whose avowed purpose was to destroy those who they believed were stock thieves and murderers. If C.S. Bell had been in Austin endeavoring to receive a captaincy in the State Police force he would be disappointed.

In addition to having a consistent paycheck and considerable authority, Helm had, as the other captains, a regular base of operations. This amounted to their residence, but was called a station. For Jack Helm his station was Concrete in DeWitt County, then in 1870 a thriving community with a two-story church building, a boarding school called the Concrete College, a post office and numerous businesses and dwellings. It was the oldest community in DeWitt County but today nothing remains of its existence; there is a highway sign alerting the traveler as to where it once had been. To assist Helm, he had James W. Cox, Christopher Columbus Simmons, Richard B. Hudson, Henry Leftage *alias* Booth, Joseph Tumlinson, Oliver H. Bennett, and J.B. Taylor (not of the Creed Taylor family). These men, all white except Henry Leftage whose real name was Booth according to census taker Willis Fawcett, were known associates of Helm before his captaincy, but citizens generally considered them deputies.[50] Helm may have used Leftage if there was a problem in the black section of DeWitt County. It is unknown if he did in fact associate much with him.

The work of Helm and his Regulators was not limited to the area of DeWitt, Lavaca, Goliad and San Patricio Counties. Cattle and horse thieves were active down in Abel Head "Shanghai" Pierce's neighborhood, Wharton, Jackson and Matagorda Counties on the banks of the Tres Palacios River, and on the coast.[51] Thieves stole and killed thousands of head, simply for the sale of their hides, the sale usually at the important port of Indianola in Calhoun County. In this area of the Texas coast Pierce had the influence, if not the amount of ranchland acreage of cattle baron Richard King in South Texas, to call on the governor and to expect results. Did cattleman Pierce appeal to the governor for help in combating cattle thieves, which appeal caused Governor Davis to send Helm there to restore order, or did Helm decide to "clean up" Matagorda County on his own? The county was one of those which would be placed within his district. The answer is uncertain, but by mid-June—a few weeks prior to his being officially a State Police captain—he and some Regulators were there. How many of Helm's men were from the DeWitt County area is also uncertain, as the available reports indicate only "a squad of citizens" had "laudably engaged in ridding the country of brigands and murderers" but failed to identify Helm as

Wharton County cattleman Abel Head "Shanghai" Pierce as he appeared in the 1870s.
COURTESY THE ROBERT G. MCCUBBIN COLLECTION

the leader.[52] One historian wrote that Capt. Joe Tumlinson was there "doggedly riding the range in search of suspicious characters"[53] and most often where Helm was there "Captain Joe" Tumlinson was as well. Helm failed to prepare detailed reports of his actions but from his sparse communications to the Adjutant General which had been summarized by his secretary we do learn at least something of his official conduct. These official records and newspaper accounts from unidentified reporters, known only by their *nom de plume*, do provide a valuable picture of the situation in the Matagorda County area in 1869 and 1870.

Helm did not do history any favors by leaving a sparse paper trail. Once he became active in the Texas State Police his actions were better recorded, although much of what he did was illegal. He quickly developed a reputation as a killer of men, causing his name to become the blackest spot on the record of the Texas State Police. Notwithstanding, he did make many arrests which did not result in a homicide. The arrest record shows he was an active policeman from the beginning. On July 18, only days after the force became a reality, Helm arrested two men in DeWitt County: William M. Moore and Jacob Johnson—the latter for assault with intent to kill—and turned them over to the county sheriff.[54] Johnson was Jacob C. Johnson who in 1871 would drive cattle up the trail to Abilene, Kansas. One of the drovers was John Wesley Hardin who soon would become a fugitive in Helm's police district. Johnson later became a good friend of Luke Short of Tombstone and Dodge City gambling fame and later as a turfman and boxing promoter.[55]

Helm wrote a letter to his superior on August 9 reporting he had been "investigating the Lunn murder cases," describing his having "a conversation with W.W. Lunn an accomplice who was mortally wounded."[56] In a follow-up letter written ten days later Helm indicated he had "sent a party to arrest the Lunn gang" but we do not know how much time had elapsed from the actual sending of the party to the communication of August 19.[57] But the Lunn gang had been essentially wiped out weeks before this, at least the principal members. Jack Helm was certainly there although we know little of his direct action in eradicating the Lunns. An item in Austin's *Daily State Journal* reported that Helm, "who was ordered, with a detachment, to Matagorda, has returned." Evidently Captain Helm had reported to Adjutant General Davidson in person, reporting that the Lunn gang had been "dispersed, and left the country." The gang had been killing stolen cattle at the rate of one hundred per day, simply for their hides. Helm had counted 1,014 dead cattle. When reporting, W.W. Lunn "one of the gang, who is badly wounded, acknowledges to having assisted in killing three men, one of who they robbed."[58]

If Helm made a detailed report of his actions in destroying the Lunns from beginning to end it has not survived, but fortunately an individual who signed his contributions, combining the two words identifying the local creek—Tres Palacios—into his *nom de plume*, as "Trespalacios," provided details on what Helm accomplished. Matagorda County in 1870 had a population of nearly 3,400 people, consisting of 1,912 blacks, presumably mostly former slaves, and 1,491 whites, according to the census enumerated by John Kemp, a black man who obviously was well educated.[59] As assistant marshal for the 1870 census one of those families Kemp enumerated on "Wilson's Creek & Tres Palacios"[60] was that of twenty-three-year-old stock raiser William Lunn. Enumerator Kemp noted his real estate was valued at $3,000 and his personal estate valued at $8,000, making Lunn an individual certainly well off. Within the household were his siblings: Annie E., twenty-two and keeping house, Benjamin, twenty-five and occupation given as "Doctor," Edwin, also raising stock, and younger sisters Mary

L., seventeen and Martha E., fifteen, both "at home." Who provided the information was not indicated but in reality it was William Wilburn Lunn who was the doctor, not brother Benjamin.[61] By reputation the Lunns were cattle thieves who operated a lucrative thieving business throughout numerous Gulf Coast counties. The Lunns and their men "had become very bold and reckless in their horse and cattle stealing, defying the laws and they were also strongly suspected of having committed one or two murders," wrote Trespalacios.

According to this correspondent, since the end of the war, numerous men and boys living on the Tres Palacios River and vicinity had been "preying" on the cattle of Matagorda and Jackson Counties, and on the horses "of a much wider range." Thousands of cattle were stolen and killed for the hides, which were then bundled up and shipped to Indianola on the Karankawa (or Carancahua) and Tres Palacios Rivers where they would be sold. The thieves were confident in their operation, so confident that they bragged they would kill eight thousand head that year. Perhaps Trespalacios was one of the "solid and respectable men . . . armed and equipped" who went to the "temporary headquarters" of the Lunns at Newel's Grove near the Jackson-Matagorda County line. There, with no apparent difficulty, the group "arrested and hung on the cross tree of the cow pen gate" three men. The three victims were identified as Benny Lunn (real name Benjamin Vastine Lunn), twenty-six years old, his brother Edwin DeMoss "Eddy" Lunn, nineteen, and John B.M. Smith, thirty years of age. Benjamin "Benny" Lunn was fifteen as of the 1860 census; Edwin was twelve during the same census so by 1870 they were hardened young men. Trespalacios perhaps knew the trio as he gave their ages, and also knew that the Lunn brothers were single men but that Smith had a wife and children who lived on the Colorado

River "16 miles above the town of Matagorda." The correct identity of John Smith is harder to confirm; we suspect he was the John Smith of the 1860 census, which records him as thirty years of age, although Trespalacios states he was thirty at the time of his death a decade later. It is suspected that this John Smith was the man who lost his life with the Lunns as his household was number 57 in 1860; that of the Lunn family was household number 55.[62] Further, he claimed he knew the Lunns were born there on the Tres Palacios River, and that their mother "was also born within a few yards of the place where her sons were hung."[63] Her parents had been among Austin's "first coast colonists." The reporter also took time to add his thoughts on what would happen, pointing out that the "fate of these young men is sad, but they had no right to expect better." Another brother, William Lunn, enumerated as William W. in the 1860 census, was wanted but he could not be found. Trespalacios concluded that perhaps he had already met his fate or was hiding out in the brush.[64]

Fortunately, Trespalacios did not conclude his reporting at that point, as on the next day, June 24, he wrote a second report to Galveston newspaper editor Ferdinand Flake. Flake headlined this communication in bold with "The War on the Cattle Thieves"— suggesting the action was taking place over a considerable period of time—giving the report prominence on page three, column one. He reported that on the twenty-third of June, some citizens, with no mention of who the leader was, surrounded a house on Jennings' Creek belonging to a black man named Joe Grimes. One report described him as "a negro, a desperate villain." Following the execution of the Lunns, some of the men "came upon" a cabin near Elliott's ferry where one of the gang was found. Regulator Edward Anderson of Wharton approached the house and called for the inmates to come out. Joe Grimes responded that he would be out in a moment as he first had to get dressed, but he did not exit peacefully. Within moments he thrust a double-barreled shotgun through the window and opened fire, killing Anderson instantly. This did not deter the vigilantes from their intended duty, as they quickly retaliated by shooting Grimes to death. There was no honor shown freedman Joe Grimes in spite of his courageous act of bravely resisting to the end, as the soul of Grimes "quit its earthly tenement by fourteen bullet holes, which penetrated his vile carcass," or so it was reported. The Regulators took the body of Anderson to a nearby church yard on the Tres Palacios and buried it, no doubt with appropriate remarks, on Friday, June 25. Again Trespalacios was inspired to provide a moral lesson following this incident: "Love of gain and the impossibility of punishing criminals in this county" he wrote, "are the principal causes of our demoralization; and it had become a question whether the robbers or the honest citizens should hold the country. I think, however, the worst throes of this disease are over, but you must not be astonished to hear, now and then, of a hanging."[65] It was only the day before that he had concluded his report: "Allow a boy to take up and brand what are called in the vernacular 'stray yearlings', and his career will terminate at the end of a rope, or some other dishonorable fate."[66]

Reporter Trespalacios was also concerned about how the public may perceive the character of Gulf Coast citizens. He hoped that "people at a distance" would not believe politics had anything to do with the troubles in Matagorda, Jackson, and Wharton Counties. As if to reinforce the notion politics had nothing to do with the situation, he assured his readers that the Lunns "were all ardent Confederates, hated a Yankee like a viper, and thought it no moral wrong to kill a nigger; and all of the known members and sympathizers of the gang . . . were at all times violent Confederates."[67]

Who were the Lunns? In 1860 the family consisted of head of household Josiah John Lunn Jr., a fifty-seven-year-old farmer born in Pennsylvania, his wife Sarah Matilda, née Keller, thirty-eight and born in Mississippi, and their six children.[68] The family then lived in Deming's Bridge, a small settlement located in the western part of Matagorda County.[69] In the 1860s there was no bridge to easily cross the Tres Palacios Creek. Edwin A. Deming commissioned W.A. Dawdy to erect a bridge "that would accommodate foot traffic as well as horse and buggy passage." The post office was established in 1858 with Edwin A. Deming the first postmaster. Later Deming's Bridge was discontinued when the name was changed to Hawley.[70] The 1870 Matagorda County census placed the Lunn household as living on Wilson's Creek and Tres Palacios.[71] At least one historian has suggested that the Lunn men earlier worked for cattle baron Shanghai Pierce, but then decided to branch out on their own.[72] The operation against the Lunns may have been the reason for Pierce to head for a safer clime. At an earlier time he had started his own herds gathering mavericks and animals that already had a brand. The idea of him having to appear in court to answer charges was perhaps the reason that with the execution of the Lunns, Pierce decided it was time to travel north to Kansas City or St. Louis.[73]

The Texas press, in reporting the results of the Lunn operation, provided considerable attention to the Regulator action, and articles about the gang's activities were even discussed in the eastern press. One gave it broad coverage: "Outlaws in Texas" headlined one lengthy report reprinted in an East Coast journal, which appeared with the sub-headline: "Whole Counties Ravaged, and Citizens Intimidated by Thieves and Murderers." According to this report the gang of outlaws had been operating for "some year or more last past" and operating on the Tres Palacios Creek, west of the Colorado

River. In their boldness they defied everyone, even writing a letter to the Matagorda County sheriff that he would be shot on sight for having accused the letter writer of having in his possession a stolen horse. So intimidating was the gang that no one dared to interfere. The gang had erected large pens in a secluded spot where they herded and slaughtered the cattle stolen from others. It was believed two freedmen had "perished at their hands" and two white men had been murdered and robbed, and their bodies sunk in the coastal waters by means of an old stove attached to their corpses.

The illegal actions of the Lunns were not secret by any means. William Prissick, a veteran of the Army of the Republic, an abolitionist who actively supported the Union during the Civil War, and who was a chief justice in Matagorda County, and who then won election as a Radical Republican to represent Brazoria, Galveston, and Matagorda Counties in the House of the 12th District, was well aware of what was happening in his area. That he knew the people he represented is unquestioned. He claimed that Peter McMahon, a twenty-six-year-old white man, had been murdered by the Lunns when he threatened to inform the authorities of their cattle-stealing operation; further, the two freedmen killed were in reality a black child and then later the child's older brother, both killed back in 1866. An additional violent act of the Lunns was the house burning of a man identified only as "Hasbroak" but whose proper name was Robert A. Hasbrook.[74] These actions of the Lunns created fear within the citizens of Matagorda County, to the extent that they "dared not move against the cattle and horse stealers for fear of being killed, or of having their house burnt down like Hasbroak [sic]."[75]

The Regulators were "a large body of armed men" who gathered at the "den of these outlaws" and captured one and chased down two others on the prairie. They were the ringleaders, carried to the "principal scene of their criminal exploits" and after confessing were "hung to the gate of the pen." Their identity of the victims was given as two brothers named Lunn and one John Smith.

The Regulators estimated there were at least 250 men engaged in the brigandage, operating in five or six counties "whose citizens had suffered from villainies of these notorious prowlers." Estimates of their "depredations" extended as far north as Austin and Washington Counties to Gonzales County in the west "and perhaps further."[76]

The contemporary newspapers reported that three men were lynched in addition to the gang member who killed Anderson being shot to death. Historian Chris Emmett wrote that five men were hung, the three Lunns, "All Jaw" Smith and a stranger whose identity was never determined.[77]

Trespalacios failed to mention Helm by name in his reports, identifying only those who lost their lives. Jack Helm was in charge of this operation, but perhaps the men he led were from the Matagorda and Jackson Counties area, not from his general area of DeWitt County, with the possible exception of Joe Tumlinson. The contemporary press provides a single newspaper item placing Helm there. Austin's *Daily State Journal*, the official publication of the E.J. Davis administration, printed a report on the doings of the State Police in August, which detailed some of Helm's actions:

> Capt. Helm, of the State Police, who was ordered, with a detachment, to Matagorda, has returned. The Captain reports to the Chief of Police that the Lum [sic] gang has been dispersed, and left the country. They had been killing stolen cattle, at the rate of one hundred per day, for their hides. Capt. Helm says he counted one thousand and fourteen dead carcasses, which had been killed for their hides. W.W. Lum [sic], one of the gang, who

is badly wounded, acknowledges to having assisted in killing three men, one of whom they robbed.[78]

Would not the stench of "one thousand and fourteen dead carcasses," the number supposedly killed in a two-week period, be overpowering? His claim certainly remains suspect.

On July 17, Columbus C. Moore, a forty-year-old Jackson County farmer from Tennessee with a wife and children,[79] sent a communication to Davidson from Morales, today a ghost town in the northwest corner of the county. He informed the adjutant general that Ed and Ben Lunn and J.W. Smith were hung by a mob, and three others were shot to death by the same vigilantes. A freedman was killed by another mob in nearby Texana; in all *sixteen men* were killed by mob action.[80] Further, but not related by Trespalacios, one of the gang, William W. Lunn, was "badly wounded" and

"Creed Taylor Springs near his residence" is how this photograph was identified. It shows a typical home on the frontier, perhaps in the early 1870s. None of the men and women are identified but the figure in the foreground is clearly Creed Taylor. Perhaps Taylor's sons, Hays and "Doboy" are among the figures. COURTESY THE ROBERT G. McCUBBIN COLLECTION.

acknowledged "to have assisted in killing three men, one of whom they robbed."[81] An additional report, possibly by Trespalacios but identified only as coming from someone in Jackson County, stated that "all is quiet, and the people intend to assist the civil authorities in maintaining the peace."[82]

Certainly after Helm's work in Matagorda County—with somewhere between three and sixteen men slaughtered by the Regulators—things were quiet, but not all the newspaper correspondents and citizens were totally satisfied with what Helm had accomplished. A reader who identified himself as D.E.E. Brama read the above-mentioned report in the August 14 issue of the *Daily State Journal* and responded, writing to the *Flake's Bulletin* editor. Reader Brama was dissatisfied with the reports coming from Matagorda County, and attempted to clarify the situation. "As false and malicious representations have been made public through the instrumentality of certain Matagorda county letter writers," he wrote, "concerning the affairs above spoken of by Capt. Helm, with an evil intent, I therefore beg that you will insert this letter in your widely circulated Bulletin, that such wickedness may be thwarted in its designs."[83] Mr. Brama failed to identify any particular letter writer of the county, but certainly the letters of "Trespalacios" gave Matagorda County a reputation of lawlessness.

5

◦—◦—◦

Feuding Against the Taylors

"Jack Helm . . . is on the war path again."
—**"Hidden Hand,"** in *Flake's Daily Bulletin,* **September 28, 1870.**

AS BOTH JOHN JACKSON HELM and to a lesser degree Charles S. Bell became deeply involved in the conflict today known as the Sutton-Taylor Feud, it is necessary to describe in brief the incident that brought them into the troubles. Creed Taylor had two sons, Philip Goodbread Taylor, known as "Doboy," and his brother John Hays Taylor, but always referred to as Hays, his name reflecting the respect his father had for Ranger Captain John Coffee "Jack" Hays. On November 14, 1867, the Taylor brothers and their brother-in-law Randolph W. Spencer, known commonly as "Ran," were at Mason, a community in the Texas Hill Country. A mile from the center of town was Fort Mason, and that is where the difficulty began with an argument between the Taylors and several soldiers. The argument led to gunplay resulting in the deaths of Major John A. Thompson and his sergeant, John McDougall. Initial reports indicated that Thompson was out riding with his wife and two children not far from J.B. Ranck's general store, which was on the town square. He observed the difficulty taking place and halted the vehicle in order for his accompanying sergeant to investigate and perhaps have the civilians arrested. What words were said is unknown but the civilians resisted arrest and drew their weapons. Major Thompson was shot through the head; Sergeant McDougall received a wound, which in a short time proved to be mortal.[1]

The trio, quickly identified by the military as "murderers" ran to their horses nearby and "fled before any attempt for their arrest could be made."[2] Later details emerged that underscore the confusion of the initial reports. In contrast, other reports placed Major Thompson inside the Ranck general store when "he was called upon to quell the disturbance which was brewing between some drunken soldiers and the Taylor boys."[3] In this version of events, Thompson indicated that after his investigation of the trouble he would determine if his soldiers were guilty and if so would punish them. But that was to no avail as the resistance of the Taylors and Spencer brought about the deaths of the two men. He may have drawn his six-shooter but both were killed before any damage was done to the civilians.[4] There were rumors that the civilian trio had been "hanging around" the fort with the intention of robbing the soldiers on pay day, and that they "at last crowned their villainy by murdering a Union officer." The trio became fugitives and substantial rewards were offered for their capture, dead or alive, although those words were not expressly stated on the reward notices. At Washington, D.C., Secretary of War John M. Schofield authorized a reward of $1,000 for the "apprehension" of the trio, or $333.33 per man.[5] Texas Governor E.M. Pease later increased the reward to $500 for each of the three, the reward to be paid upon the arrest and delivery of each to the commanding officer at Austin or San Antonio.[6] A form was prepared which began "Mr [space left blank] is authorized to arrest . . ." which may have been prepared to be issued to any number of "detectives" or "scouts," such as Jack Helm or Charles S. Bell.

Creed Taylor's version of what happened that November day in 1867 was quite different when he recalled, through John Warren Hunter,[7] that he and his sons Hays and Doboy, were at Mason for a horse race. At the Ranck store were "quite a crowd of soldiers"; some were drinking and "several were under the influence." Major Thompson was in the store as well, "chatting with Mr. Ranck and others." A "drunken soldier" began insulting Hays Taylor, even though Hays attempted to avoid any problem. The soldier called Hays a "G-d d-nd liar" which brought about a quick response: Hays grabbed the soldier by the collar with one hand and his knife in the other and demanded a retraction. The soldier attempted to draw his revolver but couldn't as the flap on the scabbard was buttoned down securely. Other soldiers now gathered around, but Doboy and Ran Spencer "with drawn pistols swore they would shoot the man" who drew a weapon. Doboy knocked down one soldier trying to draw his revolver.

By now Major Thompson was aware of the ruckus and began to leave the store, but Mr. Ranck and others urged him not to interfere. But he did and commanded "the boys" to surrender, meaning the three civilians. They responded: "Hold up major; we haven't hurt anybody very bad and what we have done was in self defense." Thompson then drew his revolver and opened fire, even though Hays called to him three times to "Hold up." Thompson ignored him as Hays Taylor raised his pistol and shot the major between the eyes. The sergeant now "made an effort to shoot Hays" but Hays was quicker and killed him. Thus, according to Creed Taylor's version, is how Hays Taylor killed both Major Thompson and Sergeant McDougall. To Creed Taylor, the father of two of the boys, it was simply a case of self-defense. Creed Taylor was fully aware of what brought about the double killing: "This unfortunate affair was doubtless traceable to the effects of whisky," he noted. "Had those soldiers been sober there would have been no trouble." He concluded: "I taught my sons, by precept and example to avoid whisky as they would a rattlesnake and to resent an injury or an insult without parley. This drunken soldier lit the flame that consumed many valuable lives and swept from my grasp the earnings of a lifetime's toil."[8]

The trio was now labeled as murderers; two men of the U.S. Army lay dead on the street of Mason. According to Creed Taylor, although not an eyewitness, Hays was the one who had killed them both, his aim being good that day. But Doboy and Ran were with him so all three became wanted men. In Creed Taylor's view, and understandably so, his sons and Spencer had unjustly been made fugitives. To him they had only defended themselves from the drunken soldiers. Adding to the problem General J.J. Reynolds who "lorded it in Austin" as commander of the Fifth Military District, now "made his infamous rule, every means calculated to humble the pride of the rebel was employed." The Taylors were declared to be outlaws and due to the happening at Fort Mason they were "placed under the ban of his displeasure and he included in his edict of extermination, all the Taylors from the Rio Grande to the Sabine [River],"[9] in other words, all the Taylors of South Texas. The Taylors now became the hunted; Jack Helm and C.S. Bell and the Regulators now the hunters.

Earlier that year Jack Helm had taken the field at the head of fifty men with a U.S. sergeant in full uniform. From the time of the Mason tragedy for months to come Helm and Bell became leading figures in the war against the Taylors; in the mind of Helm and Bell and the military the Taylors symbolized the lawless element in Texas. Helm received considerable negative criticism for his work and conduct in combating lawlessness. He knew full well that the three fugitives would not surrender peacefully, and was aware that the reward stated that if the fugitive "should be killed in resisting an arrest by lawful authority" then a like reward upon presentation of satisfactory proof of the fugitive's identity would be paid. In the mind of Helm and perhaps anyone reading the reward notice, that statement meant the $500 reward would be paid, dead or alive. This notice included others: Jim Wright charged with the murder of a black male at La Vernia in Wilson County in the autumn of 1867; and one Pinson, charged with the murder of John Trimble on the Rio Hondo. During this Reconstruction period there were many others who resisted the policies of the Fifth Military District as well as the general laws of Texas.

The violent action of the Regulators under Jack Helm as evidenced at the Choate Ranch and the reporting of Trespalacios received wide coverage in the Texas press. Following the Matagorda County action against the Lunns, Jack Helm next appeared in Gonzales, county seat of Gonzales County, the "cradle of Texas liberty," in July. The State Police bill had passed and Helm had his captaincy, although he had not yet filled the ranks of his force; he would be allowed one lieutenant and five privates, which seems a small amount of manpower indeed for the number of counties of which he would be in charge. His fearful reputation—in certain quarters—may have caused some problem in his recruitment. Gonzales had seen violence since the days before the Alamo but perhaps by 1870 citizens considered the county relatively peaceful. W. D. Cook, editor and proprietor of the *Gonzales Southwestern Index*, conversed with Helm about the situation, but whether Helm visited the *Index* office or whether the editor sought him out for an interview is unknown. Whichever was the case, Helm had an opportunity to announce his intentions, as he had not yet completed filling his force.

Editor Cook pointed out to Helm that he viewed with "utter abhorrence" the State Police law which Helm was now responsible for enforcing. But Helm "assured us that he would receive but good men." Besides his assurance that his men would be "good," his men would be "selected from all the counties of his district, not exceeding two or three from any one county." He intended to interview "old citizens of known probity for information" where he was not "personally acquainted." He assured the readers he would not receive any man who had been indicted or anyone who did not have the business capacity to make a report, "hence the ranks will not be filled with ignorant negroes [sic]." *Index* editor Cook assured Helm he apprehended no danger of resistance "so long as this force conforms its operations to the letter of the law in carrying out its ostensible designs." But, continued Cook, if Helm's force used its power "to oppress the innocent, or for purposes of private revenge, as such organizations have been used in other States, no one can answer for the consequences."[10]

The State Police force never did reach its full capacity, and one might suggest that the four initial captains had set their requirements too high. When complete the ranks would consist of the initial four captains: Helm, L.H. McNelly, M. P. Hunnicutt, and E.M. Alexander. The captains would receive $125.00 per month. There would be eight lieutenants, receiving $100 per month; twenty sergeants, to receive $75 per month and 225 "members" or privates, to receive $60 per month.[11] In addition there were "Specials," police who could work only in the county they resided in and would not receive payment for their services. The advantage of being a special policeman was that he could legally carry weapons. The state was divided into four districts: Hunnicutt, First District with headquarters in Waco, McLennan County; Alexander, Second District with headquarters in Clarksville, Red River County; McNelly, Third District with headquarters in Burton, Washington County; and Fourth District with Helm having headquarters in Concrete in DeWitt County.[12] Helm was in charge of thirty-four counties: Atascosa, Austin, Bee, Calhoun, Cameron, Colorado,

DeWitt, Dimmit, Duval, Encinal, Fayette, Frio, Goliad, Gonzales, Hidalgo, Jackson, Karnes, La Salle, Lavaca, Live Oak, McMullen, Matagorda, Maverick, Nueces, Refugio, San Patricio, Starr, Victoria, Washington, Webb, Wharton, Wilson, Zapata, and Zavala.[13]

Jack Helm was a man most comfortable in the saddle leading a group to capture fugitives from justice. But as captain of a police force with thirty-four counties to concern himself with he had to devote some time to paperwork, preparing reports, getting his mail, and dealing with it. The administrative matters began as soon as he was appointed captain. Governor E.J. Davis appointed James H. Davidson as Chief of the State Police as well as head of the State Militia.[14] Whether Helm received more communications from Austin than the other captains, due to the lawlessness in the Fourth District, is unknown, nor how often the captain picked up his mail in those years prior to instant communication, is also unknown. In his correspondence dated July 21 addressed to Captain Helm at Clinton, Davidson informed him he was sending—via George Kerlicks—a list of names of murderers, who they had killed, their probable whereabouts, names of witnesses, "and all necessary information to lead to their arrest and trial." Helm was to arrest or cause them to be arrested and have them delivered to the proper authorities. That would give Captain Helm plenty of work and even if only partially successful give positive publicity to Helm and the police force. That Davidson chose George Kerlicks to deliver these documents to Helm seems reckless. Presumably Kerlicks had been in Austin where he felt safe, as during the previous October he was involved in a shooting frenzy that cost the lives of Texas pioneer Captain Henry Gonzalvo Woods, a DeWitt County deputy named Edward Faust, and two members of his own family: William Kerlicks, and Christopher Kerlicks Sr. Five members altogether of the Kerlicks family were suspected of killing H.G. Woods and Deputy Faust, George being one of them. Now he was being a courier for the adjutant general to deliver important documents to Captain Helm in DeWitt County. George Kerlicks was by occupation a freighter. That Davidson depended on him to deliver those important documents safely indicates he was a trusted man.[15] Presumably Helm did receive the documents but it is unknown whose names were on the list, although it is likely that the name of John Kerlicks, George's own brother, was one.[16]

Nine days later, on the twenty-eighth of July, Davidson sent another letter to Captain Helm in which he ordered him to "arrest" James W. Cox and Joseph Tumlinson and "convey [them] to this office."[17] These two men were already demonstrating their enmity to the Taylor clan, and as followers of William M. Sutton would be considered leaders of the forces against them. Why did Davidson want to see this pair of policemen, presumably a conference which would have required the presence of Captain Helm as well? James W. Cox had been commissioned as a private in Helm's Fourth District on July 13, 1870, but was removed on February 13, 1871, for an unspecified reason.[18] Tumlinson was also commissioned as a private on July 13 but was discharged on April 30, 1871.[19] The feuding between the Taylors and their enemies—led by William M. Sutton—was becoming more of a concern to the administration every day.[20] The two families considered DeWitt County as their homes resulting in what has become known as the Sutton-Taylor Feud, but could be just as properly be termed the DeWitt County Feud. James W. Cox would be shot to death in mid-1873 while Tumlinson would die in bed of natural causes on November 23, 1874.[21]

About August 11 (the record is not specific) Helm arrested two men who become well known in the developing Sutton-Taylor Feud: "Buck" McCrabb and W.M. Sutton. McCrabb was John

Frederick McCrabb, known by that nickname to distinguish him from his father; the latter was William M. Sutton, each arrested for the murder of an "f. m. c." (free man of color) in Victoria County.[22] This arrest did not result in a trial for the pair and they were released, but it remains an ironic incident of Helm arresting two members of the Sutton faction.

All these concerns of being a captain of the Texas State Police may have been set aside about this time as Mrs. Helm was to deliver her first baby soon. The blessed event occurred August 21, 1870, and doubly blessed with twin girls: Emily Jane and Nancy Lee, both healthy daughters. Whether Jack was home for this event is unknown.

But Davidson wanted to see Cox and Tumlinson for a different reason, it is believed. He wanted to hear their version of a matter that had resulted in the wounding of a young girl during an attempt to arrest her father. The man was John Henry Paschal, a Tennessee-born farmer living in Karnes County with his wife Martha and seven children, one of whom was Julia, born in April, 1864.[23] Cox and Tumlinson, along with police privates John W. Smith, Henry R. Montgomery, and Edwin Weatherly, were in pursuit of several desperadoes: Buck Roland, involved in the killing of Littleton and Stannard; William Thompson, brother of the more notorious Ben Thompson, wanted for the killing of William Burke, a clerk in the U.S. Adjutant General's office in Austin; and Paschal. According to Helm, Paschal was "a bad man" and had been "harboring the Taylor Gang for a long while & is now at home after 12 months absence." Helm believed Paschal had been with about thirty desperadoes, even believing he had been involved in the murder of Captain John Littleton.[24] The police did not find Roland and Thompson but did find Paschal and attempted to arrest him. Gunfire erupted in the process and Julia Paschal—the little girl—received a minor wound. No record remains showing that Paschal was arrested or what he was wanted for. As yet no report of Cox and Tumlinson reporting to Davidson's office has been found.

On August 15 Davidson was frustrated as he had received reports that Lavaca County, adjacent to DeWitt County, was infested "with thieves of all kinds." Davidson realized full well that something had to be done. He decided Captain Helm had to go there and "*take such steps* as will remedy [the] evils."[25] Three days later Davidson again wrote to Captain Helm, a follow-up to the earlier strong request that J.W. Cox and Joseph Tumlinson report to him. Now Helm was to *order* them to Austin and meet directly with him. They were to "proceed to this place without delay."[26] Apparently Adjutant General Davidson did not appreciate the fact that traveling from Clinton in DeWitt County to Austin would take close to a day to get there, meet with Davidson, then return home—possibly resulting in a two-day trip. Cox and Tumlinson, both independent individuals, perhaps figured that if Davidson wanted to see them then he should come down to them in DeWitt County. No further information is known of this matter, if they did go to Austin and if so what the result was.

Helm reported that he was on his way to arrest the Henry Westfall "party" while waiting for Private Henry Leftage to return, who was in pursuit of the Hogan party. This time Westfall managed to elude Helm, but the fugitive was not forgotten. Leftage was also in pursuit of one Fountain, a freedman who had shot and fatally stabbed another freedman in DeWitt County. As the ranks of his command were not full, Helm had several men recommended for the fourth district: Henry Johnson, Hugh Boston, and Hugo Buschick of DeWitt County; William E. Jones of Gonzales County; and James E. Petty of Atascosa County. He also reported he had arrested

Wiley Jacobs for shooting a woman in Lavaca County. He alerted Davidson to have others be on the lookout for Richmond Anderson who allegedly had attempted to murder his wife and also be on the lookout for Russell Booth for unlawfully using a stray animal.[27]

The incident that brought greater notoriety for the Regulators/ State Police was the killing of two members of the Kelly family in DeWitt County in August 1870, nearly thirteen months following the Choate Ranch raid. Helm was not physically present at this double killing (or so he claimed) but he was in charge of the squad that did kill the pair, allegedly attempting to escape after being arrested, disarmed, and almost in the presence of family members. The Kelly family was a large one, but perhaps no larger than typical in that time and place. The members who concern us here include Wiley Thomas Kelly, born in 1844 and who lived until 1931; William B., born in 1846 and husband of Elizabeth Day Bennett Rivers, twice widowed due to tragedies in Texas; Henry, born in 1848 and who had married Amanda Jane Taylor, whose brother would become the leader of the Taylor clan; and Eugene A., born in 1850, just twenty years of age when arrested. Their sister, Mary Elizabeth "Mollie" had married James Creed "Jim" Taylor, who would carry on the feud after the murder of his father, Pitkin Barnes Taylor. The four Kelly brothers were accused of shooting up Smith's Circus in the original community of Sweet Home in Lavaca County. There is a Sweet Home today but it exists a few miles from the original, or "Old Sweet Home," which was on what is today's intersection of Lavaca County Roads 312 and 175. Today the site is a jungle of deep, near-impenetrable brush and foliage and nothing remains of the community's existence: no outlines of buildings or stores, no stones marking the location of those early settlers' homes. Only a historical marker indicates where the original Sweet Home was. [28]

Somewhere near this intersection in the summer of 1870 equestrian master Henry M. Smith set up his circus, and many citizens of the neighborhood, including members of the Kelly family, attended. The Kelly brothers and others found reason to create a disturbance there by firing off their pistols. It may have been nothing more than young men with too much alcohol and pistols ready to shoot at the moon. But the Kelly brothers and a few others took offense at something and unloaded their weapons, possibly injuring one or two of the circus workers. For this they were arrested; two of the brothers—William and Henry— were shot down, dying almost instantly, by members of a Helm posse. The date was August 26, 1870.[29]

Details of the affair are sketchy, but it is known that Henry M. Smith was a highly recognized circus performer. He was advertised as the "Grand Scenic and Principal Act Rider" as early as 1855 and was considered a well-known "equestrian director and bareback rider" during his fifty years in the business. Smith directed his circus over many cities in the United States as well as Mexico and other foreign countries.[30] Sweet Home may have been one of the smallest venues for his acts, but he also provided entertainment to the citizens of near-by Clinton. That the circus was coming to town was a popular draw for people of all ages, including young men who would become victims of the State Police as well as their families. An early report stated that the young men had "interfered with a circus performance at Sweet Home and had shot one of the performers."[31] Jack Hays Day, a member of the Taylor clan, attempted to justify the shooting by his kinsmen, writing that the show "turned out to be of the indecent variety and Henry proceeded to shoot out the lights. Of course the show was discontinued."[32] Judging from the reputation of the Smith circus the accusation that the show was of "the indecent variety" is unbelievable, but something somehow offended the brothers, causing them to shoot. Other reports stated several circus workers were wounded in the reckless shooting. Creed Taylor believed that if alcohol had not been involved at Sweet Home—just like at Mason—the tragedy would not have happened. If asked he would have expressed the same belief in the case of the Kelly brothers.

William M. Sutton, a Helm deputy; Christopher Columbus Simmons, who had been commissioned a state police private on August 13, 1879;[33] John Meador,[34] another Helm deputy, and Joseph Priestly "Doc" White, another Helm deputy made up the squad that arrested William and Henry Kelly. No one can be certain as to what actually transpired, but the two Kelly brothers were quickly killed after submitting peaceably to arrest. One authority states that Sutton killed William Kelly and Doc White shot and

Christopher Columbus Simmons, at left, as he appeared in his final years. C.C. Simmons was nominally in charge of the posse that killed the Kelly brothers. At right is his brother Napoleon Bonaparte Simmons. COURTESY PAM FANELLI.

Daniel Jefferson "Jeff" White and his family some years after the feuding in DeWitt County. He was frequently an associate of Jack Helm and the DeWitt County Regulators.
COURTESY DEBBIE BLALOCK.

killed Henry Kelly, "after which a general firing commenced."[35] The Kelly brothers had not attempted to escape as those four lawmen later claimed. After the smoke cleared and the Simmons party had left, certain family members rushed to the tragic scene. Mrs. Delilah Kelly, mother of Louisa Day, and Amanda Kelly dragged the two bodies into the shade of some trees. Louisa Day later recalled the scene: "My husband, William Day, was at home when the prisoners were murdered, but did not visit the scene of horror or give us any assistance with the dead, but left the country and is afraid to return to it, lest he should be murdered by the aforesaid Doc White and William Sutton; and I do not believe he would be safe from their depredations if he were in the country."

William M. Sutton and wife. In the album Sutton wrote above this image: "Presented to Laura E. Sutton by her husband William Sutton Dewitt Co. Irish Creek November 19th A D 1870." AUTHOR'S COLLECTION.

The bodies were taken to the house of William Day where they were prepared for burial. James Turner, a farm hand who worked for William and Louisa Day, along with Frank K. Hawks and Pat Dowlearn, went to the scene and examined the ground, noting the bullet holes.[36] William and Henry Kelly were buried in the historic Taylor-Bennett Cemetery a few miles south of present-day DeWitt County seat Cuero, although no stones mark their graves today.

According to Taylor family genealogist Eddie Day Truitt, Helm was not present at the killing of Henry and William Kelly because he was busy arresting their brothers, Wiley and Eugene, all four charged with the same offense. Wiley and Eugene were taken to Hallettsville, stood their trial and were acquitted of the charge.[37] Were they acquitted of the charge as the jury did not believe they were guilty, or were they acquitted due to sympathy for them by jury members, or as some later claimed, they were acquitted because the jury was fearful of possible repercussions from the accused if they found them guilty?

Captain Helm made no written report of what transpired that day but he did provide the bare minimum of detail for the record of arrests by the police. His "report" is in the form of an entry in the "Record of Arrests" ledger. Presumably Helm turned in some notes or made a verbal report, but the entry reads that on August 26 the four Kelly brothers were arrested in Lavaca County. In the remarks column is noted that William and Henry P. Kelly were "Killed in attempt to escape by guard [in] charge of C.C. Simmons." Their crime was "Disturbing performance of Smiths circus at Sweet Home." There is no indication in this record that anyone was wounded.[38] A later entry shows the police also arrested one John Lewis for "Shooting in Smiths circus at Sweet Home." There is no indication Lewis made an effort to "escape" or evade the guard.[39]

Although the arrest record makes no mention of any one wounded, a report in the *State Journal*, the official voice of Governor Davis, did, identifying the Kellys as "the party who attacked the circus in Lavaca [C]ounty, and wounded some of the performers and audience."[40] If accurate this would suggest several of the performers as well as members of the audience suffered by the reckless shooting of the Kellys. Unfortunately, the *Journal* did not identify any who were wounded, or indicate the number.

Was the killing of the Kellys the only double killing in Lavaca County at this time? There may have been an additional affray in which two men lost their lives. The report was that "a row occurred" at a "camp meeting" on the Cibolo Creek in Karnes County; Helm was there and attempted to "suppress" the disturbance. In making the arrest, two of the rioters were killed, or so reported a Houston newspaper.[41] This contributed to the rumor that martial law had been declared in Lavaca County. The Houston report may have been nothing more than a rumor or a garbled account of the killing of the Kellys, although it is difficult to see how the circus they supposedly shot up could be confused with a legitimate camp meeting, unless the fact that a tent was involved in both could have started the rumor and some shooting had occurred. Regardless, Governor Davis did not declare martial law in Lavaca County, although during the aftermath of the intense criticism of Helm the governor may have considered doing so.

The tragedy of the Kelly affair on August 26 proved to be the beginning of the end for Jack Helm even though he had not fired a shot at either of the brothers. Neither James W. Cox nor Joseph Tumlinson was involved. The arrest and killing of the two men for the relatively minor act of shooting up the circus was an overreaction to the complaints sent to the Adjutant General's office. Helm did not do any of the shooting but the men who did were under his control. Were they not taking steps to "remedy the evils"?

In Lavaca County Helm had arrested fifty-four men, or so he claimed. He reported the arrests but provided no names, nor any details. This also aggravated Davidson, but instead of leaving the comforts of his office and going to Helm to discuss the troubling matters face to face, he sent off another letter. This one, however, was of a positive nature.

> Your conduct in arresting 54 men in Lavaca County and your action on the affair of the Circus Company, is highly commended, and I hope to hear further of your   actions in the pursuit & arrest of criminals, as Soon as your party & horses has been rested and recuperated.[42]

He further reminded Helm he was to fully report arrests, including by whom and where and the disposition of prisoners. This information was necessary for the record, important in Davidson's opinion. To Helm it amounted to unnecessary administrative work. The captain did not concern himself with the fact that Adjutant General Davidson was required to prepare an annual report to the governor, which would be based on such details as the number of arrests, when and where and by whom the arrests were made, the number of prisoners killed, and other details. Helm may not have even been aware of such an annual report. On that same thirty-first day of August Davidson sent out another letter to Captain Helm reminding him to forward to him the names of the fifty-four men arrested in Lavaca County along with their crimes, the disposition "and any other information you can give."[43] The records do not reveal that this was done, although he did at least report that "amongst whom" in the fifty-four arrested men were the four Kelly brothers as well as Alexander Cudd and John Criswell arrested in

Fayette County, but "Rebel" Johnson had managed to escape.[44] Helm succeeded in making arrests and evoking terror in the mind of many citizens of his district, but he was obviously careless in keeping the records straight, to the distress of his superior. What Helm needed was an efficient secretary to deal with the paperwork.

Davidson was aware of the Kelly murders within days and quickly realized the negative pressure that would negate much of the good that the State Police force had accomplished. On September 6, now in the third month of the force's existence, Davidson was compelled to again address the captain of the Fourth District. His letter, partly illegible due to the fading of the ink, included this warning: "You will be held to a strict accountability for every man killed by your party. There is no justice in taking of the life of a man without [just cause]."[45] A short time later the adjutant general fired off another directive to his troublesome captain which contained this warning: "When a prisoner has been killed state all the circumstances connected with it."[46] It would not be a simple matter of reporting a prisoner killed with no further concern about it; certainly Davidson wanted evidence that the killings were indeed "justified"—at least by the perceived necessity of self-defense.

The question that many people wondered about was if the prisoner attempted to escape, did the officer in charge have the legal right to kill him to prevent that escape? Since the Simmons group had the two Kelly brothers in their charge, did they not secure them in some fashion, either on horseback or while they were on foot? Certainly they had removed any weapons which they may have had initially on their person, and certainly they had the means by which to secure them, either shackles or ropes to bind them securely, while on foot or even once on horseback. There is no evidence that any of this was done. If indeed they tried to escape then the law of the day should have been observed: that the officer had the right to use deadly force *only if the officer believed his life was in danger, or believing he was in danger of great bodily harm.* There is no evidence that the two Kellys attempted to kill any of the officers or even to do them bodily harm. Every indication points to the fact that the Kelly brothers were simply murdered by the officers who had them in their charge. The Kelly tragedy was not the first time in history that a prisoner was murdered and the excuse given that he attempted to escape.[47]

Some individuals were not afraid to state publicly (although using a *nom de plume*) that Helm was a murderer. A Victoria resident who signed his lengthy letter as "Hidden Hand," wrote to editor Ferdinand Flake on September 18, that he was not only disappointed in Governor Davis's approval of mob law, in that reports of Helm's actions proved that he had no problem with mob-like actions, but that Captain Helm was clearly a murderer. Did the governor really approve mob-law? To support his claim, Hidden Hand wrote that "[w]e see daily accounts that the chief captain of his police, in Western Texas, Jack Helm, is on the war path again, and he is at his old work shooting men down under the pretense that they were trying to make their escape. . . . The escape part we do not believe." Hidden Hand was aware of not only the killing of the two Kelly brothers, but of some half dozen others, victims he did not identify by name. Certainly among the six were the two Choates, killed prior to Helm's appointment as captain. Hidden Hand expressed his belief that so soon after the Choate killing with Helm appointed as captain, the illegal killings would then cease. He was obviously disappointed that they were continuing and that there was not yet "a new order of things." Hidden Hand admitted knowing nothing about the Kellys, but "let a man be what he may, he has a right to a trial by a jury, and these pretenses of escape are all a farce. No man or two men are going to try to escape from a posse of armed men." It could not be said in stronger terms: Helm was a murderer, and Governor Davis approved his actions by the fact that he did not bring charges of murder against him. Hidden Hand knew of many killings but mentioned only the Kellys and the Choates by name, but in closing stated that Helm's report of the Matagorda affair "is enough to damn one holding the rank of Captain of Police." Accusing Helm of nothing less than outright murder, the writer turned to mild sarcasm in pointing out that Section XVI of the Constitution "provides that no citizen of this State shall be deprived of life, except by due course of law, and we ask that this section [be] stricken out at the next session of the Legislature or have removed from office such men as have violated this section." But was it sarcasm? Hidden Hand concluded by stating he would be heard from again. Certainly Governor Davis was aware of such letters critical of not only his captain's conduct but his own in allowing Jack Helm to remain in that position.[48]

Sutton, White, Meador, and Simmons stood trial and were acquitted of the charge of murdering the Kellys. Helm, who at times failed to report his actions to Davidson in a timely manner, in this instance did report that his men were found not guilty, enclosing a statement from J.A. Abney, that the DeWitt County Grand Jury had found the killing justifiable.[49]

Rumors quickly spread that Helm had been relieved of his captaincy due to the amount of negative criticism following the Kelly killings. The *Daily State Journal* eagerly tried to squelch the rumors, informing the public that Helm had not been relieved due to the Kelly incident, but he had only been relieved *pending the investigation* (emphasis added). Besides clarifying that matter in the same column the *Journal* pointed out that Helm "has been very efficient in hunting up evil-doers in his district, and consequently has made many enemies from among that class. It is noticed, however, that the blows he has struck have always been against law-breakers of the most desperate character." The *Journal* did not explain how the Kellys were of that desperate character. Following these editorial remarks was the full statement of District Attorney J.A. Abney.[50]

Victor M. Rose, the historian who prepared the first serious work on the feud, devoted twelve pages to the Kelly tragedy in his sixty-nine-page book. He quoted the affidavits of two women who claimed to have witnessed the shooting: Mrs. Delilah Kelly, the mother of the dead brothers, and Mrs. Amanda Taylor Kelly, the wife of Henry Kelly. Their statements along with others were published in the *Daily Austin Republican* and from that source Rose obtained his material. What historian Rose did not point out, and he was certainly aware of it, was that after a "patient examination" of the wives of the deceased and other witnesses, and hearing no witnesses for the defense, the grand jury, consisting of sixteen men, the result was that under the circumstances there was no justifiable reason to present a bill of indictment against Helm, White, Meador and Sutton. And Abney concurred.[51]

Even though the killings did not result in any punishment for the men involved, there were repercussions. The incident had a tremendous effect on a number of people. For the Kelly family, two more family members had been shot and killed by a posse that included William Sutton. At this point he and Helm were considered the leaders of the forces against the Taylor family. If there indeed had been a family motto of "Who sheds a Taylor's blood by a Taylor's hand must fall," it certainly was raised again.[52] Delilah Kelly had lost two sons; Amanda Jane lost her husband. Many others now aligned themselves against Helm and Sutton who were considered by many as equal in the command of the forces against the Taylors. Jack Helm also suffered due to the reaction of the public against what he had allowed his subordinates to do. He had been commissioned a captain in the Police Force on July 1, 1870; now public outcry was so great that he was forced to resign after less than three months, on September 21, which resignation was finally accepted officially on November 30, 1870. When it became common knowledge that Helm was to be replaced, numerous citizens of the district offered names of reliable men to replace him. Alford W. Wiggenton, District Clerk of Goliad County, prepared a petition requesting that George W. Jacobs of DeWitt County become the captain "if Helm is removed."[53] The Goliad citizens had reason to prefer George W. Jacobs over other equally qualified men for the position; the county had lost Andrew Jackson Jacobs, the brother of George W., and consequently their feelings would naturally be directed for him. Their desire would never be satisfied.[54]

Those members acting under orders of Captain Helm may not have appreciated the amount of negative publicity their actions created in the Kelly affair. Certainly they were aware of the problems created in Davidson's office as well as in their home counties, but the condemnation of Helm and the State Police was not limited to Texas. Reports from Austin soon appeared in the *New York World*, which were then printed in other major newspapers, such as the *Nashville Union and American* in Tennessee. The latter publication headlined its report in bold as "Terrorism in Texas" in a lengthy page one article. The editor followed that eye-catcher with smaller headlines, also in bold: "The Murderous Operations of the Radical State Police," "Citizens Dragged from Their Homes and Cruelly Assassinated," and "Gangs of Fiends in Constant Search of Fresh Victims." The article originated from Austin and contains a great deal of hyperbole which proclaimed that such a "reign of terror" had never before been experienced in Texas. No man's life was safe from an "infamous gang of cut-throats" whose murders were legalized by commissions as State Police. The *Nashville Union* signaled out Jack Helm as the chief of the gang, describing him as "notorious . . . a merciless villain, whose heart is black with multitudes of nameless crimes, and whose hands are red with the blood of hundreds of innocent men—an ignorant man, the ready and unscrupulous tool of the wretches whom he serves—avaricious, unfeeling, without an idea of respect for law, the rights of property, or the sacred[ness] of human life." Somewhat surprisingly the name of C.S. Bell is not forgotten, although in Texas he would soon be fully overshadowed by Helm. Accordingly, Bell "shamelessly boasts of the murders of innocent, inoffensive, and unarmed men who he has slaughtered in cold blood."[55] Much of the remainder of this article focuses on Senator B.J. Pridgen's dislike for Helm as well as the killing of the Kelly brothers. In Texas it was not news, but for readers in New York and Nashville the headlines made good copy, and many people believed what they read.

The arrest of the four Kellys, although not by him personally, on August 26, was followed four days later with the arrest of Alexander Cudd and John Criswell, the former in DeWitt County and the latter in Lavaca County.[56] In the latter county Helm and party created more bad publicity for himself and by extension the entire police force, although he had not intended to do so. Following the Kelly tragedy Helm claimed to have made fifty-four arrests in Lavaca County, but he failed to identify of the fifty-four, nor what they were charged with. The date of the arrests was given as "about Augt 30" and only the charge of "Miscellaneous—offence not Stated" given.[57] It is strange that there are no details found in any record on this matter—if it occurred. Certainly, for Helm to arrest this large a group would require assistants, more than the several who had arrested the Kellys. Initially the mass arrest brought congratulations from Helm's superiors in Austin, but from some anti-Davis sources the claim was made that it was a downright lie. Senator Pridgen did not believe Helm, nor did the editor of the *San Antonio Daily Herald*. The earliest reference of the mass arrest yet found appears in the *Daily State Journal*. The article relates how the Kelly brothers, who "attacked the circus . . . and wounded some of the performers and audience," had been arrested. Two of them had been killed. After identifying several other arrests, the *Journal* continued: "Fifty-four arrests, in addition to the above, have been made in Lavaca county, all charged with various crimes. The good citizens turned out unanimously to aid the police, which [organization] is fast becoming popular."[58] The popularity of the state police of course was subject to a great deal of debate; in some circles the police force was detested. To continue the debate in the newspaper columns, the *Journal* accused the *Herald* of further falsehoods. "The statement made by the San Antonio *Herald*, and copied by the copperhead organ of this city, that Jack Helm, at the town of Sweet Home, paid for the dinner of his posse of forty-five men by levying a tax upon the principal citizens living several miles around, is a falsehood pure and unqualified."[59] In the official records no reference to Helm levying a tax on Lavaca County citizens has been located. As there is no record from Helm it becomes a matter of dueling newspaper editors. The *Herald* did claim to have proof of the taxation in the form of letters from respectable citizens. On November 19, John R. Baylor, respected Civil War hero, claimed to have been in county seat Hallettsville "and conversed with several persons living in and near Sweet Home, and was assured that such a tax was levied, accompanied by a menace or threat of punishment for all who refused to pay." Baylor explained that the tax was "to pay for the dinner of Helm and party." He further enclosed a "certificate" from William W. Boyce, a local farmer, dated November 11, saying that Clem Foster, a

Sweet Home merchant, "presented to me an order given by Helm, with a list of names, about forty in number, demanding from each person the sum of twenty-five cents, to defray the bill at the hotel of said Helm and party; against which I protested, to which Foster replied that he was ordered to report all those who refused to pay, to Helm."[60] William W. Boyce was a farmer in Lavaca County, fifty-six years old, a New York native with a wife and children helping with the work of the farm.[61] He had had no personal difficulty with Helm to report anything but the honest truth. Clemont Foster likewise, as enumerated by the census taker, was a much younger individual of Lavaca County, twenty-six years-of-age and living with his brother Thomas B. Foster and his wife. Both Fosters gave their occupation as "Retail Dry Goods Merchant."[62] There are a number of problems with this entire scenario. First, did Jack Helm and his "party" actually make fifty-four arrests and if so why did he not make an official report; if this mass arrest was true then why did not the *State Journal* make mention of it with some details? Was there a tax levied upon the citizens of Lavaca County to pay for the hotel and meal expenses of Helm, and if so was that relevant to the supposed arrest of the fifty-four individuals? The *Daily Herald* placed on page one a condemnation of Helm, stating "Some time ago we published an article in regard to Jack Helm's conduct at Sweet Home and vicinity, in levying a tax on the people by collecting it by force." The *Herald* then reported that the *State Journal* "characterizes this statement as false."[63] Three days later, the *Herald* continued the debate, reviewing the matter and then adding the fact that even though Helm was in Austin no legal action was taken against him even though there was a "copy of the indictment found against him, in Bee County, together with the sworn statement of the wives of two of his victims, were on file in the Adj. General's office, he was permitted to depart 'scot free,' to commence anew his career of horror and crime."[64] What can we make of this debate between two newspapers, one of whom was the mouthpiece of the Republican administration, the other a vehicle almost violently opposed to that administration? At least one historian claims that if Helm did tax the citizens he was within his rights as the law required citizens to cover expenses of the force while in the respective county. *This was true only if martial law had been declared by the governor* (emphasis added). This had not been done. If Helm actually levied a tax, it was not legal.[65]

Helm failed to identify those fifty-four citizens arrested around the end of August, but he was able to later, in part. In September he arrested Elijah Ratliff and John Newcomer in Yorktown, the other major town in DeWitt County; then he reported the arrest of Henry Westfall, William Dodd, and Albert Lacey, somewhere in Live Oak County, but provided no details. Davidson had learned that Westfall of "the *notorious Taylor Gang*" as Davidson expressed it, had taken refuge at the *rancho* of Sebastian Beales on the Nueces River in Live Oak County. He ordered Helm to arrest him and turn him over to the authorities in Wilson County where he was charged with murder. Davidson ordered him to report his actions, for the sake of the file and reports of course.[66] Helm did not act foolishly by going it alone. For this dangerous duty he had with him three policemen: privates William W. Black, Julio Garza, and Joseph Tumlinson, who may never have intended to report to Adj. Gen. James Davidson as ordered. Apparently Helm felt he needed dependable men with him. Lewis May and George Tesin were arrested in Bee County, and finally George McCarty, John Benham and one Chambers were arrested in Refugio County.[67] These remain essentially names only, although May was a young stock raiser living in the household of James Ryan and his family, along with the Henry Vanderrider family; since there were twelve individuals in the household perhaps the Ryans ran a boarding house. Lewis, or Louis May as the census enumerator spelled his name, was twenty-five and his wife Josephine only eighteen then.[68] The name of George Tesin has not been found in other records, but George McCarty was a twenty-three-year-old stock herder along with his brother Andrew, two years younger. The McCarty brothers were the sons of J.R. and Arminta McCarty, farmers there in Refugio County.[69] John Benham has not been further identified, although there were two Denham families living there at the time, a James Denham, eighty-seven years of age, and a Shadrick Denham, only seventy-seven years old. Nothing further has been learned about the man named Chambers. These arrests were certainly not among the fifty-four arrests Helm claimed to have made.

The exception to the above is Henry Westfall. In the remarks column it is noted that he had been sent under guard to Wilson County but was "mortally wounded evading arrest." Obviously Henry Westfall had *attempted to escape* and was shot dead.[70] At least that was the report. Apparently the others under arrest made no effort to escape from their guard. Dodd was released as no charges were filed against him. Lacey, charged with cattle theft, was turned over to the sheriff of Atascosa County.[71]

William Longworth,[72] District Clerk at Southerland Springs in Wilson County, provided a detailed report on September 7 of Helm's operation resulting in the capture and death of Westfall. Others were arrested as well, identified as Tiner, Ben Goodwin, one Applewhite, and "others in the Gang" suggesting the arresting party believed this was a group active as a criminal organization. Strangely no further information has been found on these arrested with Westfall. In addition Longworth reported that G.A. Jackson had been arrested for killing John Bell in Wilson County in May of 1870. Then the very next day, September 8, Longworth again wrote to Davidson, stressing that Helm "*Subpoenas* a posse commitates [*sic*] to go wherever he chooses even beyond County boundaries—[He makes] arrests too indiscriminately, & holds parties in arrest simply for a time."[73] Was this action even legal for Helm? Perhaps, as the General Order No. 1, entitled "An Act to establish a State Police and Provide for the Regulation and Government of the Same" stated: "when in pursuit of any criminal they [captains] will follow him, if need be, into any county in the State, and will not leave off the pursuit at the limits of their district."[74] This gave Helm the authority to deputize a person as a member of a posse and go beyond county lines in pursuit. Helm's involvement in this incident may have been legal but it brought more negative attention to the State Police. San Antonio's *Daily Herald* learned that on Tuesday, September 6, 1870, about thirty or forty armed citizens appeared on the Cibolo, "in the neighborhood of Brahan's[75] and Liner's ranches, and forced some fifteen of the citizens there to arm themselves and accompany them in the hunt" for members of the Applewhite gang. Reportedly these armed citizens entered houses and searched the premises taking arms from them "without even saying 'thank you, sir.'" Later, after "splurging about for two days and nights ineffectually, they very kindly permitted some of the planters to return home" while the original group continued on their way to the Nueces and Frio River valleys, presumably continuing to hunt for members of the Applewhite gang. The *Herald*, not keeping secret their feelings against the E.J. Davis organization, entitled its article "The State Police on the Rampage" which headline and article was quickly reprinted in the *Daily Austin Republican* as well for the benefit of legislators and other supporters of the force. The *Herald* predicted there would be further trouble with members of the State

Police being capable of searching private homes without warrant or authority of law.[76] The *Herald* reported in its issue of September 16 that Applewhite, who had been the subject of the police search with "so much fuss about of late"—meaning "impressing citizens lately on the Cibolo"—had surrendered to civil authorities on the fourteenth, was prepared to make bail and only wanted a fair trial.[77]

Helm did prove to be an effective leader of men, although his methods seemingly were based on the theory that the end justified the means. He gave, however, little if any consideration to the possible repercussions of his actions. When the police force was created, the captains were given clear instructions that the men they selected to serve under them as privates were to be selected from as many counties in their district as possible "so that every county is given satisfaction." Helm had initiated his selection from DeWitt County residents and went not much further. Just who Helm chose at this point is uncertain but his list of men submitted to Davidson for approval did not meet the grade. He had been reprimanded for using members of the military in his posses, being advised that he had "no authority to use military force for assistance" and "you will get along with your police force."[78] So the unidentified United States Army sergeant in full uniform could no longer be a part of any of Helm's missions.

In September more arrests followed: J.G. Wells and Ben Valentine[79] were taken in DeWitt County on the twenty-fourth,[80] then the record of arrests merely shows that eighteen men were arrested and charged with killing cattle for their hides and then selling them as the Lunn gang had done, or stealing hogs. One of the names appearing again was that of John Lewis who was accused of shooting up Smith's Circus in Sweet Home with the Kelly brothers.[81] No date or location was given for the arrest of these eighteen men, except it may have been done over a period of days toward the latter part of September or early part of October 1870.[82]

Whereas the record provides essentially the minimum facts about an arrest, an important newspaper item appearing in *Flake's Daily Bulletin* in Galveston provides scant information on the final fate of Henry Westfall. It references the "doings" of the "Jack Helm crowd" which provides a tone of anti-Helm certainly. It stated, in a letter from an unidentified citizen of La Vernia, in Wilson County, that Helm

> and a posse of the State Police visited this place on Monday 5th instant [September 5] in search of Henry Westfall and other alleged violators of the law. He pressed several citizens into service, who, in charge of policeman Black, of this county, moved west of the San Antonio river, remaining on the scout two or three days. We learn from good source that Westfall was killed on or near Beall's [sic] ranch, on the Nueces, by some of Helm's posse while resisting arrest.[83]

Newspaper items such as the above resulted in everyone from Galveston to San Antonio to Austin and beyond becoming familiar with the name of Jack Helm. Legitimate law officers as well as those desperadoes whom Helm claimed were only murderers and thieves who defied the law by now knew the name.

Did Jack Helm ever make detailed reports to his superiors of his actions? An item in the Goliad newspaper suggests that he may have, on rare occasion. Reportedly he had made "over one hundred arrests" although two or three had been killed resisting arrest and several had been wounded. Of course with that many arrests there was further work, as they could not simply place them all in the Goliad jail. Helm and Joe Tumlinson were "busy . . . in detailing the prisoners they brought to this place to the various counties in which the indictments have been found." The *Goliad Guard* commented further: "Among the arrests made on this last raid by the parties (Helm and Tumlinson) which met here, are several that charity would naturally regret; but Helm says he is governed by nothing but his instructions and his duty, and these he intends to carry out. If he does this all good citizens will give him credit for it."[84]

6

"Six Shooter Gentry"

"He is unreliable as well as a disgrace to your Police Corps."
—Senator B.J. Pridgen in the *Daily State Journal*, September 27, 1870.

CAPTAIN HELM'S CAREER IN THE Texas State Police was brief because of his arrogance, over zealousness, and eagerness to show the citizens what to him represented law and order—too often including murdering prisoners on the spot.

Helm's problems were not confined within the borders of the Fourth Police District. What must have been a disturbing surprise to the adjutant general's office and the governor as well was the communication from Edward M. Alexander, captain of the Second Police District in which he sent "capiases against John Helm" of the Fourth District.[1] This was dated September 3; less than two weeks later, on September 14, John S. Coffey of Sulphur Springs, Hopkins County, wrote inquiring if the indictments against Jack Helm had been received.[2] The hanging of the five pro-Unionists from the 1860s was now coming back to potentially force Helm to be tried as a common criminal.

On occasion the captain of the Fourth Police District did overstep his legal bounds. Sanders Pearce of Oakville, on September 17, 1870, wrote a letter to the adjutant general claiming that Helm had *appointed* him sheriff of Live Oak County, and thus was requesting "blank forms" but provided no further details, nor did he provide Davidson any personal information which might have

134

qualified him to be the county sheriff. This is indeed an unusual situation, as Captain Helm actually had no legal power to appoint any individual to be sheriff; the office was an elected one and only General Reynolds had the authority to appoint a sheriff. Helm must have *thought* he had the authority, and apparently the appointment was accepted as the record shows Pearce took his oath of office on October 14, 1870, before Justice of the Peace James W. Drury. Earlier, Reynolds, who did have the authority to remove elected officials and replace officials during this Reconstruction period, had appointed Chappell Spencer Boutwell by Special Order No. 72 as sheriff. Boutwell served until August 23 of 1870.[3] Then Patrick Pugh was elected but returned his commission on September 12, 1870, only twenty days later, obviously not satisfied with the position. This opened the door for Helm to appoint Pearce to the office. The act of appointing a citizen to be county sheriff may have been nothing more than a foolish act of Helm in a moment of arrogance, but the Live Oak County records show Pearce did serve as sheriff until January 1873.[4]

The new sheriff's full name was Moses Sanders Pearce. He was born in Jackson, Mississippi, on February 23, 1844. The family had moved to Texas in 1854 and remained in Live Oak County until moving to DeWitt about 1909. By occupation he described himself as a stock raiser. When the war broke out he enlisted in San Antonio on March 22, 1862, and served until war's end. By 1906 he attempted to obtain a pension, indicating he could not work to support himself because of "Old age. Bad health. Gun shot wounds." One is left to wonder: were the wounds the result of combat during his three years as a Confederate or were they received afterwards during Reconstruction? At the time he only possessed fourteen acres of land at Clinton, valued at $300 and four mules, each valued at $20. During his later years he served as a night watchman in Yorktown, where he was affectionately known as "Dad" Pearce. He died on January 12, 1929, and today Pearce rests in the Westside Cemetery in Yorktown, DeWitt County.[5]

Jack Helm received numerous reprimands from his superior in Austin, and his personality did contribute to his problems, which ultimately resulted in his removal from the police force. Victor M. Rose wrote of Helm's education as "extremely limited but his vanity was immense, while his discrimination was always muddled."[6] Perhaps this vanity led him to believe he had the authority to appoint Pearce as sheriff of Live Oak County.

Bolivar J. Pridgen, Senator of the 24th Judicial District of Texas, which included DeWitt, Jackson, Refugio, Victoria, Calhoun and Goliad Counties, was less kind than Rose. He complained of Helm in much stronger terms following the death of the Kellys, asking for a thorough investigation. On September 27 he wrote to Davidson reminding him that he had requested him to investigate the Kelly killing. He considered Helm's "cause" in DeWitt and adjoining counties as lawless and unauthorized, so much so that now he was demanding of the adjutant general to do a "prompt and immediate investigation." Pridgen knew very well that there were charges against the Kellys, using the term "bad men" to describe them, but he stressed that there were laws to provide a "proper mode of disposing of *bad men*." To Pridgen, nothing could be "more revolting to law [,] civilization and good morals than for an officer to wantonly murder prisoners in his charge and then without calling on the neighbors to take charge of the dead and have them decently buried" or call on an officer for a proper inquest. But Helm and his squad disappeared and left the bodies to be devoured by hogs or wolves. The community was so terrified that no one could be induced to visit the "scene of horrors" or to aid the women and relatives of the dead men in putting them on carts to remove them to a house preparatory to interment. Helm's "various tales" were also of concern: to Pridgen "he denied that he was present" but to other responsible and truthful citizens he had stated that he was present and witnessed all that was done. The question remained: was Helm at the scene of the Kelly brothers' death, or was he elsewhere? Senator Pridgen called the squad that killed the Kellys "six shooter gentry" whose "precedents have been to kill prisoners and conveniently alledge [sic] that they attempted to escape." Helm, he continued, was "an arrogant brainless personage, embodying only the elements of lying, bombast and cruelty, which added to his indiscretion, render him a fit subject to bring the Police bill and law into ridicule and contempt."[7] Helm may have been arrogant, bombastic, a liar and cruel at times, but he was not brainless as his few written letters do reveal a person with perhaps an above average education for that time and place.

The Kelly affair received tremendous attention in the press and became a tumultuous issue at the executive office. The family of William and Henry Kelly endeavored to find some justice but that did not come within the court system. The Kelly brothers were not the only ones killed by a guard under the command of Helm, although Helm, or so he claimed, was not actually present at either killing.

In contrast to the Kelly killings was the death of young John Smithwick, murdered sometime in mid-September 1870.[8] The details of his death did not receive nearly the attention that the killing of the Kelly brothers did, but the word of his death did reach Adjutant General Davidson in October, and there were certain similarities in that it was a case of a prisoner being killed when he "attempted to escape."[9] Perhaps Davidson even recognized the similarities and wondered if the prisoner really did try to escape; and why had he not been securely manacled or otherwise secured, which would have prevented the attempt?

Smithwick was born about 1848 in Louisiana; in 1870 he was residing in Nueces County, driving cattle.[10] He was arrested but the specific charge is not known. Sheriff Pearce, the sheriff who had been appointed by Captain Helm, identified Smithwick's murderers as "Sebe" Martin, an abbreviated form of his proper name Ceburn, and David West, with no further details, but he did add that James Martin (the father of Ceburn) claimed Smithwick was killed while trying to escape from the guard—which he hoped would mollify the guilt.[11] Sheriff Pearce, who had been appointed sheriff but had not been sworn in at the time of Smithwick's murder, conducted an investigation and reported that O.H. Bennett and a detachment of the State Guard had arrested Smithwick and had him in custody. He identified the guard members besides Bennett as James Martin, Sebe Martin, Alex Franklin, J.M. Franklin, Ralph Franklin, Charles Barker, David West "and others [who] could not be found."[12] Atascosa County rancher Peter F. Tumlinson, a brother of "Captain Joe," may have known in advance of what these men set out to accomplish. His family and the West family were connected by marriage so for all these men to be aware of a plan to rid the country of Smithwick—by fair means or foul—would not be surprising. Most significant was a document signed by Peter Tumlinson and others asking for "protection for the party who was in charge of Smithwick when he was killed (& who have since been indicted for murder) as they were acting under orders of Capt. Jack Helm." Tumlinson failed to date this document but it was received at the adjutant general's office on December 8, 1870.[13] Those men charged with the killing were apparently fearful for their own safety and wanted the state to provide protection. Davidson certainly wondered why they could not protect themselves, and just who were they fearful of?

Captain Helm had received letters from John J. Dix and James Martin referring to the death of Smithwick, which he forwarded on to Davidson.[14] Dix was a forty-four-year-old stock raiser with $2,500 in real estate and $2,000 in his personal estate.[15] The other was the forty-six-year-old Martin who was the father or uncle of the twenty-year-old James Martin, a cattle drover who resided in the household of David West, a stock raiser as was Dix. Helm enclosed the documents with his letter from Clinton, dated October 10. Live Oak County Sheriff Sanders Pearce had an interest in this killing as well. He was aware of the controversial nature of the incident, as on October 15 Davidson wrote to Pearce ordering him to arrest the parties alleged to have murdered Smithwick and deliver them to the proper authorities to be held over until the next meeting of District Court. Most telling were these lines in Davidson's letter: "You know the particulars in the case which are conflicting with the report heretofor [sic] received at this office and if your Statement is correct the parties accused should be dealt with according to law." Presumably this is a reference to the statements provided by John J. Dix and James Martin in Helm's letter to Davidson. On the same day, October 15, Davidson wrote to Dix, addressing him as "John J. Dix, Esq." of Corpus Christi. In this letter Davidson wrote: "Your letter of 9th inst enclosing statement regarding murder of John Smithwick [words illegible] Martin & David West at Dogtown on Sept 20 '70 has been received." Now Davidson got to the heart of the matter, pointing out to Dix that the report of Sheriff Pearce "differs materially" from that of James Martin. He enclosed a copy of Martin's report and pointed out that none of the parties mentioned as being members of the guard who had custody of Smithwick were state policemen. And he was to "disabuse persons who are under the impression that this was the act of the State Police."[16] It would appear that the group who "Helmized" young Smithwick led others to believe they were actually members of the State Police. This would not have been difficult to do. Were the men who were fearful for their own safety concerned because they had knowingly acted as murderers without the "blessing" of being state policemen, or were fearful of Smithwick's friends or relatives wanting revenge? It would appear both explanations were of concern.

Senator Pridgen was not yet finished with his condemnation of Helm, and it is surprising that he did not make mention of the Smithwick affair as he did the Kelly affair. In his view, Helm's actions caused citizens to feel "very insecure as to life, and so terrorized as to be unwilling to comment as to the propriety or impropriety of Helm's conduct." Supposedly Helm had stated to the senator that he had received instructions from the adjutant general and also Governor Davis "to do those things." Pridgen further claimed that Helm lied to his superiors: "I do not believe that he arrested the 54 prisoners in the County of Lavacca [sic] that he reported" and it was also "wholly untrue" that he arrested three prisoners and lodged them in the DeWitt County jail. Not yet finished with his condemnation of Helm, Pridgen stated "for brag and lying he can beat any one of my Knowledge. He is unreliable as well as a disgrace to your Police Corps."[17]

Governor Davis could not ignore this and felt he had to quickly make a response to the senator. On October 7 he instructed Pridgen to present evidence of the charges that he had made against Captain Helm. The captain had been in Austin a few days prior and he and the governor had discussed matters, including the fact that it was Simmons in charge of those who had killed the Kellys, not Helm. Did not Helm realize that even though Simmons and his men did the killing, it was still Helm's responsibility as he was his superior officer? Governor Davis instructed Helm to provide him with a full account of the Kelly matter and wanted all documents properly sworn to.[18] This "full account" by Helm, if it was made, has not yet surfaced.

Governor Davis further communicated to Senator Pridgen that Helm had accused him of "encouraging the lawless people" in his part of the country by "incendiary appeals and violent threatening against the Police &c &c." Davis made the same charge against the senator's brother, Wiley Washington Pridgen, recently arrested "for some breach of peace or offence."[19] Indeed, Helm had arrested W.W. Pridgen but he had not provided the date or place or the charge, another administrative indiscretion. Helm pointed out in his letter to Davidson that he had arrested W.W. Pridgen "for trying to influence his police against him"; also that Bolivar J. Pridgen was "working hard against him."[20] The feuding between the Pridgens and Helm would continue with words, but it was brother Wiley who eventually paid the price: in December of 1873, he was shot and killed by unknown parties, who were never fully identified and whose motives have never been determined. They were certainly men sympathetic to members of the Sutton faction, however.[21]

The notion that an officer of the court had the right to kill a prisoner while attempting to escape may have seemed justifiable to some, but certainly the attitude was anathema to others. Victor M. Rose, influential newspaper editor, was one who did not fear repercussions of his editorial statements. He found these excuses for killing prisoners worthy of headlines in October. "Killed in attempting to escape" and "Killed while resisting arrest . . . are two expressions that are fast coming to have a melancholy and terrible significance to the people of Western Texas" he began, without identifying any specific individual, but no doubt Helm was the one he had most in mind for killing prisoners in custody. "They furnish the brief epitaph to the scores who have fallen, and are falling victims to the ignorance, the arrogance or the brutality of those charged with the execution of the law, and with bringing offenders against its dignity to justice."

Editor Rose certainly could have checked his newspaper files and produced a list of men killed with those excuses, but he chose not to. Had "scores" actually been murdered while attempting to escape or resisting arrest? That may not have been the best use of hyperbole to make his point, but it may not have been hyperbole. "Never, anywhere, has there, we believe, existed so lamentable and outrageous an ignorance of their rights, duties and responsibilities as among the executive officers of the law in this State." It was clearly set out in the Constitution, that nowhere did an officer have the right to kill. "And nowhere in the statutes," Rose continued, "nor in the principle of the Common Law applicable to their construction, is to be found a word which gives even a coloring to the opinion which is prevalent, that he who attempts to escape from an officer of justice, or who resists an arrest by means not calculated to imperil the officer seriously, subjects himself to the penalty of death, and is liable to be shot like a wolf." Rose's editorial appealed to Alfred H. Longley, editor of the *Daily Austin Republican*, the major publication in opposition generally to the executive's main publication, the *Daily State Journal*. Longley, a thirty-year-old Missouri-born editor, presented a brief sidebar to Rose's lengthy reporting, entitling it "Murder Most Foul" in which he stated that "We endorse every word of the manly protest of the Advocate against this foul and cowardly system of licensed murder, for it is nothing less." Longley concluded his remarks with this thought-provoking statement: "this grave question . . . involves the life of every citizen of the State."[22] On the same day this statement appeared in the Austin newspaper, October 10, Captain Helm, at his "office" in Clinton, wrote to Davidson and enclosed the statement of J.A. Abney that the grand Jury of DeWitt County had determined "that the Killing of William and Henry Kelly by the Guard was Justifiable."[23] John Armie Abney at the time was a thirty-seven-year-old Mississippi-born lawyer practicing in Austin. He continued to be successful in all his endeavors.[24]

No mention was made of the killing of John Smithwick.

While forces were attempting to have Helm removed, others were working hard to retain him as police captain. Frederick Edward Grothaus, serving in the Texas Legislature of the Twenty-fourth District, writing at Clinton on October 14, obtained a petition signed by numerous DeWitt County citizens asking that Helm be retained, and pointed out that those who were opposed to Helm were also opposed to Governor Davis, thus treating the matter as mere political fighting.[25] Only days before, the administration had received a letter from John J. Thornton while visiting at Hackberry, Lavaca County, in which he stated that the lawless element of Lavaca County "is delighted at [the] removal of Jack Helm [,] Said to have been affected by Gen'l James Davidson while at Hallettsville."[26]

By October 19 reports began to circulate in DeWitt County that the killing of the Kellys, "by Jack Helm, was murderous, or at least unjustifiable." Reportedly the question "was brought before the grand jury . . . who, after a patient examination of the wives of the deceased, and the other witnesses for the prosecution, were unanimously of the opinion that the killing, under the circumstances, would not justify finding a bill of indictment." [27] The rumors of Helm's dismissal were finally confirmed: a few days later the *Journal* quietly reported with a single sentence: "Captain Jack Helm has been relieved from further duty on the State Police." [28]

As Helm had illegally made Sanders Pearce the Live Oak County sheriff, he had no second thoughts in appointing a man a state policeman, as he did with Cornelius V. Busby. In the latter part of October Judge D.D. Claiborne requested that Busby be officially commissioned as a state policeman for Goliad County. Busby had been "acting" as a policeman "by written authority of J. Helm" and now wanted it to be done properly so he could be paid.[29] What is most curious about this incident is that Busby had already been commissioned on August 13, 1870. He had already been serving without the realization of Helm or Claiborne. Busby served until his resignation on April 30, 1872.[30]

The Smithwick affair was not totally forgotten. On December 1 Davidson informed policeman Robert F. Haskins that he had dismissed O.H. Bennett but he had continued acting as a state policeman accompanying Judge D. D. Claiborne in his judicial district, playing the role of a bodyguard. Haskins was to investigate and of course was to then report back to Davidson. This is the last known act of Bennett.[31] Little else has been learned about the tragic Smithwick affair. The vigilante group, acting as policemen, had arrested him; certain parties became concerned that he knew too much and felt compelled to kill him to keep him from revealing information about criminal matters. Was he guilty of stock theft? Was he simply murdered or had he attempted to escape? We will never know. The adage "Dead men tell no tales" summed up his fate. He was buried in the "Boothill Cemetery" in McMullen County, near county seat Tilden, but his grave is no longer marked, if it ever was.[32]

While Helm must have been concerned with the forces who worked to have him removed, not to mention the potential for his enemies to attempt assassination, some good news did surface. Alfred Friar, the constable at Yorktown, sent to Davidson a report from Bastrop concerning the killing of Charles Taylor there by a posse led by William M. Sutton back in 1868. Helm had no connection with that incident so far as known, but since then Sutton and Helm had developed a working relationship that caused many to consider them partners. Friar stressed in his letter that the charges against Sutton had been *improperly drawn up.*[33] This perhaps was one of the little things which balanced the negative reports coming from Senator Pridgen.

Senator Pridgen continued to lambast Helm in the columns of the *Daily Austin Republican*, the Austin newspaper whose editorials frequently were in opposition to the announcements from the governor's office. He wrote to thirty-year-old newspaper editor Alfred H. Longley in reference to the Kelly affair that "the conduct of the policemen and guard are unwarranted, inhuman, and outrageous." He complained that policeman C. C. Simmons had made no report of what had happened, and had secured no legal inquest. Further, he pointed out that Simmons had "abandoned them (as prisoners generally are who are killed by the notorious Jack Helm, or his crowd) to the mercy of buzzards, wolves, and hogs." Pridgen pointed out that many citizens were afraid to speak out, "lest the wrath of his lawless crowd of prisoner-murderers and Regulators should be visited upon them." Pridgen described DeWitt County as being "completely terrorized" because Helm had made arrests without charging the prisoners with a specific crime; further, Helm levied "contributions" and unjustly taxed the people. In addition, he arrested people who were then kept in jail for weeks—and then the court turned them loose as there were no charges against them. Helm further aggravated Pridgen as he had no real office where he could deal with his mail and other desk duties; he "keeps constantly in the saddle, swinging to and fro through the country, apparently exulting in the manner in which he is terrifying the people." And there were problems with the men under Helm, who was not only "unscrupulous" but also a "liar" and was "extremely dangerous." The majority of his policemen were "not only ignorant, and can scarcely write their name, but stand charged with having shed the blood of human beings." There were criminals coming from Mexico with the intention of serving under Captain Helm, or so Senator Pridgen claimed.[34]

Senator Pridgen was not the only respectable citizen who brought serious accusations against Helm. William J. Neely was a man who developed a distinguished career in Texas; in 1868 he was Tax Assessor and Collector in Victoria County; in 1870 he was Registrar of Voters and on April 25 of that year took the oath of the District Court in Victoria County.[35] He wrote to Governor Davis reminding him that he had described the character of Helm, William Sutton, and their "co workers" before Helm had been appointed police captain, and again after the appointment. He spoke of the "outrages committed" by Helm and his party that were "so appalling." Neely wrote that Helm and his men "murder, Hang and whip" and that DeWitt County would be almost depopulated and the freedmen were all leaving. "They have been whipped and then threatened that if they went to [county seat] Clinton during Court that they would be shot. . . . Helm and his party inspect droves of cattle and collect money and demand of citizens money &c. &c." There were citizens who had left the county out of fear of Helm, White,[36] French,[37] Sutton, and others. Unless these men were arrested and put in irons, citizens would have to leave the state "for no one is safe from them in the State." Almost as an afterthought Clerk Neely added that William Sutton "has a negro [sic] with him who is worse than Sutton himself."[38]

The result of these letters of complaint to the adjutant general and the governor from respectable people was perhaps the straw that forced Governor Davis to ultimately dismiss Jack Helm. He wrote to clerk William J. Neely on October 10 that in view of the charges made against him he had relieved Helm "of the charge of his Police District." He instructed Neely to forward to his office evidence of all these charges, properly authenticated. Davis now chose Lieut. Thomas Williams of the State Police to temporarily be in charge of the fourth district.[39]

About the same time that Senator Pridgen was penning that letter to the *Austin Republican*, Alfred Belo of the *Galveston Daily News* was penning an editorial response to the news that Helm would be replaced. He pointed out that the journals were reporting that he had been removed because of the many men he had killed while resisting arrest. "Were it not for the awfully sublime information conveyed in these few words, their careless brevity and nonchalance would be amusing. But to the hundreds who weep for friends and relatives slain by order of this man since Gen. Reynolds appointed him sheriff and gave him a roving commission, they are words of awful significance, as in the dead list of a battle a few words tell of a mountain of sorrow. In no other land under the sun could such a reason be possible." And if the reader was yet uncertain just who Belo was referring to, he made it clear in the next few words: "This man, who carried terror wherever he pleased, is now removed by Adjutant General Davidson. We are glad that he has done so. He is keeping the promise that he made, and in the same manner we expect that he will remove from the State all imitators of Jack Helm's bloody deeds."[40]

Jack Helm was not the only one being dismissed at this time. In Gonzales, William E. Jones, then a special policeman, wrote Davidson reporting on his operations for the month and stressed that privates W.J. Young and Peter Haynes should both be dismissed for inefficiency and recommended Sci Jones and Nathan Busby to take their places.[41]

Although influential citizens found great fault with the law-and-order tactics of Captain Helm, there were those who viewed him differently. One of these was a highly successful merchant in Gonzales, Robert Lamar Miller, a thirty-eight-year-old Tennessean with a wife and family of four children ranging in age from less than a year to a thirteen-year-old "scholar" as the census identified her "occupation." In 1870 Miller claimed Belmont as his post office, on the western edge of Gonzales County. Whether Miller learned of Helm's work from listening to others talk or reading the *Gonzales Inquirer* is not known, possibly both, but he had a high regard for the man, so much so that he wrote to the adjutant general on October 1, 1870, stating that Helm had "done more to establish law and order in the 4th District than any other man."[42] Miller's statement was quite a compliment indeed, although it was not enough to save Helm's career in the state police. Miller no doubt felt that if a bad man was not killed, his being forced to leave the country was equally justified. Another supporter, William H. Burkhart, wrote that he "recommends also that J. Helm be retained," although if Helm had to go, Burkhart recommended William E. Jones as captain of the fourth district.[43]

Was there really such fear of Helm in the country? Yes, at least according to Senator Pridgen. He informed Davidson that William Weatherford Day and James Creed Taylor, the half-brother and brother of Amanda Jane Taylor Kelly, had left the country through fear of Jack Helm, Doc White, and Bill Sutton. The Day and Taylor families were requesting a *guarantee* from Davidson that "they will not be molested if they return."[44] This of course was hardly a guarantee that Davidson could make, but he tried. On October 31 Davidson wrote to Senator Pridgen regarding this unusual guarantee-request, stating that William Day and James Taylor could return as there would be no reason to fear "molestation or summary conduct" from Helm, White, and Sutton. But Davidson gave Pridgen a duty, that he was to inform Day and Taylor "that they may come back without fear of being molested in any way." Davidson seemed to suspect the pair had reason to fear, as he added to his admonition: "If they are guilty of any offense, they will of course be dealt with according to law but they need fear no private persecution or bodily injury. Any person attempting that Sort of conduct will be dealt with to the extent of the law."[45] That certainly sounded peaceful in Davidson's secure office in Austin, but even with these assurances the Days and the Taylors kept their weapons close.

Even after Helm was dismissed from the State Police, Pridgen would not give up on his attempts to punish Helm, although he never stated in writing that Helm should be tried and imprisoned for his perceived crimes. Pridgen had collected affidavits from various members of the Kelly and Taylor families, who claimed to have witnessed the killing of the Kelly brothers. On November 1 he forwarded

James Creed "Jim" Taylor, center, with Ed. J. Glover (left) and Ed Harris, taken at Powder Horn, Calhoun County, Texas. Jim Taylor was the "stranger" who along with John Wesley Hardin ended the life of Jack Helm. Courtesy Jack Caffall.

affidavits prepared and signed by Amanda Kelly, Delilah Kelly, Louisa Day, Pitkin B. Taylor, John W. Day, and J.K. Hawks relative to the August 26 double killing of the Kellys. He added that James Turner, "who saw the whole affair, has since disappeared" suggesting that he too may have been a victim of Helm, or possibly chose to leave the country fearing what might happen to him if he stayed. [46]

Some good news for Helm did arrive in Davidson's office when Lucas Smith, District Attorney of the 11th Judicial District, informed Davidson there were no indictments against Jack Helm in that district. On or about the same day, November 4, 1870, the communication arrived from Greenville's A.D. Roby, District Clerk of Hunt County (adjacent to Hopkins County), certifying that no indictment existed for Jack Helm. That was certainly good news, but as yet no word from Hopkins County.[47] Were Hopkins County authorities preparing an indictment for J.J. Helm?

John Chambliss also learned of the dismissal of Jack Helm from the force and now contacted Davidson about his experience. He prepared an affidavit telling how Helm had ordered State Police-men to arrest him, although the details have not been discovered. Chambliss, seventy years old at that time, resided near St. Mary's in Refugio County and farmed with his two sons, John and Walter, aged fifteen and fourteen years old respectively and his thirty-four-year-old wife Elmira. Chambliss must have had an exciting life and it is unfortunate we know so little of it. He married Elmira Jones, whose maiden name may have been Kelly, in 1854, and by 1860 the couple had located in Live Oak County, their household made up of ten young people, nieces and nephews and their own children. The Chambliss couple by 1870 had located at St. Mary's and it was there John Chambliss was arrested on orders from Helm. He received no satisfaction from the adjutant general's office as Davidson advised him he would have to deal with the matter through the court system as Helm "was no longer a member of the State Police." Chambliss received nothing from his efforts to obtain justice, and during the decade of the seventies he passed; by 1880 his widow was residing in Coryell County with her son, his wife, and their child.[48]

Senator F.E. Grothaus had come to the realization that Jack Helm might be removed and was able to recommend a replacement. He believed that a Victoria citizen, Asher P. Hammond, a thirty-nine-year-old farmer from New York, would be the man to take his place. What qualities A.P. Hammond possessed that would qualify him for the position the senator did not state, but Grothaus felt Hammond fully qualified for the position. Hammond's service record indicates he enlisted in the Union Army on September 5, 1861, in Indiana in Company B, 31st Indiana Infantry, and was mustered out January 8, 1866.[49] This New Yorker had a wife, Hannah, from Indiana and one child. In the household previously enumerated was one Thomas Ragland, who gained recognition in the feud. Henry Ragland and Thomas Ragland were related, and both saw Hammond's potential.[50]

Although by the end of 1870, Jack Helm had been ousted from the State Police force, he was still sheriff of DeWitt County, an area considered by many to be the heartland of the Sutton-Taylor Feud; some even considered the troubles would be more properly named the Helm-Taylor Feud, which evolved into the Sutton-Taylor Feud. Those who blamed him for the reign of terror in the south Texas area could not yet relax their vigilance, as he would continue that reign as sheriff of the county. He still had important men who believed in him, regardless of how he treated prisoners "attempting to escape." Besides Joe Tumlinson, there were James W. Cox, William M. Sutton, the Meador brothers, and numerous others.

But there were important and dangerous men who did *not* believe in Sheriff Jack Helm or his tactics, a group that included numerous Taylors and their friends. Among those associates were Mannen Clements and his three brothers, "Gip," Jim, and Joe, a formidable quartet; Alford C. Day, James Creed Taylor, the latter's cousin William Riley "Bill" Taylor, and George Culver Tennille. Most importantly there was among the Taylors John Wesley Hardin, a teenager who had already developed a reputation as a man-killer, filled with ruthlessness and seemingly always eager and ready to kill. It was only a matter of time before Jack Helm was on Hardin's list of deadly enemies.

And Jim Taylor would return.

George Culver Tennille, a highly respected member of the Clements-Taylor clan. He was killed in Gonzales County in 1874 COURTESY JACK CAFFALL.

Alford Creed "Alf" Day (seated) was a close associate of John Wesley Hardin and the Taylor clan. The standing figure has been identified as Jack Hays Day who later wrote a brief history of the Sutton-Taylor Feud. Courtesy Kurt House.

7

Gunfire at the Billings Store

"John Wesley Hardin Killed Thomas Holderman [sic]*"*
—**Brown Bowen**

PUBLIC PRESSURE FORCED GOVERNOR E.J. DAVIS to make the decision regarding his police captain: to remove or to retain Captain Helm. Reducing Helm in rank was not considered an option. The governor and Adj. Gen. James H. Davidson weighed the negative reports against the positive ones and determined that the negative ones outweighed the few positive. Although respected citizens had recommended Helm be retained, too much harm had been done. Governor Davis certainly had the final say, and for him, the political pressure was too much to retain Helm's services, regardless of the accuracy—or inaccuracy—of the various claims of his outrageous conduct. The question then became: who would replace Jack Helm? Whoever was chosen, the man had to be totally removed from such actions as murdering prisoners. Thomas Williams had been named captain only on a temporary basis.

Davidson chose Robert Francis "Frank" Haskins to replace the disgraced Helm. What qualities did he possess that gave him the nod over the others under consideration? Again, no notes were made for historians to later debate; but Haskins certainly possessed the qualities of courage and experience to be the new captain. As for experience, he had captained Company A 9th Regiment of the State Guards which had given him recognition in the adjutant general's office.[1] His unit was headquartered at Helena; thus Haskins had had experience not only in a command position, but was known in Karnes County where there was much lawlessness. He knew the area. The one remaining muster roll of Company A shows 105 names, one of which was James Sutton, brother of William M. Sutton whose name identified one party of the Sutton-Taylor Feud.[2] Robert F. Haskins was commissioned December 1, 1870, and qualified as Helm's replacement the same day. Few specific details of his life are known. He was born in Brazoria County, Texas November 23, 1838, and once having located in Karnes County settled there for the remainder of his life. After marriage to Ann Louisa Drake he fathered two children: son Francis Orin and daughter Emily Louise. After her husband's death the widow Haskins boarded at the John W. Ruckman home, living with her daughter and her family until her own death in Karnes County on August 23, 1930, from heart failure.[3]

By reputation R.F. Haskins was considered very competent to serve as captain of the fourth district, was of good moral character and of high standing in the community. Even Senator Pridgen had to admit that the choice for Haskins was a good one. The senator believed that Haskins was "entirely disconnected with any of the regulating or lawless cliques of the country"; no longer would the police be considered a "cause of alarm and oppression."[4] Haskins did not remain long as captain, for he resigned August 31, 1872. His health had started to fail, and he died of undetermined causes three and one half months later on December 16, 1873.[5]

As Haskins had lived and worked in the Karnes County area he and Jack Helm certainly knew each other; the pair may have even discussed the situation of the various feuding families. Just knowing each other does not imply that either one considered planning any activity together.

The brand of Jack Helm, registered December 19, 1870, preserved in the DeWitt County Historical Records. Author's Collection.

Little is known of Helm's actions following his dismissal from the police force. Besides his farming concerns he was still the sheriff of DeWitt County, although he assigned much of the sheriff's duties to capable deputies. Even as a sheriff he still had to tend to more mundane matters such as registering his brand at the courthouse. On December 17 he handled that matter, registering his brand as J Bar HE, with the top vertical lines of the "J" and the "E" connected, making what appears to be a JHE.[6] He certainly had to remain constantly on the alert as those men who were killed while in his custody, while "attempting to escape," had family and friends who might be more than willing to take revenge rather than stumble through the legal system in attempting to find a legitimate means by which to gain justice, or, more likely, revenge.

Ironically Helm also had to be concerned with the results of past actions not involving a killing while he was in charge of the Fourth District. One important matter was what had happened in Bee County; now that he was ousted, George Turner brought charges against him, claiming Helm had robbed him of $500. Davidson now instructed Haskins to arrest his predecessor. Perhaps Haskins didn't act quickly enough, perhaps taking some time to arrange his affairs now that he was a captain in the

State Police. On December 10, 1870, he wrote to Davidson that he would have Helm arrested and deliver him to the authorities in Beeville.[7] Davidson, now wanting action taken swiftly against Helm, wanted him in custody and he wanted this done promptly. By mid-January 1871 Haskins had arrested Helm but he still was not acting quickly enough to satisfy Davidson, who noted as early as January 19, 1871, that Haskins had "not yet sent prisoner Helm to Bee County." Davidson left no doubt as to what he expected Haskins to do: "You will at once place him under charge of an efficient guard and send him to Bee county turning him over to the civil authorities and taking the sheriffs receipt for him. *This must be done at once.*" Davidson underlined the last six words of his communication to emphasize his order. Davidson wondered what could be the delay, as from Helena to Beeville if traveled in a straight line the distance is less than fifty miles. Haskins should be able to deliver the prisoner to Bee County authorities before noon, and if necessary, rest riders and horses and then return in the evening. What could cause the delay?

What if the prisoner should attempt to escape?

Did this thought occur to Jack Helm, when and if he was in actual custody of the guard? Did Captain Haskins ask himself the same "what if" question? Perhaps Helm knew Haskins was not the type of man to kill an unarmed prisoner. Or perhaps Helm knew better than to even try and escape.

Of course Davidson wanted Haskins to report fully his action promptly.[8] The adjutant general was clearly under the impression that Haskins had arrested Helm on the Bee County charge, but in mid-February again wrote to his new captain: "you will at once inform me if he [Helm] has been turned over to the Sheriff of Bee county as ordered. No further delay in this matter will be allowed, and an answer to this communication will be forwarded by return mail."[9] Davidson now became more rigid in his relationship with Haskins; he did not want Helm's replacement to be so casual about reports and acting decisively on his orders. Helm was certainly not forgotten about by the adjutant general.

Captain Haskins did not fail to do his duty; after this second letter from the adjutant general, in mid-February 1871 he did arrest the disgraced Jack Helm and delivered him to Beeville where he turned the prisoner over to Bee County sheriff Thomas H. Marsden. Marsden was a young man—born in New York on July 27, 1846, twenty-five years old now—and who had served through the recent War of the Rebellion in the 32nd Texas Cavalry, Wood's Regiment, Company D, mainly in the Trans-Mississippi Department. He had been a Texan since 1854, first in Brazoria County and then in Bee County. On February 22, 1871, he had Jack Helm, now the defendant, in district court in Bee-ville facing a charge of robbery.[10]

Jack Helm did not appear alone in the courtroom to face the charge. With him were former companions from his State Police days: C.C. Simmons, the policeman who had been in charge of the squad that had killed the Kelly brothers when they "attempted to escape"; Cornelius V. "Neal" Busby, who had been commissioned as a private August 13, 1870, but who would resign April 30, 1872; and Thomas Lemuel Patton, another State Policeman, commissioned as a private October 1, 1870, but who would rank as a sergeant in April 1873 when the force ceased to exist.[11]

Helm did not stand trial on that first court appearance, but rather he made sufficient bond in the amount of $1,000. He was scheduled to appear in Bee County District Court again on June 22 but this time he failed to appear. The bond was forfeited and court costs were added.[12] This would be made final at the next term of court. A *scire facias* was issued for each: the judge ordered alias capiases issued for Helm, Simmons, Busby, and Patton in DeWitt County. Then the cause was moved to Goliad County on a change of venue. Ultimately the charge against Helm for the robbery of George Turner would be dropped; Turner received no justice. Others who became involved as sureties to maintain continuances were William Sutton, James Anderson, Richard B. Hudson, and William W. Wells. Ultimately, at the October 1873 term of District Court, the matter of George L. Turner v. Jack Helm was dismissed.[13]

Now, no longer having the blessings of the Reconstruction forces to protect him, deeds done in other counties began to catch up with Jack Helm. In March 1871, Davidson sent to Captain Haskins five capiases against Helm from Hopkins County with orders to have him arrested and to "Detail a suitable detachment of State Policemen" and deliver him to Hopkins County civil officers there for trial. Haskins was ordered to do this without delay and to report his action immediately. To show his concern in this matter Davidson added: "This order is *peremptory* and will admit of no delay." Haskins may have pondered the meaning of that word *peremptory* but perhaps he knew it meant the order was to be followed without any delay whatsoever, that it was irreversible and absolute. Haskins and Helm should leave within the hour for Hopkins County. Of course he was to report his action to Davidson.[14] His destination with prisoner Helm was nearly 400 miles north, certainly a journey of no little time and distance.

Helm may have forgotten about the hanging on Oxford's Bridge; after all, wasn't it simply an incident during the war? But the northeast Texas matter would not go away. Hopkins County was preparing to avenge the Oxford's Bridge hanging of the five men and was in the early stages of gathering witnesses. Ironically some were living in Karnes County although no explanation has been determined for this unusual situation. Davidson responded to a letter from the Hopkins County District Clerk regarding the location of certain individuals, reporting that Harrison Portwood, Barnabus Payne, William Payne, James Bartlett, William Yates, David Hemby, William Hemby, Jack Hemby, and a Miss Hemby [15] were all residing in Karnes County "where a summons will find them."[16] It is curious that various Hembys and close associates became residents of Karnes County, so close to the area where Jack

John Wesley Hardin as he appeared in Abilene, Kansas, in 1871, two years prior to his killing the sheriff of DeWitt County, Texas. COURTESY THE ROBERT G. MCCUBBIN COLLECTION.

Helm had lived and worked. In 1866, John Harrison Portwood had moved his family to Helena, Karnes County, where he established a ranch and raised horses and cattle. How long Portwood remained in Karnes County is uncertain, but twenty years later he and his family were back in Hopkins County.[17] Had they been witnesses to the hangings at Oxford's Bridge?

Little is known about Helm as sheriff compared to the abundance of material available on him as captain of the State Police. Ironically some of what we know of his work as sheriff comes directly from the memoir of John Wesley Hardin—not always accurate but always biased—as would be expected. In early 1872 Hardin for an unstated reason visited the King Ranch in Deep South Texas, some 300 miles from his home county of Gonzales. If Hardin had any legitimate business to conduct with Capt. Richard King no record is known to explain what it was. He may have been there hoping to hire out his guns as a "range detective" for the King Ranch, intending to ruthlessly rid the King range of any perceived cattle thieves foolish enough to steal livestock with the Running W brand. Years later Hardin recalled his visit to the King Ranch: "I stayed there the next day, transacted my business, and in company with Jim Cox I made my way to San Diego, stayed there overnight, and then with Cox went on to Banquetto [sic] and stayed there a day or two."[18]

Hardin's discussion with Richard King—if he even was able to meet with the cattle king—did not result in his employment so he then began the trek home to Gonzales County, but curiously he did not have to travel through the dangerous brush country, this *brasada*, alone. James W. Cox was also returning from a meeting at the King Ranch, and he lived in DeWitt County, so Cox and Hardin were both going "home" to the same general area. Had J.W. Cox also been there to offer his gun to Captain King? Cox was a deputy working for Sheriff Helm. Further he had been a private in the State Police, commissioned July 13, 1870, but removed from the force February 13, 1871, with no reason given.[19] Hardin may not have known Cox had been a State Policeman but he certainly would have known he was a DeWitt County deputy. The Sutton-Taylor Feud was raging, and Cox was a frequent companion of William Sutton and Joseph Tumlinson. Helm, Sutton, and Tumlinson were considered the leaders of the vigilante group fighting against the Taylors. Hardin certainly knew of the close association of these three men.

After a few days at Banquete, only a few miles west of Corpus Christi in Nueces County, the pair continued the journey home. Hardin was courting young Jane Bowen and was anxious to see her again; Cox presumably was anxious to return to his wife and family as well.[20] Nothing memorable happened on the way home to DeWitt County. If indeed Hardin and Cox did return together they certainly had the opportunity to discuss thoroughly the conflict between the Sutton and the Taylor forces. Cox may have even invited Hardin to join their vigilante—or Regulator—group. Nothing of substance came of it, if that offer was made, as Hardin continued his allegiance with the Taylors, although he was not related.

While he seemed to feel free to roam southeast Texas without consequences, Hardin was a wanted man, who would eventually have the highest price on his head of anyone in Texas. He was not the only one with legal problems, however: Helm as well was facing legal matters but nothing as serious as Hardin's. Presiding Justice Oliver K. Tuton;[21] Ferdinand Ploeger;[22] Justice of the Peace Little Berry Wright,[23] deputy clerk Milton V. Kinnison,[24] and J.B. Tucker gathered in the DeWitt County courthouse for important business. Also present were James Martin, District Attorney for the 17th

Judicial District, who "moved the court for an order requiring the Sheriff elect to give a new bond." It was the sixth of August 1872; the previous bond had not been filed in the time proscribed by law and was thus "inoperative and void." Secondly, the oath had not been taken until long after the bond had been filed, and was therefore doubly void. Helm was thus required to post a new bond and oath. The bond, in the amount of $10,000, was posted with Jack Helm as principal and William Sutton, Joseph Taylor,[25] J.P. Beck,[26] Joe Tumlinson, J.W. Cox, R.B. Hudson, and R.W. Thomas as sureties.[27] Presumably after the legal niceties were disposed of the gentlemen went their separate ways, although they may have been watching their backs. After all, of those eight named above three would lose their lives violently during the feud: Jack Helm, William Sutton, and James W. Cox.

Killings did occur which to us today seem totally senseless, but actually may have been directly related to the hatreds of the feud, which would have given them some meaning. The death of Thomas Jacob Haldeman[28] is such an example. On December 17, 1872, a group of men had gathered at the Billings' store at the small community of Nopal in rural Gonzales County. Nopal in 1872 may have consisted of a few stores, certainly a saloon or two, perhaps a blacksmith shop and a few homes, but not even enough to warrant a post office; today only the sign notifying its former location remains, courtesy of the Texas State Highway Department. Hardin, his now brother-in-law Joshua Robert "Brown" Bowen, William MacDonald Billings and his son John MacDonald "Mac" Billings, brothers James and John Gibson "Gip" Clements, Thomas J. Haldeman, Rockwood "Jim" Birtsell, and George Culver Tennille, father-in-law of James Clements, were among those present at the store.[29] There may have been others as well. It was a day of drinking and carousing by men who perhaps used this "watering hole" occasionally or perhaps frequently.

The group started celebrating the holidays early, as Christmas was only days away. What should have been only a day of celebration became ugly with violence. The incident had a terrible effect on many of the participants. Thomas J. Haldeman consumed too much of the ardent; he became drowsy, grabbed a blanket and lay down nearby with a tree trunk as his headboard. He promptly fell asleep. Brown Bowen, who could not have been totally sober, then saw Haldeman in this defenseless position, approached him with a pistol in hand and shot him in the head. The sleeping Haldeman never felt the bullet and died instantly.[30] Bowen initially claimed he shot Haldeman because he believed him to be a spy for the Jack Helm and Joe Tumlinson Regulator forces, of which Cox and Sutton were principal members. That at least is what Bowen claimed at first, and possibly that is what he believed. The fact that Haldeman was asleep when he was killed ruled out any possibility to claim self-defense later when Bowen was tried for murder. On trial for his life he denied any direct involvement in the killing and accused John Wesley Hardin of being the actual murderer. His statement then is noteworthy:

> John Wesley Hardin killed Thomas Holderman [sic], and he did it for the following reasons: Hardin thought Holderman was a spy who was watching him to let parties know of his whereabouts that they might capture him. J. Tomlinson, Jack Helm, and other parties were trying to get a chance to do so, as Hardin said, to kill him, and I did everything I could to keep Hardin from killing him, which Joe Sunday and Jim Birtsell know, for I went to them and told them to try to get Tom to go home, that J. Hardin was mad with him.[31]

Bowen claimed that Hardin then actually went to the home of Haldeman's parents—David and Candis[32]—and explained to the now grieving father and mother that Bowen had killed their son. Less than a month later, on January 12, 1873, State Police Sergeant Thomas L. Patton and deputy sheriff David J. Blair "and a posse of citizens" arrested Bowen, although no details as to how that was done have been learned.[33] Patton was a forty-four-year-old Alabama native who raised stock and farmed in Karnes County and would be forgotten if not for his membership in the State Police. When the force became a reality he enlisted as a private on October 1, 1870; he was promoted to sergeant on April 1, 1872, and promoted to lieutenant on April 10, 1873.[34] Perhaps his arrest of Bowen resulted in his superiors noticing him and awarded him with a promotion.

On February 10, 1873, the Gonzales District Court indicted Bowen for the murder of Thomas J. Haldeman. Unable to raise the $25,000 bail he was remanded to the county jail. He did not have to suffer the discomfort of his cell long as on March 26 brother-in-law Hardin and a dozen friends liberated Bowen from the jail. Wisely Bowen chose to leave Texas behind him and found refuge among relatives in far-off Florida. Bowen remained a free man until Florida lawmen captured him in September 1877.[35]

Jack Helm had several major concerns following his dismissal from the police force, one of which had to do with his two inventions: an improved cotton-worm destroyer and a cultivator. He perhaps sketched out his ideas and then worked on implementing them to wood and metal in blacksmith shops, at least one of which was in the little community of Albuquerque in western Gonzales County, a town established by veterans of the ill-fated Sibley campaign to conquer the southwest in the early days of the late war. How long he had worked on these inventions is unknown but

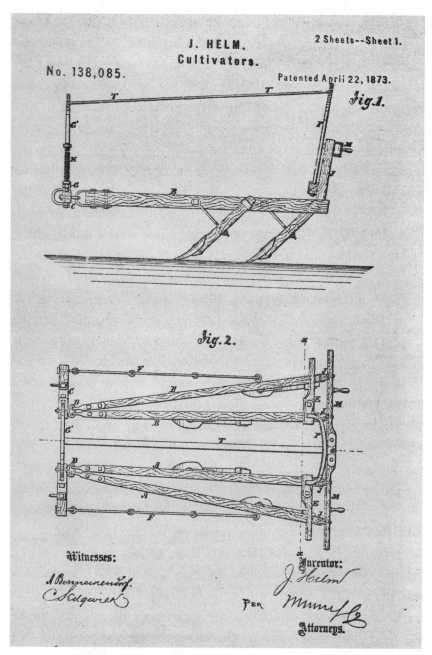

The Patent Office sketch of Helm's cultivator. AUTHOR'S COLLECTION.

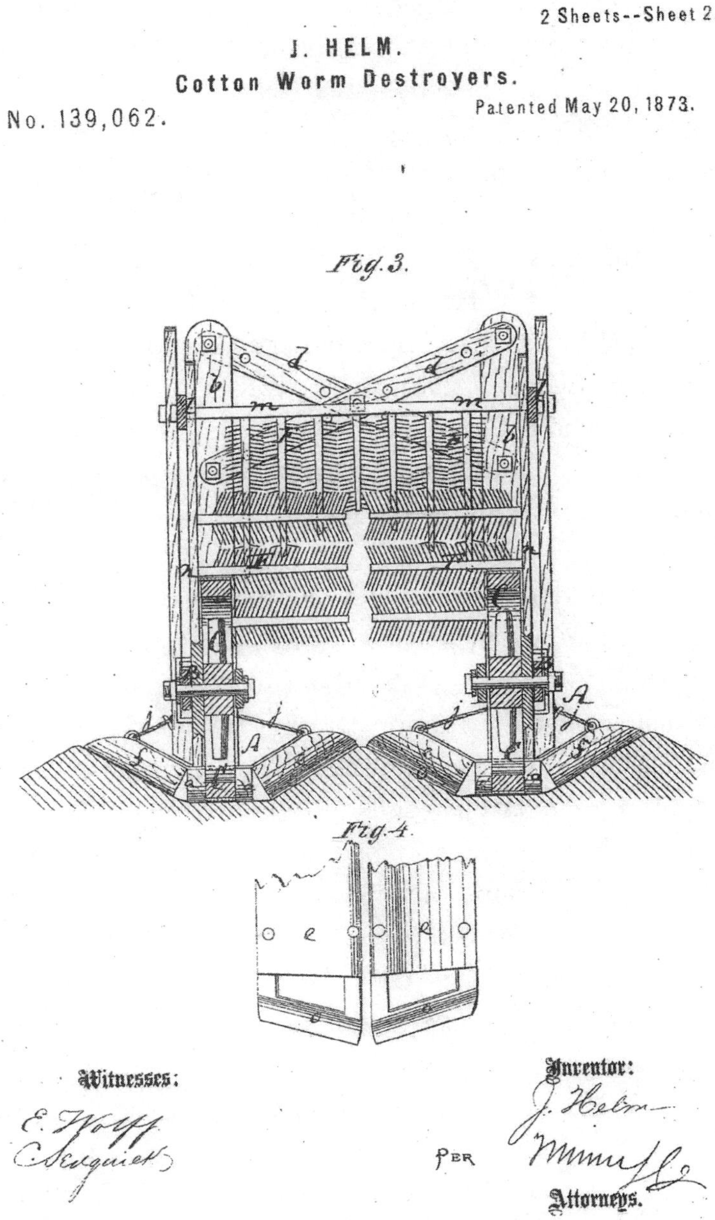

2 Sheets--Sheet 2.

J. HELM.
Cotton Worm Destroyers.

No. 139,062.   Patented May 20, 1873.

Fig. 3.

Fig. 4.

Witnesses:
E. Wolff
Sänguiet

Inventor:
J. Helm

PER

Attorneys.

The Patent Office sketch of Helm's "new and Improved Cotton Worm Destroyer" invention.
AUTHOR'S COLLECTION.

in November 1872 he applied for patents, which were issued in 1873. Albuquerque resident John Bland owned and operated the blacksmith shop there and allowed Helm to work in his shop to complete the actual modeling.[36]

In the days of horses and wagons and buggies every little community had at least one blacksmith shop, but Helm may have felt the pressures of the Taylors if he remained in his home area of Concrete and Hochheim in DeWitt County and went to Albuquerque "seeking seclusion rather than protection from the Taylors" according to local historian R.R. "Railroad" Smith who grew up in Albuquerque.[37] While working on his invention he also had to remain cautious about enemies coming to exact vengeance on him for acts committed during his time as a policeman. As a county sheriff, it was not easy to go fully armed and also tinker with his inventions. The Sutton-Taylor Feud was very much a reality and there were plenty of feudists living in Gonzales County as well as DeWitt County. As sheriff of course he had several deputies to help oversee the county. Possibly he more or less allowed them to act as they wished in dealing with lawbreakers. Sometimes his deputies created violent situations.

One such deputy was John B. Morgan, who apparently was the overseer of law and order in the newly established community of Cuero. A year before there was no Cuero, but when the Gulf, Western Texas and Pacific Railway extended their tracks from Indianola to San Antonio, the railway chose the site of Cuero to become a midway stopping point. The growing community soon became the county seat, which it is today. The saloon Morgan entered where he would have his last drink was scarcely finished. The tracks had been laid by January of 1873 but people had been erecting homes and businesses intending to establish a new community in the latter months of 1872. Whatever the appearance of the saloon was it could not have been older than a few months.[38]

Deputy Morgan instigated a difficulty in a Cuero saloon on April 4, 1873. John Wesley Hardin was also present and the trouble began when Morgan asked—or perhaps demanded—Hardin buy him a bottle of champagne. No one knows why Morgan acted as he did that day. Possibly Deputy Morgan believed he could "take" Hardin after a few drinks when he would not be totally on his guard. Hardin refused the request of course. This refusal resulted in heated words; the pair continued the argument out on the street. The result was that Hardin shot and killed Helm's deputy J.B. Morgan. By early 1873 the twenty-year-old John Wesley Hardin had developed a sizeable reputation and carried a $1000 reward for his capture. He had recently delivered brother-in-law Brown Bowen out of the Gonzales jail. Presumably Sheriff Helm informed Austin of what had happened, for in the report to the governor Adj. Gen. Frank Britton, only recently replacing James Davidson, reported that Morgan was killed on April 4 and his slayer was identified as Fred Johnson, an alias. Sheriff Helm—if he made any type of investigation—certainly knew better.[39] John Wesley Hardin was gaining a reputation *equal to that of Sheriff Jack Helm*. Adjutant General Britton was very much aware of him and wrote this in his report to the governor:

> In Gonzales County there is a strong band of thieves and murderers, headed by John Hardin, alias Wesley Hardin, alias Wesley Clements, who is reported to have committed sixteen different murders, and has threatened to kill a member of the Legislature, Hon. S.T. Robb. One thousand dollars reward has been offered by your Excellency for Hardin. . . . On the twenty-second day of March the man Hardin, with a squad of twelve men, all

armed with Winchester guns and six-shooters, rode into the town of Gonzales, and delivered the county jail of all its prisoners, threatening the guard with death if they made any alarm.[40]

Hardin of course had his own ideas about the troubles in Gonzales and DeWitt Counties, and they differed radically from Britton's view. He wrote, years later, that in 1873

there existed in Gonzales and DeWitt counties a vigilant committee that made life, liberty, and property uncertain. The vigilant band was headed by Jack Helm, the sheriff of DeWitt, and his most able lieutenants were his deputies, Jim Cox, Joe Tomlinson [sic], and Bill Sutton. Some of the best men in the county had been murdered by this mob.

John Wesley Hardin recalled as late as April 1873 he had not met the sheriff of DeWitt, although he must have known him at least by sight. That first meeting with the sheriff took place on the road to Cuero around the ninth of April. Supposedly Hardin was on his way there to conduct some business involving shipping cattle. On the way he saw a rider who acted suspiciously. Finally the two approached and, while still mounted, met; at first Hardin believed the rider was J.B. Hudson, a Helm deputy. Then the other introduced himself, explaining that Hudson was his deputy and that he was Helm, the sheriff of DeWitt County. Helm offered his hand but Hardin refused to shake it, challenging him that he now had the chance to take him to Austin as a prisoner. Hardin, who probably knew who this rider was all along, now expressed his anger: "We are man to man and face to face; on equal terms. You have said I was a murderer and a coward, and have had your deputies after me. Now arrest me if you can. I dare you to try it."

Helm knew better, realizing that he had no chance with Hardin, and pretended he did not recognize the man, acting surprised: "Are you Wesley?" and offered his hand. Perhaps now realizing he was in a dangerous situation, Helm claimed that if his deputies were hunting him they were doing so "on their own account" and not his. By now Hardin had drawn his pistol but for some reason did not shoot. Helm begged Hardin not to kill him and now pointed out that even with the governor's reward for Hardin in his pocket he promised he would never try to "execute it," that if Hardin spared his life he would be his friend. Hardin informed Helm that the actions of his deputies were his responsibility; there, the topic ended, and Helm and Hardin rode on to Cuero together.[41] This was Hardin's version of the first meeting between the sheriff of DeWitt and the deadly gunfighter. That they did not know each other by sight is doubtful; that Hardin would not shoot the sheriff is unlikely. He had killed a number of men for virtually no reason; he could have killed Helm and then made up a tale of having to defend himself. But we do not have a version of when Helm and Hardin first met other than Hardin's written years after the fact. We can only accept Hardin's description with numerous doubts. If this meeting of the two men did take place when it did, in early April, on the road to Cuero, then it is understood that members of the feuding parties at times could control their passion and refrain from violence.

In essence there existed two sides: Hardin and his associates, which included James Creed Taylor and numerous other Taylor family members, working against Sheriff Helm and his deputies and followers. At this time one could easily call the violent situation in that area of Texas the Helm-Hardin feud. In spite of the popular notion created by Hollywood westerns of enemies fighting each other face to face, each man giving his opponent an equal opportunity, frequently an ambush was preferred. Hardin planned several such ambushes, and the countryside lent itself well to such acts. One could ambush an enemy in the towns as well. One such ambush was planned to kill Bill Sutton, shooting him to death as he played cards in a Cuero saloon; the men apparently shot too fast and their intended victim was only wounded. Sutton was the object of another ambush but he and his companions—Horace French, J.P. "Doc" White, John Meador,[42] and Addison Patterson—survived. It was the common belief among the Taylor clan that Bill Sutton was responsible for the shooting of Pitkin Taylor in late 1872 but who did not succumb to his wounds until March of 1873. His son, and nephew of Creed Taylor, J.C. "Jim" Taylor, swore vengeance. Helm had been in charge of the posse which had killed Pitkin Taylor's sons-in-law—Henry and William Kelly—providing another reason for the Taylors to avenge their murders by marking Helm for death. "Anyone who did not indorse their foul deeds or go with them on their raids" recalled Hardin years later, "incurred their hatred, and it meant certain death at their hands."[43]

Sheriff Helm did not sit idle amidst these acts of vengeance. There is no evidence that he made any attempt to settle the differences between the Taylors and the Suttons. It is doubtful that he did, as none of the available literature suggests Helm ever attempted such heroic acts. But possibly there was a serious attempt made between the respective feuding parties to come to a peaceful resolution. This can be accepted only if we trust the word of John Wesley Hardin's memoir, which is frequently tenuous at best. Hardin recalled that it was shortly after the attempt to kill Bill Sutton in a Cuero billiard hall that he, cousin Mannen Clements, and feudist George Culver Tennille actually met with Jack Helm at the home of James W. Cox to discuss the situation. There was little if any progress made, as—still according to Hardin—he, Clements and Tennille would have to join Helm's vigilant committee. Joining Helm's force would be good for Hardin of course as then all charges against him could be dropped. But in return he would have to do some killing for the vigilant committee. Helm may have promised such a feat, but of course he had no authority or power to have murder charges dropped against Hardin, accused of murder in a number of Texas counties besides DeWitt where Helm did have some power. Hardin knew better, but Helm may have actually believed he could cause those murder charges to be dismissed.

If indeed this meeting did take place it is a wonder that it ended peacefully. Possibly the fact that all concerned were facing each other prevented any gun play then. Temporary truces did occur in real life. But the problem in this possible agreement was that some of the work expected of Hardin was the killing of men whom he considered to be his friends. Indeed, even if he was expected to have all charges against him dropped, he would probably have resented being considered a "hired gun." Even such a man-killer as Hardin had his standards, after all.

Hardin's rejection of this deal resulted in an unexpected reaction from the Helm party. Sometime in April 1873, Helm and a posse entered the Hardin neighborhood looking for him and certain others of his friends, mainly Mannen Clements, a first cousin of Hardin. The men folk were not at home at that time, but the women were. According to Hardin's memoir, Helm was especially abusive toward Hardin's wife, the fifteen-year-old Jane Bowen Hardin, sister of Brown Bowen who had left the state after being liberated from the Gonzales jail. Abusing Jane Hardin was a serious offense. It was one thing *to threaten Hardin*, but it was another thing *to insult his wife*. Young though she may have been the brave Jane Hardin stood up to Jack Helm, giving him no satisfaction at all, only frustration.[44]

Jack Helm then may have gone to his blacksmith shop to smolder internally and work on his cultivator or his cotton worm destroyer. Hardin, never one to smolder, sent word to the Taylors to meet with him at Mustang Mott "to concoct a plan of campaign."[45] Hardin had been too young to go into battle during the late war, but he now could become a general and develop a campaign to rid the country of "murderous cowards."[46] No uniforms would be needed in this war, which now became the Helm-Hardin Feud within the Sutton-Taylor Feud. The battlefields would be the prairies and the tangled brush of DeWitt County, or maybe even the streets of Clinton or Cuero. The mission was to eradicate the vigilantes who were destroying life, property, and family hegemony—especially among the Taylors, friends of John Wesley Hardin, and enemies of Jack Helm.

Mustang Mott was a popular gathering place some seven miles north of Cuero in DeWitt County. Early settlers found it a convenient place to stop and rest their livestock in going from Indianola to San Antonio. It once was a popular place to capture wild mustangs, hence its name by which it is known today. There may have been a grouping of live oaks or other shade-providing trees in the late 1860s and 1870s, so when Hardin called for a meeting at Mustang Mott there was no question as to where to gather.[47]

It was here that Hardin assembled his troops including Mannen Clements, George C. Tennille, James C. "Jim" Taylor, John Milan Taylor, Rufus P. "Scrap" Taylor, Alford Creed Day, and Jack Hays Day, and perhaps others. One can easily picture this group of men, all angry at their enemies led by Helm and Sutton. Hardin was perhaps the youngest, born in 1853; Tennille was the eldest, born in 1825. The group under Hardin's leadership discussed various concerns, various ways to get at their enemies. The end result was their agreement "to fight mob law to the bitter end, as our lives and families were in danger."[48] One can easily picture the group—pistol belts full of ammunition, rifles and shotguns fully loaded, eager to follow the young general and all eager to do battle.

Jack Helm became aware of this meeting of his enemies. How he learned of it and what his immediate reaction was is not recorded, but he certainly gathered some of his associates to discuss the possible change in tactics. The young Hardin would bring about a more aggressive element to the conflict. That Hardin actually wrote out a list of human targets is doubtful; perhaps, perhaps not, but James W. Cox was the first to fall. He was not alone when the bloody ambush came.

DeWitt County feudists did not choose open warfare, but rather the ambush became the preferred method of dealing with enemies. Somewhere between Helena in Karnes County—Captain R.F. Haskins' headquarters—and Yorktown—the home of Capt. Joe Tumlinson—whatever silence there may have been on that road abruptly ended. The horsemen were James W. Cox, John W.S. "Jake" Christman, Henry Ragland, and Capt. Joe Tumlinson, and possibly several others.[49] The ambush erupted with shotguns and six-shooters: Cox and Christman were hit and collapsed from their horses. The others spurred their mounts, wisely fleeing to fight another day, leaving Cox and Christman to their fate, not knowing how many shootists were hidden from view. The final act was administered quickly: the nineteen buckshot in Cox's body perhaps killed him before he hit the ground; in case not whoever slit his throat from ear to ear made sure he would not fight again. Perhaps Christman's body was treated in a similar manner. Editor Victor M. Rose of the *Victoria Advocate* learned of the incident and headlined his report with "Shocking Double Murder" but did not speculate as to who had done the deed.[50] He did point out that Cox had been with Helm in his "Regulator depredations, and no doubt he was killed to avenge some injury inflicted then." As for the others, they were riding "a few yards to the rear when the volley emptied the saddles of their companions, and thus warned, saved themselves by a hasty retreat."[51] The location of the graves of Cox and Christman, if ever marked, has since been lost.[52]

8

"Attempting to Escape"

*"I am pained to informe you that there is a verry bad State
of affairs in our County"*
—Justice L.B. Wright to Governor E.J. Davis, July 24, 1873.

JACK HELM FELT SECURE IN the blacksmith shop in Albuquerque.
It was a community in western Gonzales County, only two miles
south of where the borders of Gonzales, Wilson, and Guadalupe
Counties meet.[1] In 1873, when Helm worked at his invention,
Albuquerque was a small but thriving community; brothers-in-law
Henry S. Hastings and Samuel L. McCracken Sr. from Mississippi were considered the unofficial founders of the town. A post
office had opened in 1870 and William W. Davis was appointed
the first postmaster on September 19. Besides his postal duties he
had been commissioned a sergeant in the State Police and served
until resigning on October 31, 1872.[2] Helm and W.W. Davis first
became acquainted in July of 1870 when the police force was
organized. Along with the post office there was a cotton gin operated by Samuel L. McCracken Sr., a blacksmith shop operated by
fifty-five-year-old South Carolinian John Bland,[3] a general store, a
saloon and a school. The McCrackens operated a boardinghouse
for travelers and on occasion Jack Helm stayed there, certainly
when he was working on his inventions. Although Helm may have
conceived the implements, he chose Bland to do the modeling of
them, which required both metal and wooden pieces.[4] During the

1870s the population of Albuquerque approached the 500 mark, representing people from many other southern states. It was among the more significant towns between San Antonio and Houston. Here Helm kept busy and was among friends.

The cotton-worm destroyer invention now became his main concern, as his deputies could handle the sheriff's duties quite capably. He had received a patent not only for the cotton worm destroyer but for an improved cultivator as well. If anyone doubted his efforts he could show that the cultivator was patent number 138,085, dated April 22, 1873, and the cotton worm destroyer was patent number 139,062, dated May 20, 1873. If anyone wondered about Helm's first invention the patent began with this description:

> This invention relates to a new machine for removing the destructive cotton-worms from the cotton plants without injury to the plants, and for destroying the worms. My invention consists in the arrangement of a movable frame, which is by animals drawn over the fields to straddle the rows of cotton, and which is provided with brushes for sweeping the worms from the plants, and with jointed bottom pieces or slides, which crush them on the ground.

Helm had provided four detailed drawings which made it all clear to those at the patent office. Helm's improved cultivator patent began:

> Be it known that I, Captain JACK HELM, of Hochheim, in the county of DeWitt and State of Texas, have invented a new and improved Cultivator, of which the following is a specification: The invention consists in an improved mode of connecting eveners with a pair of gang-plows or cultivators, as herein after fully described and pointed out in the claim.

Six detailed figures explained the working of the machine. Today it is difficult to imagine a team of mules pulling such contraptions, but perhaps both of Helm's inventions would have proved to be successful in the field. No working model of either invention is known to exist. All we have today are the drawings, and we are left to wonder if Helm and blacksmith Bland ever did construct a prototype that was then put to the test. Creed Taylor was aware of Helm's invention although he probably learned of its existence second hand. In his "Literary Effort" he wrote with bitterness that Helm "was not a mechanical genius and never invented anything outside of plans to murder innocent men."[5]

Jack Helm arrived in Albuquerque on July 17, "seeking seclusion rather than protection from the Taylors" as one local historian recalled.[6] He spent the night in the McCracken Hotel (no specific name is known and it was probably referred to generally as the McCracken Place). The next day he planned to work on his invention, and due to the heat and no doubt the fact that he considered himself among friends he hung his gun belt and pistols on the hall tree at McCracken's, carelessly leaving himself unarmed. It was a dangerous act for a sheriff to do: he had plenty of enemies who wished him harm, and even if he had not been sheriff one would think he would know to be on his guard.

On that hot day in July of 1873 in that Albuquerque blacksmith shop Jack Helm tinkered with the cultivator. He was so engrossed in the workings of his invention he momentarily forgot about the troubles surrounding him. His residence was in Hochheim, a little community some twenty-five miles southeast of Albuquerque, as the crow flies. He worked there where his enemies would not easily discover his location. To work effectively here he had left behind his weapons. He now was armed only with his bowie-knife which was an essential tool and which would not interfere with his work in the blacksmith shop. Reports of the last day of Helm differ as to whether he had a shotgun or not; if he did he leaned it against a tree close to the shop.[7]

Jack Helm's final moments remain controversial. A number of people observed what actions transpired but they provided reports which are conflicting. The salient point of agreement is that Jack Helm was killed that day while the controversy remains: Who should receive credit for the killing? One early version stated that "a desperado by the name of Hardin with several others of the same stripe rode up to the blacksmith shop of Jack Helm, while he was engaged at his work, and riddled him with bullets."[8] This certainly suggests a small group of riders caught up with Helm and blasted away at their target, each taking the blame—or credit.

Hardin described what happened differently. He recalled the event over two decades later while in prison, having had time to ponder how he wished history to remember him. He recalled the event as taking place on May 17, and as so frequently in his writing his dates are a few months off. In this case the killing took place two months and a day after the date he recollected. It was only two days after the double killing of Cox and Christman. He made the remarkable statement that he was to meet Jack Helm (which name Hardin consistently spelled *Helms*) at the little town of Albuquerque, suggesting he knew where Helm was all along.

> I went there according to agreement, a trusty friend accompanying me in the person of Jim Taylor. We talked matters over together and failed to agree, he seriously threatening Jim Taylor's life, and so I went and told Jim to look out, that Jack Helms [sic] had sworn to shoot him on sight because he had shot Bill Sutton and because he was a Taylor. Jim quickly asked me to introduce him to Helms or point him out. I declined to do this, but referred

him to a friend that would. I went to a blacksmith shop and had
my horse shod. I paid for the shoeing and was fixing to leave when
I heard Helms' voice: "Hand up, you d—s—of a b —."

Hardin looked around and saw Helm "advancing" on Jim Taylor
with the large knife in his hands. Then someone shouted "Shoot the
damn scoundrel!" but Hardin gave no indication who should shoot
or who was the scoundrel, Hardin or Helm? It may have been Green
Hastings McCracken, the second-born son of Samuel L. McCracken
Sr. and who had served in the Confederate army, or his brother Samuel Lycurgus "Curg" McCracken.[9] In Hardin's mind it was clearly
Jack Helm who was the scoundrel who needed killing, and he was
taking no chances. "So I grabbed my shotgun and fired at Capt. Jack
Helms as he was closing with Jim Taylor" is how Hardin relived the
dramatic exchange, making it clear to the readers that the shotgun
was his, and not Helm's. He then "threw," meaning he pointed his
shotgun, at the Helm crowd and ordered them not to interfere.

> In the meantime Jim Taylor had shot Helms repeatedly in the
> head, so thus died the leader of the vigilant committee, the sher-
> iff of DeWitt, the terror of the country, whose name was a horror
> to all law-abiding citizens, meet his death. He fell with twelve
> buckshot in his breast and several six-shooter balls in his head.[10]

News of the death of Helm traveled quickly by word of mouth, but
additional details moved slowly. The killing occurred in the latter
part of the afternoon of Friday July 18, 1873, not May 17, 1873,
as Hardin wrote. Many later writers have continued the error,
due to their using Hardin's memoir alone as a source. Samuel L.
McCracken, a key citizen of Albuquerque, was in Gonzales later
that week and visited with friends. The Gonzales newspaperman
failed to interview McCracken but he gathered up the news as best

John Wesley Hardin's shotgun used in the fight with Jack Helm. David George discovered this weapon in a storage room many years ago. He realized its importance and it is now housed in the Buckhorn Saloon in San Antonio. PHOTO IN AUTHOR'S COLLECTION.

he could about what had happened "last Friday evening." From his reporting it is certain that the death of Jack Helm occurred on Friday, July 18, 1873, not two months earlier.

In addition to determining the exact date of the killing is the matter of how some perceived his death. DeWitt County Justice of the Peace L.B. Wright was a nervous man, and besides doing the occasional sad duties of a justice of the peace, he also dealt in general dry goods, groceries, boots, shoes, and country produce in his store in Yorktown, a town about fifteen miles from present-day Cuero. On Thursday July 24 he wrote a distressing letter to Governor E.J. Davis. As justice of the peace he had conducted the inquest on the mutilated bodies of Cox and Christman, whose deaths occurred only two days before Helm's, on the sixteenth, and now he had learned of the death of Helm. He referred to the "verry bad State of affars in our County" noting the sheriff had been killed "a few days Since." Wright pointed out that the civil authorities were wholly inadequate to restore peace and bring the contending parties to justice. He concluded his stressful letter with a hand at spelling as shaky as his penmanship: "I am wholey destitute of Power to inforce the Law. I have done all that I Can [.] our best Citizens ar[e] being Killed Evary few days."[11]

But back to the second-hand report of Albuquerque's Samuel McCracken. As the *Gonzales Index* editor learned, Helm, McCracken, and Hardin "were sitting engaged in friendly conversation" when a stranger rode up. He dismounted, and "walking up behind Helm attempted to shoot him" but the stranger's pistol failed to fire. Of course Helm, surprised as certainly were the others, turned around; now the stranger's pistol did work and as Helm stood up he shot again, the bullet wounding Helm in the breast. Helm, no coward now, at the same time rushed at him attempting to take away his pistol, grappling with him. Just at this moment, Hardin fired at Helm with his double-barreled shotgun, shattering his arm. Helm, now dying on his feet and fully realizing the deadly situation, turned to escape into the blacksmith shop but the stranger pursued him shooting him five times about the head and face. Whatever weapons Helm had left in the McCracken Place could do him no good as he there collapsed on the floor of the blacksmith shop —dead. Hardin and the stranger, James Creed Taylor, but apparently no one in Albuquerque knew his name, "then mounted their horses and rode away together, remarking that they had accomplished what they had come to do."[12]

Accepting this report as basically accurate one is presented with a strange situation: Jack Helm, apparently taking a break from his tinkering in the blacksmith shop, Samuel McCracken—whether the father or son is not stated—and John Wesley Hardin, all three sitting down taking a break and conversing quietly. If the senior McCracken then it was the Texas pioneer born June 1, 1807; if the younger Samuel McCracken it was Samuel Lycurgus McCracken, commonly called "Curg" born about 1845.[13] Helm was somewhere around forty years of age; Hardin around twenty. Hardin and Helm on this occasion at least were outwardly "civil" to each other. Was the trio innocently discussing cotton worms, and how Helm's invention would soon solve that agricultural problem? At least to an unknowing observer this was what was happening. But then the peaceful conversation was disrupted by the arrival of the "stranger" on horseback who dismounted and walked up behind Sheriff Helm, then squeezed the trigger of his pistol which failed to fire. Helm immediately forgot about cotton-worms, turned and was ready to fight this stranger who had such audacity to attempt to shoot him in the back. But this time the stranger's pistol did not misfire; Helm was now a severely wounded man, shot in the right breast. Hardin, never one to shun gunplay, now acted. He grabbed the shotgun, his own on his horse close by, and unloaded one barrel into Helm's left side. Helm at this point was bleeding badly and fighting for his life— a shattered arm and a bullet in the chest. He attempted to get into the blacksmith shop, to somehow escape; he had no weapons there as he had left his gunbelt and revolvers hanging on the hall tree at McCracken's where he had spent the night. The buckshot from Hardin's weapon and the single bullet from Jim Taylor had done their work; his struggle to escape the stranger was to no avail.

The stranger had not given up but wanted to make sure his target was dead as he followed Helm into the shop, now emptying his pistol into his head. Helm fell and was dead within seconds. Only then did Hardin and the stranger mount their horses and gallop away.

In the confusion of the moment McCracken did not learn who the stranger was, suggesting it was the senior who later spoke of the incident in Gonzales. The initial report which appeared in the Gonzales newspaper was reprinted elsewhere—in the *Bastrop Advertiser* of August 2, La Grange's *Fayette County New Era* of August 8, the *San Antonio Daily Express* of August 9, and certainly others. The stranger of course—not identified in any contemporary source—was James Creed "Jim" Taylor. He wanted the "right" to kill Jack Helm as he considered Helm responsible for the death of his father, Pitkin Barnes Taylor, shot from ambush in late 1872. It was the killing of his father that gave Jim Taylor the right to have the first chance of killing Helm. Taylor considered Bill Sutton equally responsible for killing his father, but that act of vengeance would have to wait.

Jim Taylor had never been to Albuquerque before; after all he lived down in DeWitt County. Thus it was no surprise that he was a stranger there. We rightfully may consider Hardin and Taylor had a "hit list" although they never wrote the names down on paper. They had only a few days before figuratively crossed off the names of Jim Cox and Jake Christman, and now they could cross off the name of Jack Helm. One name, perhaps the next on the list, was that of William M. "Bill" Sutton, and then Joseph Tumlinson.

From the available contemporary sources one must accept that Jim Taylor deserves the credit for killing Jack Helm, with Hardin assisting. Jim Taylor, putting four or five bullets in Helm's head did the killing damage. The Gonzales newspaper editor concluded his report with a statement which refers to the terror Helm had created within many people, but also gave him some praise.

Jack Helm had many charges laid at his door while in command of the Police, and no doubt had incurred the mortal hatred of many surviving friends of men said to be hunted down and killed by him and his party. He was nominally Sheriff of DeWitt County but had, for a long time left its duties to be performed by efficient deputies, and turned his attention to improved farming implements. He was engaged at the time of his death in manufacturing a cultivator of his own invention.[14]

This may have been the editor's outward neutral stance on Helm, presenting a "safe" conclusion to his report. But then his concluding statement leaves us wondering: "We heard of no cause of quarrel between Helm and the parties who killed him."[15] The editor certainly knew who Hardin was although he claimed to be unaware of any reason for the quarrel leading to the death of Helm. Victor M. Rose began writing his history of the Sutton-Taylor Feud in 1880. Some of what he wrote was from memory; of the Helm killing he wrote, perhaps without checking his files reporting the event: "two young men supposed to have been friends of the Taylors, rode up to the shop and announced through the throats of their revolvers the implacable message of fate."[16] Certainly dramatic prose, "the implacable message of fate," but sadly he left out so much detail which could have been reported.

Helm's body was gathered up for the inquest and carried over to the boardinghouse of Samuel and Martha McCracken, although Wilson County Justice of the Peace James W. Dickey may have conducted the inquest right there in the blacksmith shop. His actual written report, if one was made, has not surfaced, but some months later Justice Dickey turned in his bill for the inquest on Jack Helm—the amount was for six dollars, which was approved and allowed. The commissioners approved the six-dollar amount on November 20, 1873, at a "Special Term" meeting, although the matter of Dickey's bill was the last item on the agenda. Why did Justice Dickey delay for nearly four months after Helm's death to turn in the bill? There is no explanation provided in the record.[17] Following the inquest a wagon became the hearse to transport the corpse of Sheriff Jack Helm to the McCracken cemetery, not much more than a mile across open range. When the good people of Albuquerque delivered the remains to the cemetery there were fewer than a dozen marked graves in the "whites only" cemetery (a smaller section of land was reserved for blacks). Helm was "buried shallow" so it would be easy for the widow Helm or family members to exhume him if he was to be buried elsewhere. This did not happen. Someone, most likely John Bland and one of the McCrackens, marked the site of the grave with a "native red boulder."[18]

Helm's death did not mark the end of the Sutton-Taylor Feud. In March of 1874, eight months after his death, the hatred between the Taylors and Suttons still raged. On the eleventh day of that month Jim Taylor, the stranger in Albuquerque, and his cousin Bill Taylor finally caught up with their enemy, Bill Sutton. Sutton had determined he would go to Kansas, along with his wife and friend Gabriel Webster Slaughter, to get away from the feud, but he had waited too long. Jim Taylor shot Sutton to death while cousin Bill Taylor shot companion "Gabe" Slaughter to death on the deck of the steamer *Clinton* in the Indianola harbor. Hardin was not there but may have participated in the planning of the double killing. The deaths of Sutton and Slaughter resulted in such negative press concerning the state of lawlessness in south Texas that Gov. Richard Coke sent a troop of Texas Rangers to DeWitt County to settle the feud. Capt. Leander H. McNelly had thirty men under his command; he had been a former captain in the State Police as was Helm. McNelly's presence didn't end the feud but he did prevent any serious battles while he was stationed there.

One of McNelly's Rangers was a young man from Virginia who had left his native state due to a little feud of his own with a neighbor. T.C. Robinson was his name, although he went by the pseudonym of "Pidge" which he used in signing the letters he sent back to the Austin newspaper which printed them, giving history a valuable on-the-spot version of events in feud-torn DeWitt County. Pidge was no expert with pistols and Winchesters but was with pen and ink; he sent numerous letters back to Austin which appeared in the *Daily Democratic Statesman*. His letters are humorous much of the time, but he could be serious on occasion. Pidge had learned much about what had happened between the feuding factions before his arrival in DeWitt, including stories relating to Jack Helm. On November 8, 1874, Pidge wrote from DeWitt County seat Clinton of what he had learned, ostensibly with the idea of writing a book-length history of the feud (he never did). Among other topics he wrote about was the former sheriff of DeWitt County, explaining to his editor what material he might provide. "[I] Could give him the exploits of Capt. Jack Helm, who kept his helm hard down on the people of this section, until Wes. [Hardin] one day, in a playful mood, gave him a broadside and sunk him."[19] Amongst the tragedies of DeWitt County one could find a bit of humor, at least Pidge Robinson could. Even among those who may have seen Jim Taylor empty his pistol in Helm's head, thus being close to Helm's passing, it was generally considered that Hardin deserved the credit for killing Jack Helm. Apparently Pidge Robinson was unconcerned or perhaps unaware of Jim Taylor's involvement in the killing. Where Taylor was when the Rangers arrived in DeWitt County is uncertain, but Captain McNelly believed that Hardin and Taylor were both in the area and he could capture them. McNelly informed Adjutant General Steele of this but never did get close to capturing either one.[20]

It is history's loss that Pidge was not there a few years earlier to record in his particular style other incidents of the Sutton-Taylor struggles. There were numerous examples, such as Helm's raid on the Choate ranch, the Kelly tragedy, the destruction of the Lunn operation in Matagorda County, and the numerous other events when prisoners were shot and killed. The incident at Albuquerque was certainly different: Helm was not a prisoner of anyone, merely the loser in the two against one confrontation. Hardin recalled that after they were satisfied that Helm was dead he and Taylor may have remained for a short time, rather than immediately galloping off. He concluding his version that the shooting and running around the blacksmith shop "happened in the midst of his own friends and advisors" who did nothing to help Helm but "stood by utterly amazed." He then added: "The news soon spread that I had killed Jack Helm and I received many letters of thanks from the widows of the men he had cruelly put to death. Many of the best citizens of Gonzales and DeWitt counties patted me on the back and told me that was the best act of my life."[21] One is left to wonder just how many congratulatory letters Hardin received for killing Helm, as none have survived.

From analyzing the contemporary accounts, it is clear that Jim Taylor should get the pats on the back for the Helm killing. But Jim Taylor himself was killed in 1875 by a posse that included deputies of the late Sheriff Helm. He could not present his version of how he avenged the death of his father, Pitkin B. Taylor, but now in 1894 with many of the feudists dead John Wesley Hardin could, and did. In truth it was Jim Taylor who deserves the dubious distinction of killing the sheriff of DeWitt, and not the man-killer John Wesley Hardin.

The feud between William M. Sutton and his followers and members of the Taylor family did not end with the 1873 death of Jack Helm, or the 1874 death of Bill Sutton. Even after the deaths of Sutton and Slaughter in March of that year the war of attrition continued, as Sutton's followers now wanted to avenge their leader's death by ridding Texas of Jim and his cousin Bill Taylor. Bill Taylor was shortly afterward arrested and stood his trials; after some time in jail he escaped from Texas and, as best as we can tell, his life ended, ironically, as a lawman in Oklahoma in the mid-1890s.[22]

James Creed "Jim" Taylor continued his life in the DeWitt County area until the end of 1875 when in Clinton he, along with companions Mason "Winchester Smith" Arnold and former McNelly Ranger A.R. Hendricks, was surrounded by a number of Helm deputies and friends of Sutton and shot to death. They at least went down fighting, rather than being shot in the back while "attempting to escape."

The death of William Sutton and companion G.W. Slaughter brought the attention of the highest Texas administration to the situation, although it was not until three months after their deaths in March 1874 that Governor Coke sent a representative down to DeWitt County to investigate. Adj. Gen. William Steele spent some time in DeWitt County as well as other counties, such as Gonzales, Victoria, Calhoun, and Karnes. He spent considerable time in DeWitt discussing matters with the officers of the District Court. It may have come as a surprise to the governor, in opening Steele's report to read: "I find that the present state of violence had its origin in the operations of Jack Helm, a sheriff appointed by Gen'l. J.J. Reynolds, and afterwards made Capt. of State police under Gov. Davis." This was not all. Steele went on, explaining that

> From the statements made to me it appears to have only been necessary for a man should be pointed out to Helm as a cattle thief or a "bad man" to have been arrested & started off to Helena for trial by Court Martial, but the greater portion of those that started for Helena never reached that point but were reported as, escaped, though never heard of since. In one case, two young men by the name of Kelly were started to be

returned to Lavaca County, but were killed by the guard, one of whom was Wm. Sutton (whose name now designates one of the contending parties) who was with others tried & acquitted—a verdict which is not believed to be just, the fears of the jurors or other causes having overridden the testimony.

> . . . *the fears of the jurors or other causes having overridden the testimony.*

Steele continued by pointing out to Governor Coke that the Kelly brothers were related to the Taylors, and the wife of one of the Kellys was the daughter of Pitkin Taylor, "who was assassinated soon after, as is believed because he took an active part, by employing counsel to prosecute in the trial against Sutton & others."[23]

Even after the shooting in Albuquerque, Jack Helm's legacy continued to cause discontent in the area where the Sutton and Taylor forces continued their feuding. His brief experience as a soldier with the Confederacy, his involvement in the hanging of the Hembys and Howards, his experience as a leader of the Regulators, his dealings as sheriff of DeWitt County in one of the most troublesome times in Texas—all that is more or less forgotten, primarily because he was a victim of Hardin and Taylor. Perhaps we should remember that aspect of his career, that at least for a while the citizens of Lavaca and DeWitt Counties had confidence in his abilities to choose him county sheriff, rather that recalling the fact that some at least believed his actions continued the bloody conflict known as the Sutton-Taylor Feud.

At the end of Reconstruction in 1874 when Richard Coke became governor, the name of Helm was used, not in terms of honoring his memory after death but in political squabbles. During the 1880 governor's race some Democrats revolted against the re-nomination of O. M. Roberts. Some considered Roberts's platform—if he succeeded—would result in the "perpetuation of the last relic of Radical oppression and misrule."[24] A later editorial termed E.J. Davis as "the high-priest Edmund J." who was still active in Texas politics and still presiding over "Radical saints, Greenback apostles and the missionaries of the two-bit progressives." To add further shame the editor accused the progressives of sanctifying the "doctrines of state militia" as it enforced "martial law, the levying of fines upon counties, and the state police as handled, manipulated and conducted by Davidson, Jack Helm and others."[25] The name of John Jackson Helm would not be remembered as the effective leader establishing respect for law and order in a violence-ridden Texas, but as a tyrant creating terror among the people he was sworn to protect.

As Jack Helm ran into the blacksmith shop intending somehow to escape from the pair intent on killing him, did he not realize that he was now being killed in attempting to escape? Had the chickens finally come home to roost?

Helm's death as interpreted by artist R.J. Onderdonk, first published in the 1896 *Life of John Wesley Hardin*. Although inaccurate in placing the action on the street, this version remains the most frequently published portrayal of the death of Jack Helm.
AUTHOR'S COLLECTION

The late artist Jack Jackson provided a more accurate representation of the violent end of Jack Helm, which occurred in the interior of John Bland's blacksmith shop in Albuquerque, Gonzales County. AUTHOR'S COLLECTION

John Wesley Hardin as he appeared in 1875, a mere two years after the killing of Sheriff Jack Helm. This tintype was made in Florida and was preserved in his personal album. COURTESY THE ROBERT G. MCCUBBIN COLLECTION.

EPILOGUE

———◆———

The Grave of John Jackson Helm

BACK IN 1979 DR. C.L. SONNICHSEN, the *sui generis* of Texas feud historians, gathered together several essays which appeared in a book entitled *The Grave of John Wesley Hardin: Three Essays in Grassroots History.*[1] They were entitled: "Blood on the Typewriter"; "The Pattern of Texas Feuds"; and "The Grave of John Wesley Hardin." Each had previously appeared in highly respected publications, the former in *The Southwestern Historical Quarterly*; the second in *Observations and Reflections on Texas Folklore*, No. 37 of the Texas Folklore Society and the latter in *Password*, the publication of the El Paso County Historical Society. It is with honor and the highest respect that I acknowledge Dr. Sonnichsen and admit his title is the inspiration for this epilogue dealing with the burial and grave-marking of the Regulator Jack Helm.

The autobiography of John Wesley Hardin, published posthumously in 1896, provides a date for Hardin's killing of Jack Helm—May 17, 1873. (Of course Jim Taylor should get the lion's share of this killing, but when Hardin was writing his life story Taylor had been dead for two decades, so Hardin wondered, why shouldn't he take the credit? And he did, but added Taylor to the final moments of Helm's career.) But the date of May 17, 1873, is incorrect, although we should not be too critical of Hardin's mistake in memory: after all, a lot had happened in Hardin's life since the Helm killing, and being off by only two months is certainly understandable. Unfortunately, that incorrect date has been passed down and

195

numerous writers and historians have accepted Hardin's date and perpetuated the error.

Roy Sylvan Dunn in his "Life and Times in Albuquerque, Texas" accepted the date in his essay appearing in *The Southwestern Historical Quarterly*, published in July 1951; in so doing he unintentionally perpetuated the incorrect date.[2] Dunn knew about the town of Albuquerque as he had grown up in Nixon, not far from where the town had existed. As an adult he became an assistant archivist at the Texas State Library; later, at Texas Tech University he was an Associate Professor of Sociology and director of the Southwest Collection until his retirement in 1977. When the state placed two historical markers commemorating both neighboring communities of Union Valley and Albuquerque, Professor Dunn was the honored speaker.[3] Dr. James Smallwood, in his work on the Sutton-Taylor Feud entitled *The Feud That Wasn't*, perpetuated the dating error as "mid-May."[4]

Descendants of Jack Helm have ignored researching the date to verify, accepting what Hardin wrote as accurate, at least the date of his demise. Billie Rhoades Smith, great-granddaughter of Jack Helm and his wife Margaret Virginia Crawford Helm, visited with Karon Mac Smith, Albuquerque historian and unofficial caretaker of the McCracken Cemetery. She intended to locate and mark the grave of her great-grandfather.[5] In early 1973 she had come from Big Spring, Texas, to be present when the Confederate marker was to be laid in that rural McCracken Cemetery. The intent was to have the ceremony on the presumed anniversary of Helm's "untimely death." Miss Smith had read of the killing in Hardin's autobiography and accepted May 17, 1873, as the correct date.[6]

Two historical markers near the intersection of the road which leads to the McCracken Cemetery remind travelers that Albuquerque once existed. Near this site was the village which

Historical marker commemorating the community of Albuquerque, located six miles northwest of Nixon, Gonzales County, on FM 1681. Author's Collection.

was also remembered that day—Union Valley. As Professor Dunn had been at Texas Tech it was only natural that a Lubbock newspaper would report this significant event: "It was in the Albuquerque blacksmith shop that Hardin shot DeWitt County sheriff Jack Helm in 1873. The Albuquerque settlement faded when residents moved to Union as it was settled. Union in turn dwindled away when bypassed by the Galveston, Harrisburg and San Antonio Railroad." The ceremony was held on Sunday June 11, 1972. Dunn's speech is preserved as "Historical Marker Dedication—Union Valley Homecoming" in Karon Mac Smith's *On the Watershed of Ecleto and Clear Fork of Sandies*. Lubbock had received a copy of Dunn's speech prior to the event and headlined its article, "Dedication Set for Markers" in the *Lubbock Avalanche-Journal*, Saturday June 10, 1972, issue.

After 1967 Karon Mac Smith took over the task of keeping the cemetery as her aunt Karon Smith and Clyde Hastings had done before her. She and friend Gerry Sparks placed a small concrete slab on Helm's final resting place, replacing the red boulder.

In 1973 Billie Rhodes Smith, the great-granddaughter of Jack Helm, visited Karon Mac Smith in order to personally visit Helm's grave. She ordered, and received, a free government headstone after proving she was kin to the veteran; she was assisted in this effort by Karon Mac Smith due to her efforts in caring for the cemetery. This was in January or February of 1973. Using the incorrect date of Helm's death, as recorded in Hardin's autobiography as well as other historians who have

Jack Helm's grave was originally marked by a boulder which is dimly seen in the upper right corner of this photograph taken in the early 1970s by Karon Mac Smith. AUTHOR'S COLLECTION.

Historian Karon Mac Smith at the grave of Jack Helm in the remote McCracken Cemetery in Wilson County, July 1987. Author's Collection.

accepted that date, Billie Rhodes Smith and her two daughters, China and Cinnamon, and others had a brief ceremony at the placing of the government marker. The historic event was one hundred years following the death of Helm; that it was a few months off from the actual centennial of his passing was certainly not realized by anyone. [7] Today, unless the cemetery has been recently mowed and cleaned, the two grave markers of Jack Helm are difficult to find. Karon Mac Smith inventoried the graves in preparation for her books and included the grave of Margaret Virginia Crawford Helm, Jack's second wife. She gave the dates of her life as 1839 and March 18, 1877. Somewhere she had found a notice of her passing, but today her source is unattainable. We must accept that four years after Jack's burial, the earthly remains of his widow were placed next to that red boulder in the McCracken cemetery.

Today it is somewhat of an adventure just to find the grave of Helm. If one is fortunate to visit the land owners and get permission to visit the McCracken Cemetery, or "Old Albuquerque Cemetery," having the key to the gate will save many yards of walking. Once inside the pasture—and be sure to lock the gate behind you—one must walk quite a ways over rough pasture land. If not found after a hundred yards or so one must look around and explore; eventually the cemetery will be found. Then enter through the falling fence and walk a few rods to the right, and hopefully the grass will not have stretched its leaves over the flat markers covering them from view—there are two of them. If you find one, you are fortunate; if you find both you are very fortunate. You have found the grave markers of John Jackson "Jack" Helm.

APPENDIX A

◆—◆—◆

Jack Helm, DeWitt County Captain Commanding

Prior to his selection as Captain of the Fourth District of the State Police, Jack Helm was a "Captain Commanding" of a group of citizens to deal with thieves and murderers. The documents show that as early as March 1870 Helm was recognized as a leader of men and was selected for the position. The originals are in the National Archives but copies were found in the Barry A. Crouch Collection. They are as follows.

-I-

Headquarters Post of Helena
Helena Texas, April 4th, 1870

Capt. Chas E. Morse
U S Army
Secretary for Civil Affairs
Fifth Military District,
Austin, Texas

Sir:

I have the honor to transmit herewith enclosed Enrollment Lists of Citizens organized in pursuance of General Orders No. 75 of April 15th 1869 and [No.] 136 of July 23d 1869 from Headquarters Fifth Military District, in the counties of DeWitt and Karnes, together with the orders of organization, and letters of General instructions.

Very respectfully
Your obedient servant,

Geo. H. Crosman
Capt 12th Inft. Bvt. Major USA
Commanding

-II-

Headquarters Post of Helena
Helena, Texas, March 24th, 1870

General Orders)
No 11)

Under authority of General orders No. 75 of April 15th 1869 and 136 of July 23d, 1869 from Headquarters Fifth Military District,

William T. Elder is hereby appointed Captain of the enrolled citizens of Karnes County west of the San Antonio River.

Upon receipt of reliable intelligence that horse or cattle thieves or individuals or bands of men defying the civil authorities, are in their vicinity, any number of enrolled men may turn out, the Captain promptly notifying the Post Commander of their action, while out, the Captain of this enrolled men will be held strictly accountable for the sobriety and orderly conduct of his party.

The Captain upon application of the Inspector of Hides & Cattle furnish such assistance as may be necessary to enable him to properly perform the duties of his office.

By Command of
Brevet Major Geo. H. Crosman

J.T. Kirkman
1st Lieut, 10th Inft.
Actg. Post Adjutant,

To the Secretary for Civil Affairs
Fifth Military District

-III-

Headquarters Post of Helena
Helena, Texas, March 24th 1870.

Enrollment of Citizens for that part of <u>De Witt County</u> in the vicinity of
the <u>Guadalupe River.</u>
  <u>Jack Helm</u>, Captain Commanding

J.C. Sumners [Joseph Clayton]
J.M. Brooks [James Madison]
A.O. Brooks [Alpha Omega]
James Boa[?]
John H. Power
G.W. Ferguson
T.M. Field
Tobe Reeves
Edward Power
J.P. White [Joseph Priestly "Doc"]
Henry White [Henry Junius]
Jeff. White [Daniel Jefferson]
W.M. Sutton [William M.]
Buck McCrabb [John Frederick]
Huston Myers [Houston Rankin Myers]
Jacob B. Heard
Neal Busby [Cornelius Vandevere Busby]
Robert Busby [Robert Brown]
John R. Busby [John Rankin]
William Hasdorf

James Sumners
Thomas Hill
Samuel Sells
Wit. Ferguson
James [Owen] Murphree
Joseph DeMoss
Geo. W. Jacobs
Henry Ragland
Ludwick Van Roeder

I certify that the above is a correct enrollment of Citizens, organized
in compliance with General Orders No. 75 of April 15th 1869 and 136
of July 23d 1869 from Headquarters Fifth Military District.

  Geo. H. Crosman
  Capt. 10th Inft. Bvt. Major
  Commanding

-IV-

Headquarters Post of Helena
Helena, Texas March 24th 1870

General Orders)
No. 12)

Under authority of General Orders No 75 of April 15th 1869 and 136 of July 23d 1869 from Headquarters Fifth Military District, Jack Helm is hereby appointed Captain of the enrolled citizens of De Witt County in the vicinity of the Guadalupe River.

Upon the receipt of reliable intelligence that horse or cattle thieves or individuals or bands of men defying the civil authorities, are in their vicinity, any number of enrolled men may turn out, the Captain promptly notifying the Post Commander of their action, while out, the Captain of the enrolled men will be held strictly accountable for the sobriety and orderly conduct of his party.

The Captain upon application of the Inspector of Hides & Cattle [shall] furnish such assistance as may be necessary to enable him to properly perform the duties of his office.

By Command of
Brevet Major Geo. H. Crosman

J.T. Kirkman
1st Lieut, 10th Inft.
Actg Post Adjutant

To the
Secretary for Civil Affairs
Fifth Military District

-V-

Headquarters Post of Helena
Helena, Tx., March 24th 1870

Jack Helm

Captain of the enrolled Citizens of DeWitt County (in the vicinity of the Guadalupe River)

Sir:

I am directed by the Brevet Major Commanding [George H. Crosman] to instruct you not to call out your company, without authority from him, except in case of emergency.

You will not, when in pursuit of criminals, regard County lines; and should it be necessary to follow them into counties not belonging to this post, you will do so; at the same time sending notice, and a copy of those instructions, to the Post Commander in whose District you may be operating; any orders or instructions received from him by you, while in his District, will be obeyed.

Very respectfully &c &c
(signed) J.T. Kirkman
Actg Post Adjutant 1st Lieut 10th Inft.

A true copy
Geo H Crosman
Capt 10th Inft Bvt Major

APPENDIX B

――◆――

Vigilantes in Goliad County

Hd Qrs Post of Goliad Texas
Goliad, Aug. 22d, 1867

General:

I have the honor to report that on, or, about the night of Aug. 14th, 1867, a party of armed men styling themselves a "vigilance committee" composed in part of the following named persons, viz:

Wiley Pridgen of De Witt County
Thaddeus McLemore " " "
Samuel Reed " " "
James Easton Victoria "
Stanton Fields " "
John Emmerson " "
Columbus Brown " "
A.G. Brown " "
Jordan Perkins " "
Gilbert Onderdonk " "
[Henry?] Ragland " "
Jacob Dees Karnes "
— Patterson " "
Neal Brown Victoria "

Entered Goliad County, and took there from four prisoners named James Wilkerson, Martin Dickerson, a Negro and a boy, (name not known).

After taking them a short distance into Victoria County, James Wilkerson was murdered by shooting.

I have succeeding in arresting three of the party viz: A. G. Brown, Jordan Perkins and Henry Thompson.

I am satisfied that justice would not be done these men in the civil courts of either Goliad or Victoria County; and I should refuse to deliver them up until I have also a prisoner named James Patterson who is charged with a most foul murder committed in Victoria County, some time last winter, and there is least one indictment against him for robbery in De Witt County, also one in Houston. If I turn him over to the Civil Authorities to be tried for the murder in Victoria County, he will escape upon "straw bail."

The man Martin Dickson who was arrested and subsequently released by the self styled Vigilant committee is now a prisoner in my hands charged by the friends of the murderers with horse stealing. I hold him a prisoner more for his protection than on account of the affidavits of the other party, for I am satisfied he would be Killed if it were possible to prevent his giving evidence before a court.

I shall hold these men subject to your order.

I am sir,
Your Obedt Servt
P.E. Holcomb
A.A.A. Gen,

Dist of Texas—Capt 32 Infy & Bvt Maj. U.S.A.

APPENDIX C

———◆———◆———

1870 State Police Roster of Capt. Jack Helm

Two muster and pay rolls are extant giving the names of men who served under Captain Helm in the Texas State Police. The rolls show the person's name, rank, when entered and where stationed and in a very few cases remarks. Unfortunately, they do not show race or age or county and state of origin.

Helm, Jack	Captain	July 13	Concrete
Carr, James A.	Sergeant	August 27	Laredo

[Names of privates are here listed in alphabetical order.]

Baker, A.H.	Private	August 27	Victoria
Baldwin, J.H.	Private	August 1	Columbus
Bennett, O.H.	Private	August 8	Yorktown
Black, W.W.	Private	August 1	Lodi
Cox, J.W.	Private	July 13	Clinton
Cuellar, Francisco	Private	August 11	Carrizo
Delgado, Marcello	Private	August 14	Brownsville
Dignowity, A.J.	Private	August 21	Victoria
Estapa, Leon	Private	August 3	Edinburg
Florez, Vincento	Private	August 27	Laredo
Garza, Christobal	Private	July 30	Rio Grande City
Garza, Julio	Private	August 4	Lodi
Hanson, Jacob	Private	August 31	Corpus Christi
Hasdorf, W.G.	Private	August 16	Victoria
Hudson, R.B.	Private	August 24	Clinton
Leftage, Henry	Private	August 20	Clinton
Lindenberg, August	August 20	August 20	Yorktown

Lopez, Evanisto	Private	August 27	Laredo
Ohlenberger, F.	Private	August 1	Columbus
Rice, James H.	Private	August 12	Hallettsville
Rogers, Wallace	Private	July 26	LaGrange
Rosale, Sylvester	Private	July 13	Clinton
Simmons, C.C.	Private	August 23	Clinton
Taylor, Jas. B.	Private	August 23	Clinton
Tumlinson, Joseph	Private	July 13	Clinton
Vela, Cecilio	Private	August 8	Rio Grande City
Wilcox, George	Private	July 16	Clinton
Yancy, Fayette	Private	August 1	Columbus
Zorb, A.	Private	July 23	LaGrange

[Additional information on the reverse of the roll shows that captains were to receive a monthly payment of $125; sergeants $75 and privates $60. This first muster roll of the 4th police district is dated August 31, 1870. Then there are the following additional names.]

Burke, William	Sergeant	August 11	[no place]
Eberling, William	Private	August 11	[no place]
Haynes, Peter	Private	August 13	[no place]
Mitchell, J.M.	Private	August 13	[no place]
Ragland, Henry	Private	August 11	[no place]
Villanueva, M.	Private	August 11	[no place]
Young, W.J.	Private	August 13	[no place]
Zapata, Clemente	Private	July 11	[no place]

APPENDIX D

+--+--+--+

[Text of the historical marker situated on the grounds of the Goliad County court house.]

Regulators of Goliad County

When the Civil War ended in April 1865, many Texans returned to find their farms and ranches neglected, their cattle running wild and unbranded. The Federal troops sent to occupy Texas in June 1865 could not control the widespread cattle thieving and general lawlessness of the Reconstruction period.

Gen. J.J. Reynolds, commander of the Federal forces, appointed Jack Helm special marshal to the Goliad area in June 1868. A former deputy sheriff of DeWitt County, Helm captained a vigilante band of 50 men, mostly local ranchers, known as the Regulators. Based at Middletown (now Weesatche), these volunteers pursued criminals with vigor and often with cruelty. They ordered known and suspected lawbreakers to leave the state within 10 days. Those who defied the warning were shot without benefit of trial. In 1870 Helm was appointed by Gov. E.J. Davis to the newly formed State Police force but was soon discharged for his ruthlessness.

The activities of the Regulators and of the Texas Rangers, reorganized under Gov. Richard Coke in 1874, did much to restore order in this area. By 1876, most of the violators had left, and the Regulators were able to devote their time to ranching and farming. (1978)

ENDNOTES

━━◆━━◆━━◆━━

Preface

1. Jack Hays Day, *The Taylor-Sutton Feud* (San Antonio: Sid Murray & Sons, Printers, 1937), 18. Curiously the cover of this paperback shows the title as *The Sutton Taylor Feud* (no hyphen) but the title page reads *The Taylor-Sutton Feud*, with the hyphen.

2. George D. Hendricks, *The Bad Men of the West*, rev. ed. (San Antonio: The Naylor Company, 1959), 216.

3. Ann Patton Baenziger, "The Texas State Police During Reconstruction: A Reexamination" *Southwestern Historical Quarterly* 72, no. 4 (April 1969): 470–91. Ms Baenziger, now Mrs. Rose, is a descendant of State Police Sergeant Thomas Patton who worked with Jack Helm.

4. Barry A. Crouch and Donaly E. Brice, *The Governor's Hounds: The Texas State Police, 1870–1873* (Austin: University of Texas Press, 2011).

5. College Station: Creative Publishing Co., 1995.

6. El Paso: Mangan Books, 1996.

7. College Station: Texas A&M University Press, 2000.

8. College Station: Texas A&M University Press, 2008.

9. Denton: University of North Texas Press, 2009.

10. Denton: University of North Texas Press, 2013.

Chapter 1: A Nation Torn Apart

1. For the marking of Helm's grave see Karon Mac Smith, *On the Watershed of Ecleto and the Clear Fork of Sandies*, 2nd printing, with revisions and addenda (Seguin: Tommy Brown Printer, 1994).

2. The name "Jack Helms" is on panel B, line 8, with death date given as May 17, 1873, which as well as his name is incorrect. The name was added in 1994. Ironically, as May 17 is the date John Wesley Hardin gave as the date of Helm's death, other historians have erroneously accepted Hardin's faulty memory as accurate. The correct date of his death was July 18, 1873.

3. The 1860 Hopkins County, Texas Federal census shows the Hemby family consisting of head of household James W., a 35-year-old white male born in Missouri; his 26-year-old wife "Henin" (Hannah?), also born in Missouri, and children Lewis, eight; Nancy, seven; Ferdinand, four and Silas, one-year-old. All four children were born in Texas. Also in the household was a William Hemby, 29 years of age, a farm laborer, also born in Missouri. James Hemby was one of the five men waiting for the support to be removed for his hanging. His brother Jonathan and the three Howards, William Henry (born 1830), Thomas (born 1832) and James K. (born 1826) died with him.

4. Preacher Howard's final statement is from "Literary Effort" by John W. Hunter, which incorporated the memoirs of Creed Taylor. Copy in Texas State Library and Archives. Not fully paginated. Taylor/ Hunter had the quotation of Christ nearly correct. The King James version, which both were certainly familiar with, reads: "Father" instead of "Lord." *Luke*, 23:34. John Warren Hunter (1846–1915) was a teacher, historian and newspaperman. He spent his growing up years in Hunt and Hopkins Counties where he learned of the Howard-Hemby hanging. Too young to fight in the Civil War, he drove cotton wagons to Brownsville and spent part of the war in Mexico. Fascinated with Texas history, he founded *Hunter's Magazine*, and then with his son J. Marvin founded *Frontier Times*, which is a valuable resource of Texas history. "John Warren Hunter" by his son J. Marvin Hunter in *The New Handbook of Texas*, 3: 787–88.

5. David Pickering and Judy Falls, *Brush Men and Vigilantes: Civil War Dissent in Texas* (College Station: Texas A&M University Press, 2000), 56. Hereafter cited as Pickering and Falls.

6. Creed Taylor was born in Alabama, one of nine children born to Josiah and Hepzibeth Luker Taylor in 1820. By 1824 the family had moved to Texas and settled in DeWitt's Colony. His life was made up of engaging various enemies in deadly conflict, from Mexicans to Comanche to Union soldiers and finally to fellow Texans. At the age of fifteen he helped the Gonzales citizens defend their "Come and Take It" cannon. Prior to the fall of the Alamo he had gained valuable experience as a participant in the battle of Concepcion, the Grass Fight, and the siege of Bexar. After the fall of the Alamo he helped his family to safety in the Runaway Scrape, then caught up with the Texian army and fought in the Battle of San Jacinto. In 1840 he fought in the battle of Plum Creek against a large band of Comanche. Joining John Coffee Hays's Texas Rangers, he fought the Comanche again, then joined Capt. Samuel H. Walker's company during the Mexican War. As a Confederate he served under Colonel John S. "Rip" Ford. His first marriage was to Nancy Matilda Good-bread who gave him two sons and a daughter. After her death he married Lavinia Spencer and they had several children. He dictated his memoirs to James T. DeShields, which were published in 1935 in *Tall Men with Long Rifles*. Taylor died December 26, 1906, and is buried in the Noxville Cemetery in Kimble County, Texas. A historical marker was erected there by the Texas Centennial Committee in 1936; in Cuero his name is listed twice on the Centennial Marker as a soldier in the Texas army in 1836 and as a participant in the battle of the Salado in 1842. "Creed Taylor" by Dovie Tschirhart Hall in *The New Handbook of Texas*, 6: 215.

7. "Literary Effort."

8. Pickering and Falls, 35–37.

9. 1860 Lamar County, Texas Census, 167. 1860 Lamar County Slave Schedule, 54.

10. E.L. Dohoney, *An Average American* (Paris, TX: Self-published, 1885), 134.

11. Ibid.

12. At the time of the execution Charleston was located in Hopkins County, but when Delta County was formed its location was in that county. Vista K. McCroskey, "Charleston, Texas" in *The New Handbook of Texas*, 2: 48–49.

13. Pickering and Falls, 55.

14. Ibid., 58.

15. "Literary Effort," 21–22.

16. *Dallas Weekly Herald*, September 16, 1865, citing an article originally appearing in the *Paris Press* of August 26, 1865.

17. Ibid.

18. Some have claimed he was born in Franklin County, Virginia, but there is evidence the Jacob Helm family was in Montgomery County, Virginia, directly north when G.W. was born. The 1810 census of that county lists Jacob Helm with one white son between the ages of ten through fifteen—the right age for his son George.

19. An obituary headlined "Old Texan Dies" appearing in a Dallas newspaper of Tuesday, October 19, 1904, states that George W. Helm "died last Friday," which would have been October 15, 1904, at his home in Charleston, Delta County, "in the ninety-sixth year of his age." The obituary also noted that Helm was a "noted Indian fighter" and sat on the first jury ever impaneled in Lamar County with "the court being held under a tree." Helm was the father of seven children, all of whom survived him, except one son "who was killed while serving sheriff of DeWitt County, in southwest Texas." See *Dallas Morning News*, October 19, 1904. This important obituary confirms the name was Helm, not Helms, in spite of later writers, and this George W. Helm was the father of the subject of our study, "Jack" Helm.

20. Jacob Helm, George W.'s father, was a native of Franklin County, Virginia, and was among the first colonists settling on the James River. He became an active Mason and fought in the War of 1812. Jacob Helm wed Nancy Webb, also a Franklin County native, and the couple gave five children to the world: Sebird, George W., John

J., Sarah or "Sallie," and Ann S. Sometime during the decade of the 1820s the Jacob Helm family located in Patrick County, Virginia. Occasionally the name is spelled "Helms" but the correct spelling is Helm. This error of spelling did not take place with Jacob Helm, as the censuses of 1820, 1830, and 1840 all spell his name correctly. The other household members in the censuses of 1820, 1830, and 1840 remain nameless, as only the sex and age are given of both whites and slaves. No author, *Biographical Souvenir of the State of Texas* (Chicago: F.A. Battey & Co., 1889), 385–86; Patrick County, Virginia census of 1830, 157; of 1840, 54.

21. Jordan R. Dodd, *et al. Early American Marriages: Virginia to 1850* (Bountiful, UT: no date).

22. "Harrisonville Town Records," Journal A from the Office of the County Clerk. Transcribed in *Earliest Records of Cass County, Missouri, 1836–1861*, compiled by Marjorie Pearce Buckner, (Pleasant Hill, MO: NP, No date), 54–55.

23. *First Settlers of Lamar County, Texas*, Edited by Gifford White, published 1982, no pagination. Records from the originals in the General Land Office and the Texas State Archives.

24. Jack's siblings were Adeline Effinah, born in 1832 in Missouri; James W., born in 1839 but who died as an infant; Marshall Williams, born 1841 and who also died as an infant; Sarah Ann, born August 9, 1842, in Lamar County, Texas, and who died on June 22, 1934, in Childress County, Texas; Virginia Emily, born September 17, 1845, in Lamar County and who survived until October 17, 1919; and another daughter also named Adeline born in 1851, suggesting perhaps the first-born daughter had died. Sarah Ann Helm's official death certificate # 26388 of Childress County shows she was 91 years, ten months and thirteen days old when she died. Death was caused from "shock from fall on June 18th, no injury" with the contributory factor of "old age."

25. The children who became the half-siblings of Jack were Charlotte Joy, born 1859 in Lamar County; Aletha Isabell, born February 8, 1860, and who survived until 1922; Harriet W. born about 1862 but

who died about 1868, and Robert Edward Lee Helm, born in 1863 in Charleston and who lived until 1935. Genealogical information courtesy Marc Coker; *The Burnetts and Their Connections* compiled and published by June Baldwin Bork in 1989, volume one.

26. G.W. Helm is shown to be a fifty-one-year-old farmer from Virginia with wife Charlotte, a decade younger, born in Kentucky. Their children are shown as Virginia, 14; William T., 12; George W., six; and Leatha J., one-year old. Those four children were born in Texas. Next listed are the Chapman children of the former Mrs. Charlotte Madden Chapman: Mary C. is 13 and born in Indiana; James W. is 16 and working on the family farm, followed by Pennia E., nine years of age. Daughter Tilda A. is seven and born in Texas. Then there is Benjamin H., five years old, also Texas-born. Two others make up the household: Martha Burnett, the mother of George W. Helm's first wife, caring for the nine children as best she could, then 72 years of age, born in Virginia, and Henry J. Roberson, a 21-year-old farm laborer, born in Texas.

27. 1860 Hopkins County, Texas Census, 155. Their post office is shown as Charleston.

28. 1860 Hopkins County, Texas Census, Slave Schedule, 575.

29. Frances Arnold Ellis and Skipper Steely, *First Church of Paris* (Paris, TX: First United Methodist Church, 1985), 57–58.

30. James E. Tuck, *Civil War Shadows in Hopkins County, Texas* (Sulphur Springs, TX: NP, 1993).

31. James A. Mundie Jr. *et al. Texas Burial Sites of Civil War Notables: A Biographical and Pictorial Field Guide*, 258. Sims was born December 19, 1829, and died February 28, 1889. His grave is in the Oakwood Cemetery at Jefferson, Marion County. *Texas Burial Sites* includes a photograph of his grave marker.

32. Confederate Pension Application # 15512 for Lorenzo D. King; his application was approved.

33. Douglas A. Albright, "Criminal Cases of Delta Co." with "Helm Genealogy" in the Barry A. Crouch Collection, Victoria Regional

History Center, Victoria College/University of Houston-Victoria Library, hereafter the Crouch Collection, VC/UHV Library.

34. The Civil War record of Helm is available through the Library of Congress; "Literary Effort," 23.

35. "Helm Genealogy" in the Crouch Collection, VC/UHV Library and e-mail from Sandra Glenn, April 23, 2016.

36. Jack's and Minerva's son George was listed as two years of age in the 1860 Hopkins County census. He is frequently confused with Jack's father's other son who was named George also. Family sources indicate that George W. Helm, Jack's brother, was born September 14, 1863, and died July 26, 1926. He married Sarah Elizabeth Sheppard, who lived from January 21, 1858, to January 15, 1960. They are buried together with a double headstone in the Oaklawn Cemetery in Cooper, Delta County, Texas.

37. Homer L. Kerr. *Fighting with Ross' Texas Cavalry Brigade C.S.A.: The Diary of George L. Griscom, Adjutant, 9th Texas Cavalry Regiment* (Hillsboro, TX: Hill Jr. College Press, 1976), Appendix A. No pagination. See also Pickering and Falls, 64.

38. Various authors would have us believe Helm killed his unfaithful wife with no substantial evidence. Michael D. McCown presented a history of the family indicating Minerva was the seventh child of Roger and Ada Bradley McCown. In this essay Minerva is shown to have been born in 1840 and passed—with no details whatsoever—in 1862, "in either Fannin or Lamar County." "Roger McCown" in *Fannin County Folks and Facts* (Dallas: Taylor Publishing Company, 1977), 258–59. A statement in the Helm Genealogy, however, gives the date of her death as March 18, 1877, but gives no further information as to where or how this date was determined. This date is believed to be the date of death of Helm's *second* wife, Margaret Virginia Crawford Helm.

39. G.D. Albright to Attorney Clark Hurd, correspondence dated December 2, 1978. Letter in the Falls Collection, Texas A&M University-Commerce. George Douglas Albright died December 9,

1990, in Delta County. He is buried in the Oaklawn Cemetery in Delta County.

40. G.D. Albright to Mrs. Gloria Kosco, correspondence dated May 18, 1981. Letter in the Falls Collection, Texas A&M University-Commerce. In this letter Albright states that Helm, upon his return (after deserting) "killed his brother in law, A.L. Leech because his sister, Sarah Ann reported to her brother that his wife was unfaithful with Leech." It was then that Helm went to South Texas.

41. Federal Pension Application # 43389. Born August 9, 1842, in Lamar County and dying on June 23, 1934, in Kirkland, Childress County, Texas, she had an exceptionally long life for that era. Her attending physician was John L. Bubblis.

42. The bureau was properly termed the Bureau of Refugees, Freedmen, and Abandoned Lands and existed from 1865 to 1870. In Texas it operated from September 1865 until July 1870. In the five years of its existence five men held the position of assistant commissioner: Edgar M. Gregory, Joseph Kiddoo, Charles Griffin, Joseph J. Reynolds, and E.R.S. Canby. Cecil Harper Jr., "Freedmen's Bureau" in *The New Handbook of Texas*, 2: 1166–67.

43. Douglas A. Albright, tape recording for Judy Falls, Christmas, 1968. Transcript in the Crouch Collection, VC/UHV Library.

44. Chris Emmett. *Shanghai Pierce: A Fair Likeness* (Norman: University of Oklahoma Press, 1953), 53.

Chapter 2: Troubles on the DeWitt-Lavaca County Line

1. "Literary Effort," 20.

2. Ibid. It is believed, however, that these are not actually words from Creed Taylor as it is doubtful he was aware of such terms as "egotism." The actual description first appeared in Victor M. Rose's book on the Sutton-Taylor Feud, *The Texas Vendetta*, which Hunter was undoubtedly familiar with, and chose to include that by putting it in the mouth of Creed Taylor. Compare with Rose's description of

1880: "Jack Helm was about five feet nine inches high, rather heavy, but altogether well made, with black hair and eyes, and dark complexion. His appearance was agreeable, but his conversation was directed too much upon himself and his exploits to be entertaining. His education was extremely limited, but his vanity was immense, while his discrimination was always muddled." Rose, 13–14.

3. Thomas Ripley, *They Died with their Boots On* (Sydney, Australia: Angus & Robertson Ltd., 1936), 115. This was first published by Doubleday, Doran & Co., of Garden City, New York, in 1935. This American edition featured numerous photographs from the N.H. Rose Collection.

4. As yet there is no solid biography of Ben Thompson. The best biography of Longley is by Rick Miller, *Bloody Bill Longley: The Mythology of a Gunfighter* (Denton: University of North Texas Press, 2011).

5. "Literary Effort," 23.

6. The town of Clinton was located on the west bank of the Guadalupe River southwest of present-day Cuero, now the county seat. Early settlers Richard Chisholm and Andrew Lockhart both experienced tragedy: Chisholm's son was killed in the early years of the Sutton-Taylor Feud, and Lockhart's daughter Matilda was kidnapped by a band of Comanches. She was later rescued but the ordeal caused her an early death. Clinton became the county seat in 1850 with a frame building erected in 1855 and a two-story building erected in 1858 as the courthouse. When the railway bypassed Clinton, settlers located to the nearby community of Cuero, across the Guadalupe River. Clinton soon dwindled and today there is only the cemetery, although still very much an active cemetery, to remind people the town once existed. "Clinton, Texas" by Craig H. Roell in *The New Handbook of Texas*, 2:163–64.

7. For a biographical sketch of Griffin and his problems with the administration of the sub-district see Barry A. Crouch, *The Freedmen's Bureau and Black Texans* (Austin: University of Texas Press, 1992), 27–32.

8. Petition to General Charles Griffin, undated but in mid-1867. Original in the National Archives; copy in the Crouch Collection.

9. The letter is not in Helm's handwriting, and presumably it was dictated to an administrative assistant. James Oakes was born April 6, 1826, in Pennsylvania. After graduating from West Point in 1846 he served in the Mexican War. He then continued in military service during the Civil War. He was brevetted brigadier general in March 1865. After the war he commanded the Freedmen's Bureau in the northern frontier of Texas. He retired from active duty on April 29, 1878. He died November 27, 1910, in Washington, D.C. and is buried in Arlington National Cemetery. Biographical information from www.findagrave.com and Heitman, *Historical Register and Dictionary of the United States Army*, 1: 754.

10. J.J. Helm, Deputy Sheriff of Lavaca County, to Brigadier General James Oakes, July 15, 1867, from Austin.

11. Sammy Tise, *Texas County Sheriffs*, 157.

12. The 1870 Calhoun County Census shows Wesley Ogden as a 51-year-old District Judge from New York. In his household were a 31-year-old female, E.H., (his much younger second wife, Elizabeth H. Chichester), and children: Charles, an 18-year-old law student; Lilian, eight; Mary, five and Alma, three. Their post office was "Lavaca," today known as Port Lavaca. Judge Ogden died at his home in San Antonio on June 15, 1896, according to an item in the *Colorado Citizen* and reprinted in the *Galveston Daily News* of June 29, 1896. Calhoun County census and further biographical information from Robert Henry Brown's *Indian Wars and Pioneers of Texas* (Austin: L.E. Daniell, Publisher; reprint by State House Press, 1988), 517, and *Memorial and Genealogical Record of Southeast Texas*, reprint by Southern Historical Press, 1894 edition, which contains a portrait of Ogden.

13. Report of P.E. Holcomb, Captain 32nd Infantry, Headquarters Post at Goliad, Texas, August 22, 1867, to General J.J. Reynolds.

14. Ibid.

15. This term was used by Senator B.J. Pridgen in a letter to the *Austin Republican*, November 23, 1870.

16. "Communication from Governor E.M. Pease of Texas, Relative to the Troubles in that State," in *House Miscellaneous Document # 127*, 40th Congress, 2nd Session, May 1868, p. 22 entry # 375.

17. "Caldwell County" by Vivian Elizabeth Smyrl in *The New Handbook of Texas*, 1: 896–98.

18. The Helm-Crawford marriage license, number # 819, is on file today in the courthouse at Cuero, DeWitt County. The license was issued December 28, 1868, and witnessed by James L. Crawford Jr., her older brother. The groom's name appears in full as John Marshal [*sic*] Jackson Helm; the bride's as Miss Margaret Virginia Crawford. She was the daughter of Virginia-born James Alexander Crawford and Tennessee-born Rachel Sawyers Crawford. In 1860 James A. was 59, his wife Rachel was age 53. Crawford's real estate was shown to be $16,248 and personal estate as $5,000. Their children were James A. Jr., 23, born in Tennessee; son Pleasant Alexander, 23, born in Tennessee; Margaret 21, also born in Tennessee; Emily (Rachel Emily) 19, born in Arkansas; Isaac C., 15 born in Arkansas; Nancy J., 12, born in Arkansas and Thomas E., 11 born in Texas. James A. Crawford Sr. died October 17, 1861, and is buried in the small but well-kept cemetery at Hochheim, DeWitt County, Texas, with other Crawford family members.

19. James Alexander Crawford Sr. was born November 17, 1800. Wife Rachel Sawyers Crawford was born August 18, 1806, and died August 10, 1879. On the recently placed double headstone in the Hochheim Cemetery are their names and dates and this inscribed on the stone: "Rachel Crawford donated 5 acres of land for Hochheim School and Cemetery." Notes and photograph of headstone from personal visit.

20. Family Tree in Karon Mac Smith papers collected by Judy M. Falls preserved in Texas A&M-Commerce Library.

21. O.P Coppedge "To the Sheriff or any Constable of DeWitt County", January 26, 1869, Texas State Archives, Box 301–58 Folder 55.

22. Jack Helm to Governor E.M. Pease, undated but January 1869, included with Coppedge notice of January 26, 1869.

23. *Galveston Daily News*, April 21, 1869, reprinting an item from the *Gonzales Inquirer* of April 16. This article dated the incident as "Monday last," or April 12, 1869. The original article spelled the name "Helms" which was often the case.

24. Perhaps this is Jesse J. Pullen, born January 1847, and according to the 1880 Gonzales County census was farming there, listed as son-in-law of Sarah A. Babbitt. His wife is incorrectly listed as daughter but certainly his wife, eighteen years old. Both are shown to be born in Texas. 1880 Gonzales County Census, 526. In 1900 Pullen is living as a boarder in Kerr County.

25. Sheriff George W. Jacobs to Commander U.S. Forces, Helena, Karnes County, April 30, 1869, written from Clinton. National Archives Record Group 93, Part V, Records of U.S. Army 1821–1920 Civil Affairs. Letters File 1869–1870, Post of Helena, Texas.

26. Letter to Governor E.M. Pease, dated June 30, 1869, Box 301–58. Texas State Archives.

27. Victor M. Rose, *The Texas Vendetta; or, The Sutton-Taylor Feud*, 13. Facsimile by Ed Bartholomew and the Frontier Press of Houston, 1956; originally published by J.J. Little & Co. of New York, 1880.

28. George W. Jacobs was born in Jasper County, Mississippi, in 1823 although the exact date is unknown. The Federal census of 1850 shows him as a 27-year-old farmer with 25-year-old wife Eleanor, both born in Mississippi. By 1860 the Jacobs couple and their three children resided in DeWitt County, Texas, raising stock. G.W. Jacobs is buried in the Runge Cemetery in Karnes County; his grave has recently been marked but has no birth or death dates. 1850 Jasper County Census, 58; 1860 DeWitt County Census, 476.

29. E.M. Pease to General J.J. Reynolds November 16, 1868. Box 2014.076–7. This was followed by Special Orders No. 15 on January

18, 1869, "George Jacobs to be Sheriff, *vice* James F. Blair, resigned." Box 401–860.17.

30. The document is entitled: "Enrollment of Citizens for that part of DeWitt County in the vicinity of the Guadalupe River [.] Jack Helm Captain Commanding." See appendix 1. These men were stock raisers or farmers and in their twenties and thirties, living mainly in DeWitt, Goliad, or Victoria Counties. A.O. Brooks was perhaps the youngest at age twenty; Joseph DeMoss and James J. Sumners were both twenty-one; John Power may have been the oldest at the age of thirty-eight. Some information has been gathered from census records, which of course are not always accurate. Many were related by blood or marriage. James Madison Brooks, born in 1843, and Alpha Omega Brooks, born in 1850, were sons of George Washington Brooks Sr. Some of these twenty-nine men would carry on their allegiance to Helm and Sutton when the Sutton-Taylor Feud brought about treaties of peace. Among the signers of the August 12, 1873, treaty were R.B. Busby, Edward Power, J.W. Ferguson, Cornelius "Neal" V. Busby, Richard Power and Henry Ragland. Another treaty of peace was deemed necessary and on January 3, 1874, men lined up again to sign, including William Sutton, J.W. Ferguson, John F. McCrabb, Edward Power and his brother Buck Power, John H. Power, W.J. Ragland [Henry?], Joseph DeMoss and J.A. McCrabb.

31. General Orders No. 12 dated March 24, 1870, Headquarters, Post of Helena, Karnes County, recapitulating General Orders number 75 of April 15, 1869 and number 136 of July 23, 1869, from headquarters Fifth Military District. Copy of orders and enrollment list (both dated March 24, 1870) in the Crouch Collection, VC/UHV Library.

Chapter 3: The Choate Ranch Raid

1. A.J. Jacobs to commander, post at Helena, March 27, 1869. Copy from District Clerk's office, Goliad, and in unpublished biography of gunfighter A.Y. Allee by Gary P. Fitterer.

2. In 1860 the Peace family (spelled incorrectly as "Pease" by the census taker) resided in household 364. The next residence visited was that of the A.J. Jacobs family, 365. A.J. Jacobs, misidentified as "H.A." in the same census, was identified as a farmer, as was the Peace family. 1860 DeWitt County Census, 479.

3. *Galveston Daily News*, June 23, 1869, reprinting an item from the *Gonzales Inquirer*, June 19, 1870.

4. Goliad County Mortality Schedule, 1870, entitled "Persons who Died during the Year ending 1st June 1870, in the County of Goliad, State of Texas, enumerated by me, Edward S. Roberts, Asst. Marshal." Roberts gave Jacobs's age as fifty, his occupation farmer and from Mississippi. In remarks he noted "Murdered." Goliad County, Texas Census, 367, enumerated by Edward S. Roberts. When Roberts enumerated the Jacobs family in 1870 he found widow Mary with only $100 in real estate and no personal estate; her children were William, 16; Georgiana, 12; Cordelia, 9; Harriet, 6, and Ava, four years old. During the following decade Georgiana married Robert Lafayette Tumlinson; the 1880 census shows Tumlinson as a 28-year-old stock raiser with Georgiana keeping house along with their two children, William T., two years old and Robert R., two months old. Mary Jacobs's occupation is given as "keeping house." Sister-in-law Mary Jacobs was shown as 49 years old and listed as a boarder. Her children William, Cordelia, Harriet, and Ava are the other in-laws boarding with her. By 1900 Ava Jacobs, now 34, had married Jesse Simpson and was living in Wilson County. With Jesse and Ava are their three children and Mary Jacobs, the mother-in-law, identified as a 71-year-old widow. Mary Jacobs died in 1905 and is buried in the Marcelina Baptist Church Cemetery in Floresville, Wilson County. Her simple headstone reads "Mary Jacobs/ 1830–1905/ Grandmother of the Simpsons." What a memoir she could have told.

5. Goliad County 1870 Mortality Schedule shows he was murdered in June but does not give a specific date.

6. 2nd Lieut. William Thompson to Captain C.E. Morse, Secretary of Civil Affairs, June 21, 1869. Letter written at Helena, Karnes County. Letter in the Crouch Collection. VC/UHV Collection.

7. Senator B.J. Pridgen letter to *Austin Weekly Republican*, November 23, 1870.

8. Milton W. Stapp was born July 11, 1792, in Scott County, Kentucky, and died in Galveston August 2, 1869. The family had spent many years in Indiana prior to their moving to Texas and purchasing land in Goliad County. The death of James Stapp received considerable attention by the press partly due to the prominence of the father. The *Courier-Journal* of Louisville, Kentucky, as well as the *New York Herald* reported the son's death. The latter reported: "James Stapp, the son of the United States tax collector, General Milton Stapp, was murdered on June 11 at Goliad, Texas. His body was found on Sunday, perforated by eleven bullets. No clue to the murderers." See *New York Herald*, July 8, 1869; *Courier-Journal*, Louisville, Kentucky, June 28, 1869; *Galveston Daily News*, Galveston, Texas, August 6, 1869. The murder of James Stapp perhaps contributed to his father's death so soon after.

9. Were George W. Jacobs and A.J. Jacobs brothers? Probably, but some available records do not show the relationship conclusively. George W. was born in Mississippi in 1823 and by 1870 was sheriff of DeWitt County. Andrew J. was born in 1819 in Mississippi and by 1869 was sheriff of the neighboring county of Goliad. In an unpublished manuscript biography of A. Y. Allee, Gary P. Fitterer of Kirkland, Washington, shows both brothers were from Mississippi, married sisters, and then located in Texas in the 1850s. This seems too much to be coincidental if they were not brothers. See Jacobs family records provided by Noveda Ashley Metzger of Montgomery, Texas, and Ginger Rae Allee of Friendswood, Texas.

10. Lieut. William Thompson to Capt. Charles E. Morse, Secretary of Civil Affairs, Headquarters Fifth Military District, Austin, June 21, 1869. Letter in the Crouch Collection, VC/UHV Library.

11. Lieut. William Thompson letter to Capt. George Gibson Huntt, 4th Cavalry, from Headquarters, Post of Helena, Karnes County, October 18, 1869. Copy in the Crouch Collection, VC/UHV Library. G.G. Huntt served throughout the Civil War, beginning with the rank of 2nd Lieutenant, 1st Cavalry in March 1861; by February 1870 he held the rank of Major. He retired with the rank of Colonel, May 31, 1898. Francis B. Heitman. *Historical Register and Dictionary of the United States Army, from Its Organization, September 29, 1789, to March 2, 1903.* Washington, D.C.: Government Printing Office, 1903; reprint 1988, I: 559. Huntt, born September 1, 1835, died in 1914.

12. *Galveston Daily News*, June 25, reprinting an item from the *Goliad Guard* of June 19, 1869.

13. 1860 Goliad County Census, enumerated by L. Thurmond. James Stapp was kin to Hugh J. Stapp whose father Achilles had married Mary Jane Taylor, in DeWitt County in 1848. Mary Jane Taylor was the youngest child born to Josiah and Hepzibeth Taylor, thus there may have been a connecting link to the feud with this killing of James Stapp.

14. Clifford R. Caldwell and Ron DeLord, *Texas Lawmen 1835–1899: The Good and the Bad*, 146, 383.

15. Special Order No. 131, reported in the *Galveston Daily News*, June 11, 1869. The report duly noted "vice Andrew J. Jacobs removed." Apparently neither Reynolds nor the newspaper chose to say he had been removed by assassination.

16. From lengthy newspaper item quoted in Rose, 16. Rose had erred in dating this article from the *Victoria Advocate* of September 23, 1868, but obviously it was 1869.

17. 1870 Goliad County, Texas Census.

18. Sessions is more mysterious than many others involved in the troubles at this time. His name has not been found on a mortality schedule. In 1860 a John G. Sessions resided in DeWitt County, Texas-born, 22 years old, who farmed, with $1,200 and $5,100 in

real and personal estate. His wife was Martha A., 22 years old and from Mississippi; they had a one-year-old daughter, Elizabeth G. In the same household a 22-year-old John Sessions resided, but with no indication of place of birth. His occupation was given as teamster. Is either of these John Sessions the one killed by Lunsford? 1860 DeWitt County, Texas Census.

19. Senator B.J. Pridgen letter to *Weekly Austin Republican*, November 23, 1870.

20. 1880 Bosque County, Texas Federal Census.

21. James C. Bell was 27 years old when "shot by vigilantes" according to the 1870 Goliad County mortality schedule prepared by census enumerator Edward S. Roberts. Bell's family at the time of his death consisted of his wife Frances Harriet Busby and their children who ranged in age from 11 years to three months: Mary, Elizabeth, Jane, Emma, Robert and the new-born Harriet. Ironically Mrs. Bell, the former Busby, was a sister to state policemen Cornelius V. Busby, John Rankin Busby and Robert Brown Busby. The family tragedy continued when son Robert Ed Bell was killed in a bloody affray in Sanderson, Texas, along with a companion Henry Scudder Biggs, both killed by Deputy R.C. McMahan, in 1903. It was the result of a family feud. The widow Busby died in San Antonio on January 21, 1925.

22. An item in the *Houston Times* which was reprinted in the *Daily Austin Republican*, August 10, 1869.

23. Policeman C.V. Busby to Davidson, December 17, 1870. State Police Correspondence Ledger 863/21, entry # 1518, 210. Busby was commissioned August 13, 1870 and resigned April 30, 1872. *The Governor's Hounds*, 259.

24. The deaths of James Bell, Charles Moore, Rutland [sic, Russell] Jones and Tobias Poole are as Pridgen reported them in his lengthy letter to the *Weekly Austin Republican*, November 23, 1870. Without giving dates one wonders if he was working strictly from memory, although these deaths did occur in June and July.

25. *Galveston Daily News*, July 24, 1869, reprinting an item from the *Lavaca Commercial* of July 22, 1869.

26. Photographs of marker and personal research trip to Goliad, July, 2015.

27. *Galveston Daily News*, August 1, 1869, citing a letter from "Western Texas" which may have been no further west than Atascosa or Bexar County, written in Gonzales July 23, 1869.

28. Helm's version of events appears in Rose's *The Texas Vendetta*, 15–19. His lengthy statement was made for the purpose of "enlightening the law-abiding citizens as to what I have done, and why I did it."

29. Rose, 16–17, citing an article from the *Victoria Advocate* of September 23, 1868 [sic, 1869].

30. In the feud literature Fulcrod seems to always be just "Fulcrod" as if he was known only by his surname. Research has pointed to Mathias Fulcrod as the man, born December 22, 1800, in Pennsylvania and who married Elizabeth Crownower, born February 2, 1798, and who died May 10, 1860. The 1850 Goliad Census shows the couple in household # 21 with a Martha Pool[e], age 20 and her son William, four years old; also a Maryann Fulcrod, seventeen and her two siblings: Catherine, age 16 and Philip, age 13. The Fulcrods had three children prior to the above, all daughters. The 1860 Goliad Census shows Mathias Fulcrod farming with $18,500 real estate and $21,200 personal estate, a wealthy man indeed.

31. The others who were supposedly among those at the Choate ranch remain names only, as no further reference to the Broolans, Doughtys, Gormans, or Perrys in the context of alleged thieves in South Texas has been found. Certainly there were individuals with those names in 1870 in Texas and some in South Texas but without first names it is now impossible to identify who Helm means. James M. Smallwood, in his *The Feud that Wasn't*, states that these individuals "had indictments in the various counties throughout Taylor country." Page 61. In the appendix "Members of the Taylor Ring

Conspiracy (197) Men" he has them in each case as "two brothers" suggesting he had some knowledge of them, but indicates, in the index, their first names were unknown.

32. Helm intended to convey the idea that Choate had provisions which would allow him to survive a siege of fifty days by fifty men. Rose, 18.

33. Rose, 15.

34. The Martin Choate household consisted of Martin, his wife Mary, 45, and their children: William, Rubia, Charlie, and George. None could read or write. 1870 San Patricio Census, 102. Even though their county was San Patricio, the post office was in Refugio, Refugio County.

35. Letter of Senator B.J. Pridgen in the *Weekly Austin Republican*, November 23, 1870.

36. Rose, 18.

37. Ibid.

38. Ibid., August 13, quoting the report from the *Goliad Guard* of August 7, 1869.

39. Skidmore Family Group Sheet appearing in the *Texas Genealogical Society Newsletter* 2, no. 2 (Summer 1990): 33. The 1860 San Patricio County census is more informative. Samuel Coil Skidmore, the father, is shown as 39 years old while his wife Elizabeth is 37. The children are sons Calvin, 16, and Marcellino, 14. Daughter Martha is 12; son Francis is 11, and Charles is six years of age. One-year-old Otis is the remaining family member listed. The father S.C. Skidmore died August 3, 1883, in Oakville, Live Oak County. 1860 San Patricio County Census, 376.

40. The San Patricio County Mortality Schedule, prepared by the same individual who prepared the Federal census for the county—R.A. Upton—carries the names of only five men who died in the previous year of 1869. They were John and Crockett Choate, 51 and 28 years of age respectively, both "Stock Raisers," in the remarks column, both "murdered." The other three were Jesus Garcia, Juan

Domencio, and Casmer Cravahal (Cravajal?), all "Stock Drover" and "murdered." Their deaths came in January. If Kuykendall died at the Choate Ranch his name would have been included in the San Patricio County mortality schedule. However, there is a John Kuykendall listed in the Goliad County Mortality Schedule who is identified as being 34 years of age, a stock raiser, "shot by vigilantes" in August 1869. He obviously was a victim of the Regulators instead of Choate. A John Kuykendall resided in Goliad County in 1860, a 24-year-old farmer from Texas with a 22-year-old wife from Tennessee and one daughter. It is believed this John Kuykendall of the 1860 Goliad County was with Helm at the Choate Ranch raid, was severely wounded and returned to Goliad where he then succumbed to his wounds. That is why his name is on the Goliad County 1870 Mortality Schedule and not in the San Patricio County schedule. The Mortality Schedules were prepared by the same individual who conducted the Federal census. In the case of Goliad County, Edwards S. Roberts was the enumerator.

41. Rose, 24.

42. Ibid., 25. Dr. E.M. Downs resided in neighboring Refugio County so it would not be a difficult ride from his place to the Choate ranch. The 1870 Refugio County census shows the doctor as a 59-year-old native of Scotland with wife Caroline, 46 years old and from New York, with their four children. 1870 Refugio County, Texas Census, 161.

43. Rose, 26.

44. *Galveston Daily News*, July 4, 1874.

45. 1870 Refugio County, Texas Census. The W.C. Dickey family appears on pages 161A and B; Dr. E.M. Downs is enumerated on page 161B; thus they were perhaps close neighbors regardless of how the enumerator made his rounds. Her later marriage and children information is from an e-mail to author courtesy Michael A. Howell, November 25, 2013. Catherine A. Dickey Choate Wallace died November 8, 1884 "reportedly at Rockport, Texas"; William Warren Wallace died April 12, 1915.

46. Nueces County, Texas Marriage Records, Book C, 498–99. Her marriage to John Choate was in Refugio County Marriage Records, Book A, 45.

47. *San Antonio Daily Herald*, October 30, 1870.

48. *Galveston Daily News*, November 2, 1870.

49. Jo Ann Morgan, "Vigilante Justice (?) Accounts for Two of Rockport's Oldest Graves" in the *Newsletter* of the Aransas County Historical Society 10, no.1 (March 2013). It is believed that Dr. Downs assisted in the arrangements for the burial. The wounded Skidmore was removed to Rockport where the widow Choate later located; Rockport was the residence of the doctor. This article is essentially a reprint of an interview with James Huckman Sr. who witnessed the Regulator action against the Choates.

Chapter 4: Action in Matagorda County

1. Jack Helm to Maj. Milton T. Callahan, August 17, 1869, written from Mission Hill, Victoria County. Record Group 393, Part V. Records of the U.S. Army, 1821–1920. Civil Affairs Letters, February 1869–1870 Post of Helena, Texas.

2. Brevet Major General Charles Griffin to Governor J.W. Throckmorton, January 21, 1867, written from Galveston Headquarters, District of Texas.

3. Nicknames of these individuals are sometimes difficult to understand. "Ran" Spencer was Randolph Spencer, and Hays Taylor was John Hays Taylor, named after the famous Texas Ranger John C. Hays; his brother was Phillip Goodbread, the middle name from his mother's maiden name. The nickname "Doboy" or "Dobey" could also be based on the term to describe a young calf, a "dobie." Certain historians have written his middle name was DuBois, which thus eroded into Doboy, but this obviously was not the case.

4. "Communication from Governor Pease of Texas, relative to the Troubles in that State." 22, entry # 386. In *House Document 127*, 40th Congress, 2nd Session, May 11, 1868.

5. *Galveston Daily News*, August 13, 1869, written from DeWitt County, August 7, 1869.

6. Report of C.S. Bell to Captain C.E. Morse, from Campbell's Ranch near Helena, August 23, 1869.

7. Bell expressed himself frequently with a literary flair. This is not surprising as he later contributed articles and stories to the *New York Ledger* dealing with his adventures in the Civil War. Gathering and editing all of Bell's literary contributions could prove to be an interesting study.

8. *Galveston Daily News*, September 4, 1869.

9. Report of C.S. Bell to Captain C.E. Morse, from Campbell's Ranch near Helena, August 23, 1869.

10. C.S. Bell to General J.J. Reynolds, August 23, 1869, from Campbell's Ranch.

11. Reward notice of Governor E.M. Pease, October 28, 1868. Pease stipulated that "the reward for the *arrest* and *delivery* of *Each* of the *Persons* so charged to the *Commanding Officer* of the *Post* at Austin or San Antonio, or if *Either* of them should be killed in *resisting arrest* by lawful authority, then a *like reward* upon the presentation of Satisfactory proof that *Either* of them was so Killed." Words in italics were underlined in Pease's document. Besides the two Taylors and Spencer the reward was notification that Jim Wright was also wanted for the murder of a man in La Vernia, Wilson County; and a man named Pinson was also wanted for the murder of John Trimble. Copy of document in the Crouch Collection, VC/UHV Library.

12. "Literary Effort."

13. Ibid.

14. George Callison did not long enjoy the narrow escape from C.S. Bell's actions. In December 1869 he was killed, probably by vigilante action, although no details have been determined. 1870 Gonzales County Mortality Schedule, cited in *The Ties That Bind*, by Marjorie Lee Burnett, 60.

15. C.S. Bell to Colonel Clay Wood, August 26, 1869. Copy in the Crouch Collection, VC/UHV Library.

16. *Galveston Daily News*, September 4, 1869.

17. Ibid., August 13, 1869.

18. "Persons who Died during the Year ending 1st June, 1870" is how the Mortality Schedule is entitled. No pagination.

19. 1870 Goliad County, Texas Census. Their post office was Middleton, Goliad County and 1870 Goliad County Mortality Schedule.

20. The phrase, "Fellow citizens, this is the last resort," was omitted in *Flake's Daily Bulletin* of August 26, 1869, with no explanation given.

21. This version is from the *Galveston Daily News* August 24, 1869. The phrase is also omitted from Rose and it is abbreviated as well. The Rose version also appears in Taylor/Hunter's "Literary Effort" further indicating it was another item copied from Rose's book. It is not surprising that Rose borrowed newspaper items for his book *The Texas Vendetta; or, The Sutton-Taylor Feud*, as he was editor and publisher of the *Victoria Advocate* from 1869–1873, prior to becoming editor of the *Laredo Times*.

22. *Galveston Daily News*, September 1, 1869.

23. Ibid., September 10, 1869, commenting on an undated item in the *Goliad Guard*.

24. Charles A. Wikoff to Capt. Charles E. Morse, September 16, 1869. Copy in the Crouch Collection, VC/UHV Library.

25. Kreisle was appointed to the office of Goliad County Judge by Reynolds's Special Orders No. 195 dated November 1, 1867. He replaced William S. Gorman who had been removed. Records of the Fifth Military District, Texas State Archives, Box 401–860–folder 8.

26. Judge M. Kreisle to General J.J. Reynolds, November 3, 1869. Document in Crouch Collection, VC/UHV Library. Kreisle was born in Wurtemburg about 1830, although when he arrived in Texas is unknown. The 1870 census identifies him as a successful merchant of Goliad with a wife and four children. His real estate and personal

estate each was valued at $10,000. 1870 Goliad County Census, enumerated by Edward S. Roberts, 363.

27. Martin Taylor was born February 16, 1843. He married Sophronia Morris, born March 22, 1848, a daughter of W.B. "Dave" Morris, on May 29, 1867. The Martin Taylor daughter was "Molly" and born on February 23, 1870, shortly after her father's death. On February 15, 1982, the Bureau of Reclamation removed and then reburied the remains in the Tilden Cemetery, "beside other family graves." The workers explained what they found during the operation: "two shoes in good shape, metal coat buttons, some skull parts, nails, parts of a leather heel, knife, and other small items." Rev. Fleming Martin, retired Methodist minister, married to a great-great-granddaughter of the two deceased men, conducted the graveside services. A.E. Adlof's article, "Reburial Services for Taylor and Morris," first appeared in the *Beeville-Bee Picayune*, February 18, 1982, and then reprinted in the *Taylor Family News* 8, no. 1 (February 1998): 2.

28. Jack Hays Day, 12.

29. Ibid., 13.

30. Ibid.

31. McMullen County History, 1982, 412–13. No place. No publisher. Presumably this work was an effort of the McMullen County Historical Society.

32. Smallwood, 86.

33. Karen Holliday and John D. Tanner Jr., "Lon Oden: The Rhymin' Ranger," *Old West* 34, no. 4 (Summer 1998): 10–14. The bodies were originally buried on the Snoga Ranch in Live Oak County.

34. *Galveston Daily News*, October 5, 1874; this same article appeared in the *New York Times* of October 5, 1874.

35. C.S. Bell to Capt. C.S. Morse, Secretary for Civil Affairs, November 28, 1869. Copy in the Crouch Collection, VC/UHV Library.

36. *The Daily Herald*, (San Antonio), Tuesday, December 7, 1869.

37. General Orders No. 18, Headquarters 5th Military District, dated February 1, 1870.

38. Helm to Governor E.J. Davis, June 14, 1870.

39. Ibid. This is a very remarkable statement for Helm to make, that he had worked over much of the state. At best perhaps he could claim to have worked over the northeast and south central portions of the state.

40. Helm to Governor E.J. Davis, June 26, 1870.

41. *Galveston Daily News*, June 15, 1870.

42. "John Leal Haynes" by Alwyn Barr in *The New Handbook of Texas*, 3:517. Haynes was born July 3, 1821, in Bedford County, Virginia, and died April 2, 1888, in Laredo, Texas.

43. No serious treatment of the career of Charles S. Bell yet exists. Concerning the violence in which he was involved, this item is of interest, from a report after Bell had left Texas. "Bell, the swift witness before the Congressional Committee, has been boasting that he killed six men while he was operating in Texas. We think it highly probable, especially if he was a member of E.J. Davis's Bandit Police." *The Daily Herald* (San Antonio), April 13, 1876.

44. *Galveston Daily News*, June 28, 1870.

45. 1870 DeWitt County, Texas Census.

46. A significant contribution to Reconstruction history is *The Governor's Hounds: The Texas State Police, 1870–1873* by Barry A. Crouch and Donaly E. Brice, published in Austin by University of Texas Press, 2011.

47. Hunnicutt also proved to be unworthy of continued work in the police. Commissioned as captain of the First District on July 6, 1870, his commission was revoked on September 1, 1870. See *The Governor's Hounds*, 273. The *Daily State Journal* reported the news, pointing out the reason for his dismissal was "for inefficiency and general worthlessness. Other removals have been made, and still others are impending. The police force contains no berth for

sluggards, knaves or fools. General Davidson is about starting on a somewhat extended tour of duty. He proposes to visit the disorderly sections of the State, and ascertain the evils that actually exist, and apply the proper remedy. He knows that there is a stimulus in actual presence, which official instructions cannot communicate; and it is his fixed and steadied purpose to leave untried no agency, that can be used to repress violence and desperadoism, in our borders." *Daily State Journal*, September 18, 1870.

48. This blank oath is in the Texas State Archives, Adjutant General's Files.

49. *Report of the Adjutant-General of the State of Texas, from June 24, 1870, to December 31, 1870* (Austin: Tracy, Siemering & Co., 1870).

50. "State Police Stations" in *The Texas Almanac for 1870, Emigrants Guide to Texas* (Galveston: Richardson and Company, 1870), 227. "Leftage, (Booth) Hy" is how the *Almanac* identifies him. Willis Fawcett enumerated him in 1870 as a 34-year-old black male, native of Virginia. His Georgia-born wife, Maria, 26 years old, and daughter Francis, nine, were classed as mulattos while son Moulton, five, was classed as black. Both children were born in Texas. 1870 DeWitt County Census, 240.

51. The 1870 census shows A.H. Pierce and household: he was 37 years old, a native of Rhode Island, and identified as a stock raiser. He is shown to be living with his wife Fannie, 32 and a native of Texas, his children and employees: eight drovers, a cook, and a hostler. That his real estate was valued at $4,000 and personal estate valued at $41,300 indicates he was perhaps the wealthiest man in that area. 1870 Matagorda County Census, enumerated by John Kemp, 481.

52. *Flake's Daily Bulletin*, July 6, 1870. Article entitled "The War on the Cattle Thieves."

53. Emmett, *Shanghai Pierce, A Fair Likeness*, 57.

54. "Report of Arrests," 32–33.

55. See *The Notorious Luke Short: Sporting Man of the Wild West* by Jack DeMattos and Chuck Parsons (Denton: University of North Texas Press, 2015).

56. State Police Ledger, 401–985, Captain Helm to Davidson, page 34, entry 171.

57. Ibid., Helm to Davidson, page 45 entry 228.

58. *Daily State Journal*, August 14, 1870.

59. A line-by-line examination of the 1870 Matagorda County, Texas, census reveals that enumerator John Kemp occasionally wrote "W" and "M" (for mulatto) interchangeably, but the numbers are certainly accurate in the main. For Kemp there were whites, blacks, and mulattos. He noted one Indian residing in the county. Kemp's self-enumeration shows he was then 38 years old, a black male residing with Rose Kemp, a 28-year-old black female. 1870 Matagorda County, Texas Census.

60. This is how the census taker identified the area. The river that provided the inspiration for the contributor's *nom de plume* rises near El Campo in Wharton County and runs southeast to the Tres Palacios Bay in Matagorda County. The town of Tres Palacios, also known as Tidehaven, was an important port as early as the 1830s.

61. 1870 Matagorda County, Texas Census. William Wilburn Lunn in reality was a doctor; born in 1846 in Mississippi; it is difficult to imagine him having anything to do with the cattle thieving ring of his brothers. He then graduated from Jefferson Medical College of Philadelphia in 1874 and continued his practice until death which occurred on February 24, 1909, at the age of 62 years. He is buried in the Old City Cemetery of La Grange, Fayette County, Texas. Thomas L. Stedman, Editor, *Medical Record: A Weekly Journal of Medicine and Surgery* 75 (New York: William Wood & Company, 1909), 445.

62. The 1870 Matagorda County Census shows John B. Smith as thirty-eight years of age, a white male with occupation as "Wheelwright"

with only $100 worth of real estate and $330 of personal estate. The other six members of the Smith household include a 23-year-old Madeleine Barre identified as "Housekeeper" and her (their?) two children, a 19-year-old Ephie Murray, with occupation as "Asst Housekeeper" with her two children.

63. Their mother was Sarah Matilda Keller who married Josiah Lunn on January 11, 1844, in Wilkinson County, Mississippi. The mother was born in 1822 but death date is unknown. Josiah, born March 6, 1803, died February 22, 1868. *Historic Matagorda County*, Vol. 1 (Houston: D. Armstrong Co., Inc., 1986). E-mail from Paul M. Spellman, October 29, 2014.

64. Report from Trespalacios of June 23, published in *Flake's Daily Bulletin* of Galveston, July 12, 1870.

65. Report from Trespalacios, written June 24 and published in *Flake's Daily Bulletin*, July 6, 1870.

66. *Flake's Daily Bulletin*, July 12, 1870; this communication was headlined "Letter from Matagorda County" and was written June 23.

67. Ibid., July 6, written June 24, 1870. This was headlined "The War on the Cattle Thieves."

68. The children were: eldest Benjamin Vastine was fifteen, William Wilburn, thirteen, Edwin DeMoss, twelve, and daughters Catherine A., ten, Mary L., eight, and Elizabeth M. (or Martha Elizabeth), five. The first four children were born in Mississippi, but Mary L. and Martha Elizabeth were born in Texas, suggesting the family did not arrive in the Lone Star State until the early 1850s.

69. 1860 Matagorda County, Texas Census.

70. Matagorda County Historical Commission, *Historic Matagorda County*, vol. 1 (Houston: D. Armstrong Co., Inc., 1986), 183. *Texas Escapes* Online Magazine indicates that all that remains of Deming's Bridge is a "supporting beam" of the original bridge span that gave the community its name. The beam and historical marker are located in the very back of the Old Hawley Cemetery.

See also "Hawley, Texas" by Rachel Jenkins in *The New Handbook of Texas*, 3:513.

71. 1870 Matagorda County, Texas Census. The 1870 census listed all who resided in that household as of June 1, 1870. They all were residents on "Wilson Creek & Tres Palacios" and claimed Matagorda their post office. William Lunn, now the head of household, is shown as a Mississippian by birth, a stock raiser by profession, and twenty-three years old. He claimed $3,000 worth of real estate and $8,000 worth of personal estate. His 22-year-old wife Annie E. was Texas born. In the same household were Benjamin, 25 and also raising stock; brother Edwin, 22, also a stock raiser, and siblings Mary L., seventeen, and Martha E., fifteen. On the following page is listed a John B. Smith, 38-years-old, occupation given as "Wheelwright" and his family. This may be the man identified as "All Jaw" Smith.

72. *Matagorda County History*, 183.

73. Chris Emmett. *Shanghai Pierce, a Fair Likeness*, 59.

74. The 1860 Matagorda County census enumerated Robert A. Hasbrook as a 24-year-old native of New York living alone, with occupation as "Stock Raiser"; his real estate was valued at $1,000 and personal estate valued at $10,000. His post office was Deming's Bridge, 493. He has not been found on the 1870 census but in 1880 he was a resident of Refugio County with a family, and occupation given as "Clerk in store." His wife is shown as 30-year-old Susan, born in Texas, and their five children, all born in Texas. 1880 Refugio County Census, 335.

75. "The Matagorda Murders" article and letter from William Prissick in the *Daily State Journal*, July 8, 1870; also Laurie E. Jasinski, "William Prissick," *Handbook of Texas Online*, accessed November 29, 2014, Published by the Texas State Historical Association; and 1860 Matagorda County Census, showing Prissick as a boarder in the residence of James T. Chambers, 506. He then was a 54-year-old butcher with $3,000 worth of real estate and $800 worth of personal estate.

76. Worcester, Massachusetts *Evening Gazette*, July 29, 1870, reprinting the *Galveston Daily News* article. This indicates the story of the Lunn hanging and their operations received considerable national publicity.

77. Chris Emmett, *Shanghai Pierce, A Fair Likeness*, 58.

78. *Daily State Gazette*, August 14, 1870.

79. Columbus C. Moore and wife V. [Virginia?] had five children in 1870 when the Jackson County census was enumerated. Henry Duncan, a 22-year-old mulatto male labored on the farm. 1870 Jackson County Census, 464.

80. State Police Correspondence Ledger, C.C. Moore to Davidson, page 14, entry 58. The ghost town of Morales is located on State Highway 111 in Jackson County. During Reconstruction it experienced considerable lawlessness and for that reason the railroad bypassed it. Today there is a cemetery and some existing foundations. 1870 Jackson County Federal Census, enumerating the Columbus C. Moore family, 464. T. Lindsay Baker, "Morales," in *Ghost Towns of Texas* (Norman: University of Oklahoma Press, 1986), 90–91.

81. The 24-year-old William W. Lunn may have been wounded and took to the brush but did survive nearly two decades after his narrow escape from the Regulators. He later continued his medical practice in the Matagorda County area until his death on February 24, 1909. He is buried in the "Old LaGrange City Cemetery" in Fayette County.

82. *Daily State Journal*, August 14, 1870. Of interest, Pickering and Falls, in their study *Brush Men and Vigilantes: Civil War Dissent in Texas*, wrote that Helm and his Regulators raided Bee, San Patricio, Wilson, DeWitt, and Goliad Counties but made no mention of Matagorda, Jackson, or Wharton Counties.

83. *Flake's Daily Bulletin*, September 3, 1870. Unfortunately, efforts to identify further this correspondent, D.E.E. Brama, have not been successful.

Chapter 5: Feuding Against the Taylors

1. Julius E. DeVoss, "Some Fort Mason Personnel," in *Mason County Historical Book Supplement* (Mason: Mason County Historical Commission, 1994), II:21.

2. *Tri-Weekly Austin Republican*, November 23, 1867, citing a report from the *San Antonio Express*.

3. *Houston Daily Telegraph*, November 30, 1867.

4. Ibid.

5. E.D. Townsend, Assistant Adjutant General, War Department, Washington, D.C. to Brevet Major General R.C. Buchanan, commander Fifth Military District, New Orleans.

6. Official reward notice dated October 28, 1868, from Governor Pease, $500 for the arrest and delivery of each to the commanding officer of the Military Post at Austin or San Antonio.

7. John Warren Hunter was born in Alabama in 1846 but the family had moved to northeast Texas before the Civil War. As a teenager he witnessed the hanging of one of his friends by Confederate soldiers, which caused him to avoid fighting for the Confederacy. He soon found refuge in Mexico. He later wrote of his experiences in the book *Heel-Fly Time in Texas*. Later he spent two years in Lavaca County farming. He failed as a farmer but began to find success in the field of teaching and then journalism. He established a number of newspapers. Notably he founded the magazine *Frontier Times* which was published for many years in Bandera, Texas. "John Warren Hunter" by J. Marvin Hunter in *The New Handbook of Texas*, 3: 787–88.

8. "Literary Effort."

9. Ibid., 24. This is one of the numbered pages.

10. *San Antonio Daily Herald*, July 27, 1870, reprinting an article from an undated *Gonzales Southwestern Index* but probably July 23, 1870.

11. *San Antonio Daily Herald*, July 29, 1870.

12. *The Governor's Hounds: The Texas State Police, 1870–1873*, 31.

13. Ibid., 197 and in Adjutant General "General Orders No. 1" Ledger, dated July 4, 1870, signed by James Davidson.

14. Davidson's middle initial is rarely seen. An article in a leading Galveston newspaper of late 1870 discussing the removal of Helm from the Captaincy of Police in the Fourth District identifies the Chief of Police as "J.H. Davidson." Article "Jack Hem" in *Galveston Daily News*, December 13, 1870. Crouch and Brice in *The Governor's Hounds* did not include this middle initial.

15. E-mail from Cheryl Lynn Highley to Parsons, February 3, 2015, concerning the Kerlicks family.

16. James Davidson to Helm, July 21, 1870, 63. "No. 1 Police July 1 1870 to Jany. 18 1871" Ledger 401–1030. For details on the Kerlicks shooting and tragedy see *The Sutton-Taylor Feud: The Deadliest Blood Feud in Texas* by Chuck Parsons, 83–84. The Kerlicks are buried in the Jonischke Cemetery located off FM 119 south of Yorktown. It is visible from the Alvis Road. Henry Gonzalvo Woods is buried in the Woods Cemetery midway between Cuero and Yorktown on State Highway 72.

17. "Police" Ledger 401–1030, 85.

18. Barry A. Crouch and Donaly E. Brice, *The Governor's Hounds: The Texas State Police, 1870–1873*, 261.

19. Ibid., 294.

20. C.L. Sonnichsen identified Sutton as William E. Sutton in his first book on Texas feuds. He wrote that Sutton had "a hearty laugh and liked to crack jokes," one of which was that the initials W.E.S. stood for "watermelon, eggs and sugar" (32). I accepted, in my book on the Sutton-Taylor Feud, what Dr. Sonnichsen wrote but in further research into the troubles of Reconstruction Texas I found several references from contemporary documents that the man was William M. Sutton. Sonnichsen erred, as I did in accepting what he wrote, and perhaps numerous other writers. Now the question remains: what did the middle initial "M" stand for? See Sonnichsen, *I'll Die Before I'll Run: The Story of the Great Feuds of Texas*.

21. A brief item in the *Hallettsville Herald and Planter* of Lavaca County printed an item from the *Cuero Star* stating that Captain Tumlinson would be buried November 24, 1874, suggesting his death occurred the day before. This did not appear in the Hallettsville newspaper until its issue of December 10, 1874.

22. Ibid. McCrabb survived the shootings of the feud only to be killed in a runaway team accident near Thomaston, DeWitt County, on August 23, 1909. His death certificate, # 15541, states "Killed by his team." He was 63 years and five months old when the accident happened. He had married Cora E. Augustine on March 31, 1883. McCrabb is buried in the McCrabb Cemetery near Cuero. His single tombstone carries his name on one side, his wife on another, and his son on another.

23. State Police Correspondence summaries, Helm to Davidson, August 8 and Helm to Davidson, August 10, 1870, p. 34 entry 171 and p. 36, entry 179. 1860 Karnes County Census, 5 and 1870 Karnes County Census, 14. According to his pension application, Paschal had served in Company I, 2nd Texas Cavalry. His 1st Lieutenant was William A. Spencer; his commanding officer was Capt. John Little-ton. Ironically, William Addison Spencer was a brother of Randolph Spencer who was a companion of the Taylor brothers when they killed Major Thompson and Sergeant McDougall; Captain Littleton was killed by a group including Hays and Doboy Taylor, Randolph Spencer, Buck Roland, Jeff Clark, and Fred Pell. Sworn statement of William A.G. Lewis in communication from George H. Crosman, September 9, 1869, Headquarters Post of Helena, Karnes County. Of this group at least four died violently: both Taylors by gunshot, Spencer by *lightning*, and Fred Pell by gunshot as well. Pell was born about 1848 in Prussia, although when he came to the United States is unknown. He settled in Karnes County and raised stock. Apparently he misappropriated other stock raisers' cattle and was arrested in Travis County. James W. Cox reported on May 9, 1870, that Fred Pell "was killed by a guard of citizens, while on transport from Austin, to De Witt Co. Tx." Cox informed a Justice of the Peace of the

fact, "in order that he might hold an inquest over the body." Report of Cox to George H. Crosman, Capt. 10th Infantry, Headquarters, Post at Helena. Microfilm Record from National Archives, "Letters Received and Endorsements" provided by Lynn Highley.

24. Jack Helm to Davidson, written from Concrete, DeWitt County, August 9, 1870. "Index to Letters Rec'd 1870 Police" Ledger 401–985, page 34 entry # 171.

25. "No. 1 Police July 1 1870 to Jany. 18 1871" Ledger 401–1030, 136.

26. Ibid., Davidson to Helm, August 18, 1873, 147.

27. Helm's communication to Davidson summarized in Ledger 401–985, written at Clinton, August 19, pages 45–46, entry # 228.

28. The Sweet Home community that exists today is not where the original community was, but a few miles removed. No photograph, drawing, or even a plat of the original community is known to exist. Thanks are due Lavaca County historian Doug Kubicek for guiding us to the site and touring the surrounding area.

29. The Kelly Family consisted of parents Robert and Delilah Oldham Kelly. Nine of their ten children were born in Mississippi. The ten children were: Franklin C., born 1835; James, born 1837; Louisa, born 1839; Robert, born 1841; Wiley T., born 1844; William B., born 1846; Henry Peter, born 1848; Eugene A., born 1850; Emmett D., born 1852, and Mary Elizabeth "Mollie," born 1854, the only child born in Texas. Mollie Kelly married James Creed "Jim" Taylor who became the leader of the Taylor clan after the death of Pitkin B. Taylor, his father. Eddie Day Truitt, *The Taylor Party* (Wortham, TX: Privately printed, 1992), 76.

30. The *New Orleans Times-Picayune*, December 19, 1855; the *New York Clipper*, January 8, 1870; the *Galveston Daily News*, September 22, 1870; Smith died on March 30, 1886.

31. *Flake's Daily Bulletin*, September 7, 1870, printing a report from the *Lavaca Commercial* printed in Hallettsville, August 31, 1870.

32. Jack Hays Day, *The Sutton-Taylor Feud*, 13.

33. Christopher Columbus Simmons was born in Jefferson City, Missouri, in 1844; the family came to Texas about 1850 and resided in Goliad County. As a Confederate he enlisted on October 8, 1861, and served until 1864. On his application for pension he stated he was sent home on furlough due to sickness but the war "closed before my return." He had served in Beaumont's Company, Company B, Buchel's Regiment. On returning home he became a farmer and apparently that was his life's choice, except for that brief period as a state policeman, having resigned on April 1, 1872. During the Sutton-Taylor Feud Simmons did sign one of the treaties of peace. On August 12, 1873, he was one of 39 men who signed their name, or their "X," as did "Captain Joe" Tumlinson. Simmons did not sign the treaty of peace of January 3, 1874, perhaps having returned to Goliad County leaving the feud behind him. Years later, indigent and suffering from rheumatism, Simmons became a resident of the Confederate Home in Austin in 1916. There he died in bed on July 21, 1918. He was buried in the Texas State Cemetery; his grave is marked.

34. John Meador may have been with the Simmons party to prevent initial concern among the Kellys. According to the sworn statement of Pitkin B. Taylor, Meador had been "induced" to accompany the posse "as Meador and William Kelly were such intimate and good friends." P.B. Taylor statement sworn to before Justice of the Peace Oliver K. Tuton, October 15, 1870, and printed in the *Daily Austin Republican*, November 1, 1870; reprinted in *The Texas Vendetta*, 49.

35. *The Governor's Hounds: The Texas State Police, 1870–1873*, 46.

36. Affidavit of Louisa Day, wife of William Day, sworn to before DeWitt County Justice of the Peace Oliver K. Tuton, October 15, 1870.

37. Eddie Day Truitt. *The Taylor Party*, 69–70.

38. "Record of Arrests" Ledger # 401–1001 in Texas State Archives, 34–35.

39. Ibid., 40–41.

40. *San Antonio Daily Herald*, September 4, 1870, citing a report originally appearing in an undated *State Journal*.

41. *Houston Daily Times*, September 20, 1870, in article entitled "Martial Law."

42. Davidson to Helm, August 31, 1870. Ledger 401–1030, 190 and Ledger 401–985 entry 71 page 17.

43. Davidson to Helm, August 31, 1870. Ledger 401–1030, 191.

44. Helm to Davidson, page 56 entry 289. State Police Communication Ledger 401–985.

45. Davidson to Helm, September 6, 1870, Ledger 401–1030, 218–19.

46. Ibid., 220.

47. Clarification on the question of "killed while attempting to escape" courtesy County Attorney of Bell County, Texas, Rick Miller (retired), e-mail to Parsons, April 25, 2013.

48. "Hidden Hand" to Editor, *Flake's Daily Bulletin*, (Galveston) written at Victoria, September 18 and printed in issue of September 28, 1870. Could the writing of "Hidden Hand" be the work of the *Galveston Daily News* correspondent John J. Hand? In 1870 he was the correspondent who covered Austin, and thus was in a position to be familiar with the doings of the State Police. John J. Hand was born in Donard, County of Wicklow, Ireland, on September 20, 1834. Beginning his career in Quebec, Canada, he learned there the printing trade and then went to New Orleans in 1847 where he continued with the trade. On a trip to New York in 1855 he met the woman he would marry, Laura Sophie Sawtelle. In 1867 he located in Galveston and soon became a leading member of the staff of the *Galveston Daily News*. Obituary in the *Galveston Daily News*, July 17, 1888. The *Austin Weekly Statesman* also provided an informative obituary, describing him "as a whole-souled gentleman, and was universally esteemed for his excellent and generous qualities of head and of heart, and his death is deeply regretted by all classes." *Austin Weekly Statesman*, July 19, 1888.

49. State Police Communication Ledger 401–985. Helm to Davidson, October 10, 1870, page 93, entry 527.

50. *Daily State Journal*, October 23, 1870.

51. Ibid.

52. This statement appears in Rose's study of the feud, *The Texas Vendetta*. The quotation appears as a chapter title, page 10. Crouch and Brice's endnotes cite the *Weekly Austin Republican*, September 14, November 2, 1870; the *Daily State Journal*, October 19, 1870, and Rose's *The Texas Vendetta*, 40–48.

53. State Police Communication Ledger 401–985. Wiggenton to Davidson, no date but received in office October 13, 1870, page 95 entry 536. At this time Wiggenton was the District Clerk, having been an Austin lawyer then residing in Goliad. His son Alford Jr. was County Judge and son James was Deputy District Clerk. 1870 Goliad County, Texas Census, 359.

54. Little has been learned about George W. Jacobs. He is buried in the public cemetery at Runge with a simple stone showing only his name: "George W. Jacobs." There are no dates but presumably he lived in the area after his period as a sheriff and remained there the rest of his life.

55. *Nashville Union and American*, Nashville, Tennessee, November 18, 1870.

56. "Report of Arrests," 34–35. Cudd was perhaps A.R. Cudd, a DeWitt County stock raiser, 35 years old and born in Georgia. He was head of household with Susanna Estes and her five children. 1870 DeWitt County Census, 292. Criswell has not been located.

57. "Report of Arrests" 34–35, Ledger 401–1001.

58. *Daily State Journal*, September 2, 1870.

59. Ibid., October 13, 1870.

60. *The Daily Herald*, (San Antonio) November 22, 1870.

61. 1870 Lavaca County, Texas Census, 501.

62. Ibid., 499.

63. *The Daily Herald*, (San Antonio) November 22, 1870.

64. Ibid., November 25, 1870.

65. James M. Smallwood, *The Feud that Wasn't: The Taylor Party, Bill Sutton, John Wesley Hardin, and Violence in Texas* (College Station: Texas A&M University Press, 2008), 95.

66. "Police No. 1" Ledger 401–1030, Davidson to Helm, August 2, 1870, 117.

67. "Report of Arrests," 38–39.

68. 1870 Bee County, Texas Census.

69. 1870 Refugio County, Texas Census.

70. Henry Westfall was the son of Gabriel and Eliza Jane Westfall, Kentucky natives, born around September 1850. The Bexar County census of that year shows the family with Henry listed as two months old, born in Texas. Besides the parents there was the 16-year-old son Lycurgus, also born in Kentucky. 1850 Bexar County, Texas Census.

71. "Report of Arrests," Ledger 401–1001, Texas State Archives.

72. William Longworth of Sutherland Springs, in 1870, was a 45-year-old New Yorker, then a District Clerk with $1,000 in real estate and $500 in personal estate, post office Lodi, Wilson County. 1870 Wilson County, Texas Census, 473.

73. State Police Communication, Longworth to Davidson, September 7. Ledger 401–985, page 64 entry 337 and September 8, 1870, page 64 entry 338.

74. Adj. Gen. James Davidson, Chief of Police, General Orders No. 1: "An Act to Establish a State Police . . ." issued July 1, 1870, 5–6.

75. This refers to the ranch of Robert Weakley Brahan, a Tennessee-born physician, who located in Texas in 1852 and settled on the Cibolo Creek in Guadalupe County, Texas. Ranching and farming was not his only occupation as he was also a doctor who "continued to practice his profession for his friends and neighbors as a pleasure and not for profit" according to one obituary. On passing on April 16, 1885, he left behind his wife, Martha E. Haywood, whom he

had married May 1, 1832, and five children. There is a cenotaph for him in the La Vernia Cemetery although he is actually buried in City Cemetery # 2 in San Antonio. *San Antonio Express-News*, April 17, 1885 and Ancestry.com. No information has been located about Liner's Ranch.

76. *San Antonio Herald*. September 11, 1870, headlined "The State Police on the Warpath." This was later reprinted in the *Daily Austin Republican* of September 14, 1870

77. *The Daily Herald*, (San Antonio) September16, 1870.

78. Davidson to Helm, August 15, 1870, 130. Ledger 401–1030 "No. 1 Police July 1 1870 to Jany, 18 1871."

79. The census spells this man's name as Volentine. Benjamin Volentine was a 26-year-old farmer born in Texas with wife Mary A. and two daughters. 1870 Lavaca County, Texas Census, 506.

80. "Report of Arrests," 40–41.

81. Ibid., 42–43.

82. The eighteen men arrested by Helm were George W. Jacobs, Barter Gorman, William Campbell, D. Dryden, who escaped from the guard; Wiley Pridgen, who will be shot to death by persons unknown in December 1873, a senseless act of the Sutton-Taylor Feud; Jabe Lewis, Les Green, Manuel Green, Simon Wallace, Sam Wallace, Isham Henrys, Jesse Henrys, L. Henrys, A Harrison, William Rhodes, William Cram, W. and Boone Fly. The Greens, Wallaces and Henrys were arrested for stealing hogs; Harrison and the two Flys were arrested for killing cattle, presumably to skin and sell the hides and tallow. What the others were arrested for is not shown. "Record of Arrests" Ledger, 401–1001, 42–43.

83. This originally appeared in the San Antonio's *Herald* and then reprinted in *Flake's Daily Bulletin* of Galveston, September 22, 1870.

84. Item in the *Goliad Guard* of September 24, reprinted in *Flake's Daily Bulletin*, October 1, 1870.

Chapter 6: "Six Shooter Gentry"

1. Police Communication, E.M. Alexander to Davidson, ledger 401–985, page 60, entry 312.

2. Ibid., John S. Coffey to Davidson, September 14, 1870, page 71, entry 378. Coffey's primary business was as a grocer but he may have been working part time as a clerk in the district clerk's office. 1870 Hopkins County census shows him as a 24-year-old white male boarding in the household of William Sickles, 48.

3. Sammy Tise. *Texas County Sheriffs*, 342.

4. Ledger 401–985, which is a summary of letters received in the office of the Adjutant General, page 75, entry 407. Sammy Tise, *Texas County Sheriffs* points out that there were no entries in the State Election Register from September 7, 1870–July 15, 1872, 342. See *The History of the People of Live Oak County Texas 1856 to 1982*, by Live Oak County History Book Committee, Mrs. Carolyn Bateman, Central Chairman. [George West, 1982], 40.

5. McMullen County Census 1870 and Live Oak County Census 1880; Pension application # 15050; "Moses Sanders Pearce and Mary Emma Alford" by Mrs. Willie Lucille Meyer in *The History of DeWitt County, Texas* by the DeWitt County Historical Commission (Dallas: Curtis Media Corporation, 1991), 650–51. Obituary in the *Yorktown News*, January 17, 1929. Pearce's grave in the Yorktown Cemetery is marked with a government military headstone. Widow Mary Emma Pearce survived until June 3, 1943.

6. Rose, *The Texas Vendetta*, 14.

7. This is from a letter of Senator Bolivar J. Pridgen written at Clinton, September 27, 1870, to Adj. Gen. James Davidson recorded in the Executive Record Book, Secretary of State Papers, Record Group 307, 443–45. Also printed in the *Daily State Journal*, September 27, 1870.

8. The earliest reference to this killing is from James Martin's letter to Davidson of September 21, 1870, written at Dogtown, in which he

explains that Smithwick attempted to escape from the guard and was killed. Ledger 401–985, page 79, entry # 435.

9. In fact, no contemporary newspaper article has yet been uncovered concerning the death of John Smithwick. The probable reason is that so few early newspapers of this area of the state were preserved.

10. 1850 United States Census. Natchitoches Parish, Louisiana. John is listed as a two-year-old; the family consisted of mother Elizabeth Anne —"Betsy" —and older siblings Sara and Simon living in the household of their grandparents A.J. and Sara Gough. Additional family information from Ancestry.com. 1860 Census, Nueces County, Texas showing John Smithwick as one of eleven boarders in the household of John R. Peterson, 295. Eli Smithwick and Elizabeth Gaugh (pronounced "Goff") were married in Natchitoches Parish, Louisiana, on January 15, 1842, by M.A. Simkins, Minister of the Gospel. Of interest is the existence of a marriage license between John's mother Elizabeth Ann Gough Smithwick and Richard Delaney, the marriage taking place in Nueces County on December 3, 1862. The father Eli obviously is missing and presumed dead, although if he was killed in the Civil War or by some other cause is not known.

11. Statement from Pearce to Davidson, undated. Letters summarized in Ledger 401–985, page 92, entry # 522.

12. Ibid. Statement from Pearce to Davidson, communication from Oakville, November 1, 1870. Ledger 401–985, page 131, entry # 764. These men were all identified by census records as driving or raising stock; it is likely they believed Smithwick was stealing cattle, and thus targeted him for death for that alleged offense. James Martin was a 46-year-old stock raiser from Louisiana with a family, one of whom was their son Ceburn, twenty-one years of age. His occupation was so typical for a young man at that time and place: driving cattle. Oscar Hamilton Bennett was a 50-year-old farmer and stock raiser from Kentucky with a wife and nine children. His record as a state police private is not impressive. He was commissioned on July 26 under the command of Captain Helm; he was discharged

October 1 but then reinstated December 30. He was discharged for good on March 14, 1871. Alexander Franklin was forty years old, raising stock, claiming no real estate but his personal estate was valued at $5,000. He was from Mississippi. J.M. Franklin and Ralph Franklin were two of the half dozen or more children of Allen Franklin; John, certainly the census enumerator's "J.M.," and Ralph, were twenty-six and twenty-three years old respectively. No occupation was listed but as their father Allen was a stock raiser certainly they drove and raised cattle as well. Nothing has been learned of Charles Barker but in all likelihood his occupation would have been given as stock raiser or cattle drover also.

13. Peter Tumlinson to Adj. Gen. James Davidson, no place, no date, but received December 8, 1870. Ledger 401–985, page 182, entry # 1213.

14. Captain Helm to Davidson, in which he enclosed letters regarding the Smithwick killing. Unfortunately, these letters were not preserved or summarized in this ledger. Ledger 401–985, page 93, entry # 526.

15. 1870 Nueces County Census, showing John J. Dix as a 44-year-old stock raiser, from Michigan, with his wife Cynthia, from Florida. Their children were all born in Texas. He was an exception as nearly all the other ranchers and stock raisers in this area, this *brasada* between the Nueces and the Rio Grande, were from southern states. Page 156. Their post office was shown to be Corpus Christi.

16. Dogtown was once a thriving community in McMullen County. The county was organized in 1862 but few settlers arrived due to the bandit activity in the area. By 1870 the settlers who had stayed called the main settlement Frio Rio, but gradually the name became Dogtown, which was later moved to the Frio River Crossing where the community became Tilden, now the county seat. The probable inspiration for the name of Dogtown was that those early ranchers used dogs to herd their cattle and sheep; another belief which may be just as plausible is that on one occasion drunken cowboys shot as many dogs as possible on the streets.

Renee Pierce Smelley, "McMullen County History"; John Leffler, "Tilden, Texas" in *The New Handbook of Texas*, 6: 497. Smelley spelled the town as one word, "Dogtown" whereas the *Handbook* spells it "Dog Town."

17. Executive Record Book, 444.

18. Ibid., 445.

19. Ibid., 445.

20. "Adjutant General Letters Received, a summary of letters received providing a brief summary of contents, date written, etc." Helm had written this letter on September 27, 1870. He claimed Pridgen was "working hard against him." Page 85, entry # 473.

21. Wiley W. Pridgen was killed the night of December 30–31, 1873, by a group of men frequently associated with William Sutton. According to historian James M. Smallwood, the group included William Meador, brothers "Doc" and Jeff White, Edward Parkinson, and Addison Patterson. They were arrested for the killing but at trial were released. See Smallwood's *The Feud that Wasn't*, 134. In contrast Taylor historian Jack Hays Day who survived the feud but did not record his memoir until the 1930s, wrote that Pridgen's killers were John Goens (or Guynn), James Mason, *alias* Long, Sutton, and the White brothers, Joseph Priestly "Doc" White and brother Daniel Jefferson "Jeff" White. *The Sutton Taylor Feud*, 68–69. Day gave the date of the killing as January 1, 1874. According to the *Cuero Star*, Pridgen "was perfectly riddled with buckshot." The death was a mystery then and remains so today. *Cuero Star*, December 31, 1873. Probably W.W. Pridgen was killed in retaliation for his brother, Senator Pridgen's, efforts to have various Sutton force members placed on trial for their actions against Taylors and related family members. The White brothers are generally linked together in any action during the feud. Curiously although there were at least two different "treaties of peace" signed by members of the feuding factions, neither White brother signed either. Addison Patterson, Edward Parkinson, William Meador, and John Guynn did sign the treaty of January 3, 1874.

22. *Daily Austin Republican*, October 10, 1870.

23. Captain Helm to Davidson, October 10, 1870, in "State Police Correspondence Ledger," 401–985, page 98 entry # 527.

24. John A. Abney obituary, which appeared in the *Lampasas Leader*, February 13, 1903. Abney left Travis County and worked in Lampasas County and Johnson County before moving to Chaves County, New Mexico, where he died on February 6, 1903. The obituary noted that the writer "knew Judge Abney intimately from 1884 to 1889, and formed a very high opinion of his character. He was a wonderfully versatile man, one who had studied theology, law, political and domestic economy, and had made a success in life, despite all untoward circumstances." Abney is buried in the South Park Cemetery, Roswell, New Mexico.

25. "State Police Correspondence Ledger," 401–983, page 95 entry #538.

26. Ibid., page 92, entry # 523.

27. *Daily State Journal*, October 19, 1870.

28. Ibid., October 22, 1870. This brief statement was placed on page one, whereas the result of the grand jury investigation into the Kelly killing was placed on page three.

29. D.D. Claiborne to Davidson, written at Beeville on October 20, 1870. "Index to Letters Rec'd 1870" Ledger 401–985, page 118, entry # 683.

30. *The Governor's Hounds*, 259.

31. Davidson to R.F. Haskins, December 9, 1870.

32. Renee Smelley, "History of Boothill Cemetery," copy in author's collection. This cemetery originated with the burial of a suicide in the late 1850s. Through the years, others who died, many with their boots on in a violent confrontation, were buried here. In 1877 the cemetery was abandoned and many marked graves were lost. In 1955 the recently organized Cenizo Garden Club chose to clean up the cemetery, clearing away brush and placing stones around the identifiable graves. A further note in the history indicates that the

murderer of Smithwick "was later shot by another person seeking revenge for the murder of Smithwick." A state historical marker at the entrance to the cemetery was unveiled in June 2006.

33. A. Friar to Davidson, October 29, 1870, from Yorktown. State Police Correspondence Ledger 401–985, page 148, entry # 888. The census shows Friar as a boarder in the household of William M. Meiskell, a wagoner by profession, and his wife Sarah and child Alfred, a 15-year-old stock hand. Also in the household are Henrietta Anderson, daughter of William M. Meiskell, 18 and her two-year-old son Wyatt. Henrietta had married Richmond Anderson in 1857 but the couple was divorced by 1870 when the census was enumerated. 1870 DeWitt County, Texas Census, 259. Mary Anderson, a sister of Richmond, had married William P. "Buck" Taylor who was killed with Richard Chisholm by members of the Sutton faction. Marjorie Lee Burnett, *Fuel for a Feud*, 85.

34. *Austin Daily Republican*, October 29, 1870. When Pridgen made these accusations he was in his second year as a senator from the 12th Legislative District, serving from 1869–1872. He openly favored the Taylors and found great fault with Helm's tactics. During the feud, his brother Wiley W. Pridgen was murdered by (at least so he believed) members of the Sutton faction; Abram Bryant, his former slave, was murdered because he would not reveal where B. J. Pridgen was. He continued his feud with Helm until Helm was dismissed from that office.

35. Texas Bonds and Oaths of Office, 1846–1920, Secretary of State Oaths of Office, Texas Stare Library and Archives.

36. Joseph Priestly "Doc" White remains somewhat of a mystery figure in contrast to Sutton, Helm, and French. He was the son of Daniel Jefferson and Elizabeth White; by 1860 the family, consisting of the parents and children Josephine, Henry J., Joseph P, then 12, and Jefferson, then nine years old, were in DeWitt County, as enumerated by John R. Foster. They were household #156. Two households later Foster enumerated the Pitkin B. Taylor family with wife Susan and daughter Amanda Jane and son James C., then

eight years old. The Whites and Taylors would become enemies. Doc White was with Sutton, French, and Sumners on Christmas Eve in Clinton when they became embroiled in a fight with Richard Chisholm and William P. "Buck" Taylor; the latter two were killed. Also, Doc White was one of the group that killed Wiley W. Pridgen, according to Jack Hays Day. Doc White's final fate is undetermined. His brother, Daniel Jefferson White, born August 27, 1845, married Rachel E. Walling on December 2, 1884, and lived in DeWitt County. They later moved to Corsicana, Texas, where he lived for many years prior to his death there on Monday, July 23, 1928. His obituary indicated he was survived by four sons and four daughters. Apparently Mrs. White had predeceased him. *Dallas Morning News*, July 25, 1928.

37. Horace G. French was the son of Joseph H. and Hannah Ann Wilkins French, born in New Jersey March 4, 1848. On November 16, 1881, he married Ida B. Wilson in Austin, Texas. He died in San Antonio on July 5, 1912, of "acute indigestion" according to death certificate # 16831 and is buried in City Cemetery No. 1. He was with William Sutton the night Richard Chisholm and William P. "Buck" Taylor were killed, which renewed the enmity between Sutton and the Taylors.

38. Executive Record Book, 450–51.

39. Executive Record Book, 451. Police Captain Thomas Williams was the antithesis of Helm. For his tragic demise see David Johnson, *The Horrell Wars: Feuding in Texas and New Mexico* (Denton: University of North Texas Press, 2014), 31–41.

40. *Galveston Daily News*, October 29, 1870.

41. Ledger 401–985, which is a brief summary of letters received at the Adjutant General's office, date written and date received and identity of letter writer. Jones's letter of October 30 is summarized on page 125, entry # 729. Their records do suggest they were not completely serious about being members of the police force, once they were in. W.J. Young, about 26 years of age, white, was first assigned to the Albuquerque area of Gonzales County; he was then dismissed

and then reinstated and then resigned completely on June 10, 1871. Haynes's record is similar: the 22-year-old black man was commissioned August 1, 1870, then dismissed, then reinstated and finally resigned on January 30, 1873. Crouch and Brice, *The Governor's Hounds*, Young, 198; Haynes, 270–71.

42. Ibid., page 91 entry # 513. Miller's letter is summarized here. The Miller family was enumerated as residents of Belmont, Gonzales County, in August 1870 by M.H. Beaty, 451.

43. Ibid. Burkhart to Davidson, written from Hallettsville, November 17, 1870, page 165, entry #1041. William Henry Burkhart, at the time of writing this letter, was a resident of Matagorda County, with a wife and family. By occupation he was a lawyer, and it would be interesting to know if he was in Hallettsville on a business trip or was he there in a matter relating to Helm's actions against the Lunn gang. Burkhart was born April 11, 1838, married Mary Anne Goldbraith in Wharton on July 8, 1864, and continued successfully in the law profession. He died February 22, 1900. The 1870 Matagorda County Census shows Burkhart with wife Mary A. and four children. Burkhart was born in Pennsylvania and wife Mary A. in Mississippi. All their children were born in Texas. See also "Widow's Application for Pension," # 17953 Form B.

44. Ledger 401–985, Pridgen to Davidson written November 1, 1870. Page 126 entry # 730.

45. Davidson to Pridgen, October 31, 1870. State Police Correspondence, Letter Press Book, 401–1030, # 456.

46. James Turner was a 22-year-old white male farm hand who boarded in the William W. Day household. 1870 DeWitt County, Texas Census, 243. Others in the household were Day's wife, Louisa Kelly Day, who had married Thomas H. Hawks in Lavaca County in 1853. Others were three-year-old Willie Day, and two stepsons Frank Hawks, fourteen, and Thomas, twelve. Then farm hand Turner and three others: Harriet Andrews, 25, Nancy Andrews, 12 and Susie, three, black domestic servants.

47. District Clerk A. D. Roby to Davidson, November 4, 1870; Lucas Smith to Davidson, "Index to Letters Rec'd 1870 Police" Ledger 401–925, page 153, entry # 930 (Roby) and page 151 entry # 911 (Smith).

48. Davidson to John Chambliss, December 8, 1870, summary of letter in Ledger 401–1030, Letter Press, 738. St. Mary's once was a thriving port, rivaling Indianola in importance. The town declined when the railroads bypassed it; various storms did further damage and today it is a ghost town with only a well-kept cemetery to mark its existence. Some grave markers date from the early 1860s. Federal Census records: 1850 Lavaca County for James Jones and wife Elmira, 316; 1860 Live Oak County, 369; 1870 Refugio County, 148; and 1880 Goliad County, 354.

49. "1890 Veterans Schedule: 11th Census of the United States— Special Schedule of Surviving Soldiers, Sailors, and Marines and Widows, Etc." Ed Sitterle, Enumerator. Available on line through Ancestry.com.

50. 1870 Victoria County Census, 272, showing Thomas Ragland in household # 449 and A.P. Hammond in household # 450.

Chapter 7: Gunfire at the Billings Store

1. When Governor Davis took office he organized three separate groups to deal with any type of civil unrest: the State Police, the State Guard, and the Reserve Militia. All males between the ages of 18 and 45 who voluntarily enrolled made up the State Guard; all those who were liable for military service but not in the State Guard became part of the Reserve Militia. The State Police was to deal with lawlessness and protect citizens and property, while the State and Reserve militia was to deal with foreign invasion and assist state, county, or local police. All were under the command of the adjutant general. Haskins had proved to be competent to replace Captain Helm due to his experience as an officer in the State Guard. Crouch

and Brice, *The Governor's Hounds* and personal communication from Brice to Parsons June 15, 2016.

2. "Muster Roll of Company A 9th Regiment State Guards Headquartered at Helena, Karnes Co." No date. Archived in the Texas State Archives.

3. Karnes County Federal Census for 1900, 1910, 1920 and 1930 and death certificate # 61523 of Karnes County. Kate Ruckman provided a brief Haskins family history; she is the great-great-granddaughter of R.F. Haskins.

4. Pridgen's comments on the choice of Haskins to replace Helm are from an "Address of Senator Pridgen" directed to the citizens of the Twenty-fourth District appearing in the *Daily State Journal*, December 22, 1870.

5. Haskins was born November 23, 1838, and died December 16, 1873, in Karnes County. His wife, Ann Louisa Drake, was born July 6, 1845, and survived him until her death on August 23, 1930, at the age of 85 years, one month and 17 days. Upon entering her widowhood she resided with the John W. Ruckman family. She died in Karnes County and is buried next to her husband. Her death certificate, # 61523, states she died of heart failure. His grave was "discovered" by James A. Mundie and this author by accident while searching for the grave site of Captain Littleton and Stannard who were killed during the Sutton-Taylor Feud. The graves of Haskins and his wife are above ground tombs, now sadly broken by the various elements, whether by man or by nature. The small cemetery is still in use, an "active cemetery" as it were, although much of the foliage has overtaken certain areas. It is located across the road from the historic Helena courthouse-museum in Karnes County, Texas, located at the triangular intersection of Farm to Market Road 81 and State Highway 80. The graves of Littleton and Stannard have not yet been found.

6. DeWitt County Marks and Brands, Book 1, 126. County Clerk's Office, Cuero.

7. Haskins to Davidson, December 10, 1870. "Index to Letters Rec'd 1870 Police," Ledger 401–985, page 204, entry # 1449.

8. Davidson to Haskins, January 19, 1871 in "No. 2 Police Jany 3 71 to Apr 25 71," Ledger 401–1031, 112.

9. Ibid., Davidson to Haskins, February 13, 1871, 302.

10. "Brazoria County Biographies: Thomas H. Marsden" in "Genealogy Trails History Group" accessed May 25, 2015. Additional biographical information on Marsden courtesy research of Donaly E. Brice and Dave Johnson. Marsden died February 19, 1910, in Lampasas, Texas, and is buried in the Live Oak Cemetery in Brady, McCulloch County. An obituary in Brownwood's *Daily Bulletin* described him as "one of the pioneer citizens of McCulloch county and a well known man throughout this section of the state." *San Antonio Daily Express*, February 20, 1910 and the *Daily Bulletin* of Brownwood, Brown County, February 21, 1910. Both these newspapers reported the death of Marsden, and both originated in the *Lampasas Leader*.

11. District Court Records, Minutes, Bee County, Book A, 124. Crouch and Brice, *The Governor's Hounds*, 285.

12. District Court Records, Minutes, Bee County, Book A, 135.

13. Ibid., 309–10.

14. Davidson to Haskins, March 20, 1871, in "No. 2 Police Jany 3 71 to Apr 15, 71." Ledger 401–1031, # 605.

15. The identity of this "Miss Hemby" remains a mystery. Possibly she was Nancy Hemby, the daughter of James Wesley Hemby, born about 1854. If this is the "Miss Hemby" who was in 1870 in Karnes County she would have been about sixteen. In the 1870 census she is shown to be 17; in 1880 she has married a Mr. Bostick, but who is not living in the Hemby household. 1860 Hopkins County Census, 136; 1870 Delta County Census, and 1880 Delta County Census, 526. In the 1880 census she was 26-years-old and her occupation was given as domestic housework.

16. Adj. Gen. James Davidson to Hopkins County District Clerk May 2, 1871. "Police Ledger No. 2," 401–1032, Letter Press book page 49.

17. 1860 Hopkins County Census, 168; 1880 Karnes County Census, 21; Dora Portwood Jackson, "A Pioneer Texas Woman" in *Frontier Times*, September 1944, 21: 2, 462–63.

18. Hardin, *The Life of John Wesley Hardin*, 64–65. Hardin and Jane Bowen were married on February 29, 1872. Their marriage license is preserved in the Gonzales County Courthouse.

19. Crouch and Brice, *The Governor's Hounds: The Texas State Police, 1870–1873* (Austin: University of Texas Press, 2011), 261.

20. Kentuckian James W. Cox had married Arena Wofford on September 7, 1848. When she passed is unknown but by 1870 widower Cox was in Texas raising four children: Frank, 17; William, 15; Melessie, 12; and Perry age 10. 1860 DeWitt County census, 213. James W. Cox was killed in a Taylor ambush directed by John Wesley Hardin.

21. Oliver K. Tuton, born about 1805 in North Carolina, farmed in DeWitt County. In 1870 his household was composed of himself and wife (or possibly daughter), Christian, and nine children. He was one of the signers of the treaty of peace between the feuding factions on August 4, 1873. 1870 DeWitt County Census, enumerated by Willis Fawcett, 212.

22. Ferd Ploeger, Prussian born, was both a farmer and justice of the peace when enumerated by Willis Fawcett in 1870. He was 52 years-old with wife "Ottittie," 49, keeping house, and their four children. 1870 DeWitt County Census, 274.

23. Little Berry Wright was born in Perry County, Alabama December 4, 1830. On November 4, 1858 he married Ann E. Tumlinson, the daughter of "Captain Joe" Tumlinson, a leading figure in the feud. At his death on June 15, 1882, he was buried in the Upper Yorktown Cemetery, not far from where Dr. Philip H. Brassell and his son George are buried, both killed by followers of Sutton. In the same cemetery is the unmarked grave of Charles Heissig, another feud victim. Recently a new headstone was placed on L.B. Wright's grave showing besides the birth and death dates a Masonic symbol indicating his Masonic membership. During 1873 he had the unpleasant

duty of conducting the inquest of several men who had been killed in the feud: James W. Cox, J.W.S. "Jake" Christman as well as that of Jack Helm. His letters reflect the worry he experienced daily as his father-in-law, Joe Tumlinson, was occasionally the target of the Taylor forces.

24. Milton V. Kinnison was a 33-year-old Mississippi-born lawyer according to the 1870 Lavaca County census, 510. No post office is shown.

25. There was more than one Joseph Taylor in the area but it is believed the one referred to here was born June 6, 1833, and died May 23, 1923, and is buried in Goliad. He married Elizabeth Ann Silkriggs on January 19, 1856, and served in the Confederate Army.

26. The 1870 DeWitt County Census shows J.P. Beck as a twenty-two-year-old "Stock Raiser" and his wife A.P., 23. Their household was # 219. The next household visited was that of Abram Williams, a 59-year-old black man who worked for Senator Bolivar J. Pridgen. Later he would be murdered for refusing to tell Sutton followers where Pridgen was. A few households before, in number 215, resided the Pitkin B. Taylor family; he would be killed in the feud. P.B. Taylor and wife Susan were with their two children: James Creed, then eighteen, and Mary Elizabeth, then sixteen. In August of 1873 J.P. Beck signed one of the two treaties of peace arranged by civil authorities in DeWitt County.

27. Robert W. Thomas, according to the 1870 DeWitt County Census, was born about 1843 in Mississippi. The census shows him as a "Stock raiser," then boarding with the F. Julius Gohmert family. This was household # 10; in household # 14 lived the Martin V. King family, King a few years later would also be killed in the feud.

28. The surname is seen spelled in a variety of ways: Haldeman, Halderman, Holderman. I have used the spelling which appears on the several family headstones in the Salt Creek Cemetery in DeWitt County. The middle name of Jacob is from Robert Muschalek's *Davy: Old Salt Creek Community, Its Beginning, Its Development, Its People* (Privately printed, 2010).

29. Nothing definite has been located about this individual, and it may have originated as a clerk's error. In 1870 a "Rufus Birdsell" resided in Erath County along with his seven children. The Birdsell/Birtsell name is unusual to say the least.

30. Haldeman was buried in the family plot in the Salt Creek Cemetery near Old Davy in DeWitt County. Besides his birth and death dates is the following message: "Remember, friends, as you pass by/As you are now,/ So once was I./ As I am now,/So you will be,/ Prepare for death,/ And follow me."

31. *Gonzales Inquirer*, April 13, 1878. Bowen was hanged on May 17, 1878. Curiously, the date of May 17, 1873—five years earlier to the day exactly—was the date Hardin wrote that he had killed Jack Helm. Was this a mere coincidence or a psychological quirk at work?

32. The 1870 census shows the Haldeman family. David Haldeman, a farmer, was 61 and a native of Kentucky. His wife Candis, 51, was born in Tennessee. Their three children living at home with them were John T., 24; Thomas J., 23, and Jesse B., 19. All were born in Texas and then were listed as farm hands. A seven-year-old, William Walter, was shown to be "at home." Their post office was Clinton. See 1870 DeWitt County Census, 268. An older sister had left the home when the census was taken; she was Mary E. Haldeman, born about 1839. John T. was born March 4, 1846, and died May 22, 1918. His marker was erected by the Woodmen of the World. Thomas Jacob was born August 1, 1848 and was killed December 17, 1872. Jesse B. was born 1851 and Joseph born 1858.

33. The arrest of Bowen is from Patton's letter to Adjutant General Britton, dated January 14, 1873 in Letter Press Ledger 401–703 "Letters Received." A separate report identified the men who arrested Bowen as DeWitt County Sheriff Green DeWitt and Deputy Richard B. Hudson. Perhaps the four together: Blair, Patton, DeWitt and Hudson comprised the posse which made the arrest.

34. Information on Patton from *The Governor's Hounds*, 285; personal interview with Ann Rose, a Patton descendant, February 5, 2015. Patton married Lucy Virella Wells on April 16, 1857, in Gonzales,

license # 456. Patton died March 16, 1878, of unknown causes and is buried in the Harmony Cemetery near Gillett, Karnes County. His grave is marked.

35. For details on the capture of Hardin and brother-in-law Brown Bowen two works are essential: *Bowen and Hardin*, by Chuck Parsons and Marjorie Parsons (1991), and *Bounty Hunter* by Rick Miller (1988), the biography of professional detective and Texas Ranger John R. "Jack" Duncan. Both were published by Creative Publishing Company of College Station, Texas.

36. Karon Mac Smith, *On the Watershed of Ecleto and the Clear Fork of Sandies*, 302 (Volume 1). At the time this volume was printed, a collection of her newspaper articles which appeared in the *Nixon News* and the *Stockdale Star* as well as other unpublished writings, author Smith did not know if there would be a second volume. There is no indication which articles may have appeared in which newspaper. Karon Mac Smith was the daughter of Cole Frohock Smith and Ada B. Cecil Smith. At her death she was buried in the McCracken-Smith Cemetery.

37. Letter from R.R. Smith to Dr. C.L. Sonnichsen, dated October 1, 1943, cited in Karon Mac Smith, *On the Watershed of Ecleto and the Clear Fork of Sandies*, 1:301.

38. Craig H. Roell, "Cuero, Texas." *The New Handbook of Texas*, 2: 432–33. Clinton remained the county seat of DeWitt County until 1876.

39. Frank L. Britton. *Report of the Adjutant General of the State of Texas for the Year 1873* (Austin: Cardwell & Walker, Printers, 1874), 116.

40. Ibid., 122–23.

41. *The Life of John Wesley Hardin, As Written by Himself*, 77–79. I have used the University of Oklahoma Press edition with the Robert G. McCubbin introduction for any quotations from Hardin.

42. This man's name is spelled in a variety of ways but the spelling I have used appears on a stone entrance at the McCrabb Cemetery in

DeWitt County where presumably several members of the Meador family are buried, although none now have a separate stone.

43. *The Life of John Wesley Hardin, As Written by Himself*, 80.

44. Ibid. This description of Helm's abuse of Jane Hardin is from pages 81–82.

45. Hardin, 82.

46. Ibid., 81.

47. Laurie E. Jasinski. "Mustang Mott, Texas," *Handbook of Texas Online*, Published by the Texas State Historical Association. Today Mustang Mott exists as a small convenience store on Highway 87 mid-way between Gonzales and Cuero. A life-size statue of a wild mustang greets the traveler although there are today few trees to mark it as a "mott."

48. Hardin, 82.

49. The identity of those in the group who were ambushed varies, but an article in the *Galveston Daily News* and then reprinted in the *New York Times* of October 5, 1874, dealing with the upcoming trial of Bill Taylor for the murder of Sutton and Slaughter, gave the survivors of the ambush as W.W. Wells, Henry Ragland, and Joe Tumlinson. Some sources identify the others as W.C. "Curry" Wallace and one Griffin. A reporter attempted to give a brief history of the Texas vendetta and this ambush was one of the incidents he noted. The reporter continued: "During the same year Mark [*sic*, Martin] Taylor was killed by a party with whom Jack Helm was, and in the same year Helm was killed in Atascosa County [*sic*], it was believed by some of the Taylor gang." *New York Times*, October 5, 1874.

50. Victor M. Rose, *The Texas Vendetta: or, The Sutton-Taylor Feud* (New York: J.J. Little & Co., 1880; reprint by Ed Bartholomew, The Frontier Press of Texas, 1956), 80; and the *San Antonio Daily Herald*, July 23, 1873. Rose, who was editor of the *Victoria Advocate*, unfortunately did not provide the date of the issue which carried the "shocking double murder" headline.

51. Rose, 29–30.

52. The Clinton Cemetery today is physically divided into two parts: the front part which faces the highway is still in use and kept neat and clean. The back part, which is allowed to become overgrown although occasionally cleaned, is known as the "old section." For years it was nearly inaccessible due to the amount of undergrowth. Recently members of the DeWitt County Historical Commission cleaned the old section and then erected a large sign listing the names of many who are *believed* to be buried there. The sign lists the names of 72 individuals in the old section; some of those have a homemade headstone with only a name scratched thereon; most have no stone. Among the names on the sign is that of "Jim Cox" with no further information. If this is our James W. Cox shot to death in 1873, then it is highly probable that his partner in death —Jake Christman— is also buried there. The names of Richard Chisholm, Kute Tuggle, and James White are listed as well; Chisholm of course was shot to death with Buck Taylor in Clinton and White and Tuggle were taken from the Clinton "jail" and lynched in 1874 in the aftermath of Hardin's killing of Brown County Deputy Sheriff Charles M. Webb.

Chapter 8: "Attempting to Escape"

1. For years it was believed that Albuquerque was in Wilson County but a new survey in 1914 corrected the error, placing it just within the Gonzales County line. It is generally accepted that the name of Albuquerque came from survivors of General H.H. Sibley's failed invasion of New Mexico in February 1862.

2. Crouch and Brice, *The Governor's Hounds*, 262. The date of the postmaster appointment is from "Appointments of U.S. Post Masters, 1832–1921," Microfilm roll, 1004.

3. John Bland at this point in time was about fifty-five years old and living in the household of Samuel McCracken Sr. Bland was born in South Carolina. He and the McCracken family and the Louis Wiley

family all resided in household # 430 when the Wilson County census was enumerated. Possibly the McCracken household actually was the hotel of Albuquerque: there were seven McCrackens enumerated, Bland, and eight members of the Louis Wiley family, a total of sixteen individuals ranging in age from ten years (George Wiley) through sixty-three (Samuel McCracken Sr.). Wilson County Census, enumerated August 24, 1870. Their post office was listed as "Knockenut" [sic, Nockernut].

4. R.R. Smith letter to Dr. C. L. Sonnichsen, October 1, 1943, printed in Karon Mac Smith's *On the Watershed of Ecleto and the Clear Fork of Sandies*, 302.

5. "Literary Effort" no page number.

6. *On the Watershed of Ecleto and the Clear Fork of Sandies*, 301.

7. *San Antonio Daily Herald*, July 31, 1873, in the "Local Affairs" column. This item, based on the report of a gentleman "just arrived in town from Guadalupe County" was a follow-up to the earlier report that Helm had been killed by Hardin and several others. In this latter report it clearly states *Helm had leaned or placed his shotgun against* "a neighboring tree." Unable to reach the weapon, he drew the only weapon within reach, his bowie-knife, with which he "endeavored to defend himself."

8. *San Antonio Daily Express*, July 25, 1873.

9. R.R. [Ralph Roy, nicknamed "Railroad"] Smith to C.L. Sonnichsen, letter of October 1, 1943, concerning early events in and around Albuquerque. Letter printed in Karon Mac Smith's *On the Watershed of Ecleto and the Clear Fork of Sandies*, 215.

10. Hardin, 80–84.

11. L.B. Wright to Gov. E.J. Davis, July 24, 1873.

12. *Bastrop Advertiser*, August 2, 1873, reprinting an article from an undated *Gonzales Index*.

13. Historian Karon Mac Smith, who lived in the Albuquerque area much of her life, and today lies buried in the McCracken Cemetery where many other McCracken family members as well as Jack

Helm are buried, suggested it was the senior McCracken who was visiting with Helm and Hardin that day. She grounded her belief on nothing more than a hunch, although we tend to believe it was the younger one, Curg McCracken. He had troubles with the law although not nearly as severe as did Hardin, and perhaps notified Hardin that Helm was often in Albuquerque to work on the invention. Karon Mac Smith, *On the Watershed of Ecleto and the Clear Fork of Sandies* (Seguin, TX: Tommy Brown Printers, 1983), 1:215. A McCracken descendant believes it was Samuel Lycurgus "Curg" McCracken who was associated with Hardin and Taylor and thus was seated with Hardin and Helm when Taylor arrived intending to shoot Helm in the back. E-mail from Ken McCracken to Parsons, June 30, 2014. Curg McCracken, who may have on occasion associated with Hardin, ultimately was convicted of horse theft and sentenced to fifteen years in prison. Jailed temporarily in Cameron, Milam County, on May 17, 1884, he and three others broke jail but were recaptured. Later, after his prison sentence, he farmed near Leesville in Gonzales County. In mid-April 1895 he was shot and killed by a hidden assassin. He was plowing in his field and when turning at the end of the rows he was shot twice by someone with a Winchester. His brother, Green, was nearby, but chose to return to the house, not knowing if he was the next to be killed. *Dallas Morning News*, April 24, printing an item dated Leesville, April 19, 1895.

14. *Gonzales Index*, August 2, 1873.

15. Ibid.

16. Rose incorrectly gave the date of Helm's death as taking place shortly before the State Police act went into effect. This of course is incorrect as Helm was named one of the first four captains in July 1870. Rose, 37.

17. Karon Mac Smith's article "There was an inquest" in an undated clipping from the *Gonzales County Free Press* alerted me to the existence of this record. The original handwritten entry is found in the Commissioners Court Minutes of Wilson County, Book A,

229. This is a large heavy ledger book; thanks to Assistant County Clerk Frances Cherry the original was located after some difficulty in the county clerk's office at Floresville. James W. Dickey was born in Mississippi on July 6, 1842, and was in Texas at least by 1860 as a single man. He married Martha Jane Gillette on April 9, 1865, and spent the remainder of his life in the Wilson-Gonzales Counties area. He obtained bond for the position of Justice of the Peace on May 7, 1870, and took the oath two days later. In 1880 he was a Wilson County Tax Assessor living in Floresville with his wife and five children. He died August 3, 1895, at Floresville and is buried in the Floresville Cemetery. His grave is marked.

18. Karon Mac Smith, *On the Watershed of Ecleto and the Clear Fork of Sandies*, 1: 111.

19. Pidge's letter was written November 8 and published in the *Austin Daily Democratic Statesman* of November 12, 1874.

20. Captain McNelly to Adj. Gen. William Steele, September 30, 1874, written from Clinton.

21. Hardin, 84.

22. For a discussion on the mysterious end of Bill Taylor see this author's article, "The Dangerous Career of Bill Taylor: Death in Oklahoma for a Texas Fugitive?" in the OKOLHA *Journal* (Oklahoma Outlaws Lawmen History Association) 7, no.4 (Winter, 2010): 1–6.

23. Adj. Gen. William Steele to Governor Richard Coke, July 10, 1874.

24. *Austin Weekly Statesman*, March 25, 1880.

25. Ibid., April 1, 1880.

Epilogue: The Grave of John Jackson Helm

1. C.L. Sonnichsen, *The Grave of John Wesley Hardin: Three Essays in Grassroots History* (College Station: Texas A&M University Press, 1979).

2. Roy Sylvan Dunn, "Life and Times in Albuquerque, Texas," *The Southwestern Historical Quarterly* 55, no. 1 (July 1951): 62–76.

3. Roy Sylvan Dunn was born in Nixon in 1921 and passed in 2010 in San Antonio but is buried in the Nixon Cemetery. The obituary provided by Nixon's Finch Funeral Home provided an excellent résumé of his life and accomplishments.

4. James M. Smallwood, *The Feud that Wasn't: The Taylor Ring, Bill Sutton, John Wesley Hardin, and Violence in Texas* (College Station: Texas A&M University Press, 2008). The death of Helm appears on pages 130–31.

5. Billee Rhodes Smith (Mrs. Dale Smith), also spelled Billie, was the daughter of William Hiram and Myrtle Fay Jones Rhodes; William Hiram, (January 6, 1908–1968) was the son of Hugh Lindin and Rachel Ruth Helm Rhodes; Rachel Ruth Helm was the daughter of John Jackson "Jack" and Margaret Virginia Crawford Helm, born September 8, 1872, in Bee County, Texas. Rachel Ruth Helm Rhodes, who had married Hugh Lindin on April 22, 1894, died August 12, 1955. Their daughter Billie Fay Rhodes died March 20, 1977. It was she who came to Albuquerque to be present at the marker dedication.

6. Myers Monument Company of Stockdale, in neighboring Wilson County, installed the flat military marker.

7. Karon Mac Smith, "Gravesite of Jack Helm" in *On the Watershed of Ecleto and the Clear Fork of Sandies*, 11–12. Billie Rhodes Smith to historian G.D. Albright, December 1, 1972. In this letter she wrote: "I contacted Dr. [Robert] Shook by letter—he gave me a 'rough' idea of where the grave was. I met a Karon Mac Smith—she jumped into her pickup—we sloshed through the mud (rain) through two pastures and there it is—she had just had a small concrete marker made for a number of unmarked graves—John Jack was among them—it says 'Jack Helm killed by John Wesley Hardin in Albuquerque'—I had the *privilege* of paying for the marker. I am the only one in the family who knows where he is buried." Letter in the Judy Falls Collection, Texas A&M Commerce. This letter reminded me of the first time I visited the grave of Helm. It was in the summer

of 1977, and it was through the courtesy of Karon Mac Smith. I too was able to "jump" into her pickup and drive to the cemetery, although there had been no recent rain so there was no sloshing through mud. It was a rough road with ruts and mesquite tree limbs to avoid but the cemetery was easily found. There had been a fence but it was broken; the several horses which were in the cemetery paid us no mind.

SELECTED BIBLIOGRAPHY

◆——◆——◆

United States Census Reports:
Texas

Bee County, 1870

Bexar County, 1850

Bosque County, 1880

Calhoun County, 1870

Delta County, 1870, 1880

DeWitt County, 1860, 1870, 1880

Erath County, 1870

Goliad County, 1860, 1870, 1880

Gonzales County, 1880

Hopkins County, 1860, 1870

Jackson County, 1870

Karnes County, 1860, 1870, 1880, 1900, 1910, 1920, 1930

Kerr County, 1900

Lamar County, 1860

Lavaca County, 1850, 1870

Live Oak County, 1860, 1870

Matagorda County, 1860, 1870

McMullen County, 1870

Nueces County, 1860

Refugio County, 1870, 1880

San Patricio County, 1870

Victoria County, 1870

Wilson County, 1870, 1880

Other Census Schedules

Jackson County, Mississippi, 1850

Mortality Schedule: Goliad County, 1870;

Mortality Schedule: San Patricio County, 1870

Natchitoches Parish, Louisiana, 1860

Patrick County, Virginia, 1830, 1840

Slave Schedule Hopkins County, 1860

Slave Schedule Lamar County, 1860

Texas Veterans Schedule 1890

Newspapers

Austin Weekly Republican

Bastrop Advertiser

Brownwood Daily Bulletin

Courier-Journal, (Louisville, Kentucky)

Cuero Star

Daily Democratic Statesman (Austin)

Daily Express (San Antonio)

Daily Herald (San Antonio)

Daily State Journal (Austin)

Dallas Morning News

Dallas Weekly Herald

Evening Gazette (Worchester, Massachusetts)

Express-News (San Antonio)

Flake's Daily Journal (Galveston)

Gonzales County Free Press

Galveston Daily News (Galveston)

Gonzales Daily News

Gonzales Daily Inquirer

Hallettsville Herald and Planter

Houston Daily Telegraph

Lampasas Leader

Lubbock Avalanche-Journal

Nashville Union and American (Nashville, Tennessee)

New Orleans Times-Picayune

New York Herald (New York)

New York Times (New York)

Texas State Gazette (Austin)

Tri-Weekly Republican (Austin)

Victoria Advocate

Weekly Statesman

Yorktown News

Books and Periodicals

Anonymous. *Biographical Souvenir of the State of Texas*. Chicago: F.A. Battey & Co., 1889.

Anonymous. *Fannin County Folks and Facts*. Dallas: Taylor Publishing Company, 1977.

Anonymous. *McMullen County History*. No place. No publisher. 1982.

Anonymous. *Historic Matagorda County*. Vol. I. Houston: D. Armstrong Company, Inc., 1986.

Anonymous. *Delta County History*. Cooper, TX: Delta County History Book Committee, 1991.

Baenziger, Ann Patton. "The Texas State Police During Reconstruction: A Reexamination." *Southwestern Historical Quarterly* 72, no. 4 (April 1969).

Baker, T. Lindsey. *Ghost Towns of Texas*. Norman: University of Oklahoma Press, 1986.

Bateman, Carolyn, chair. *The History of the People of Live Oak County, Texas 1856 to 1982*. No publisher. [George West, Texas, 1982]

Bork, June Baldwin, complier and publisher. *The Burnetts and Their Connections*. Apple Valley, CA: NP, 1989.

Brown, John Henry. *Indian Wars and Pioneers of Texas*. Austin: L.E. Daniell. Reprint, Austin: State House Press, 1988.

Buckner, Marjorie Pearce, and Hazel Jennings Myers, comps. *Earliest Records of Cass County, Missouri 1836–1861*. Pleasant Hill, MO: Privately printed, No date.

Burnett, Marjorie Lee. *Fuel for a Feud*. Smiley, TX: Sandies Creek Press, 2008.

Caldwell, Clifford R., and Ron DeLord. *Texas Lawmen 1835–1899 The Good and the Bad*. Charleston, SC: The History Press, 2011.

Crouch, Barry A. *The Freedmen's Bureau and Black Texans*. Austin: University of Texas Press, 1992.

Crouch, Barry A. and Donaly E. Brice. *The Governor's Hounds, The Texas State Police, 1870–1873*. Austin: The University of Texas Press, 2011.

Day, Jack Hays. *The Taylor-Sutton Feud*. San Antonio: Sid Murray & Sons, 1937.

DeVoss, Julius. "Some Fort Mason Personnel" in *Mason County Historical Book*, Supplement II. Mason County Historical Commission, 1994.

DeWitt County Historical Commission, Editors. *The History of DeWitt County, Texas*. Dallas: Curtis Media Corp., 1991.

Dodd, Jordan R., et al. *Early American Marriages: Virginia to 1850*. Bountiful, UT: NP, No date.

Dohoney, Eben L. *An Average American*. Paris, TX: NP, 1885.

Dunn, Roy Sylvan. "Life and Times in Albuquerque." *Southwestern Historical Quarterly* 55 (July 1951): 1.

Ellis, Frances Arnold, and Skipper Steely. *First Church of Paris*. Paris, TX: Privately printed by First United Methodist Church of Paris, 1985.

Emmett, Chris. *Shanghai Pierce: A Fair Likeness*. Norman: University of Oklahoma Press, 1953.

Gammel, H. P. N., Compiler. *The Laws of Texas 1822–1897*. Austin: The Gammel Book Company, 1898.

Goebel, Patsy, and Karen Gohmert. *Cemetery Records of DeWitt County, Texas*. Vol. 3. NP: Privately printed, 1992.

Hardin, John Wesley. *The Life of John Wesley Hardin, as Written by Himself*. Norman: University of Oklahoma Press, 1961.

Heitman, Francis B. *Historical Register and Dictionary of the United States Army*. Washington, DC: Government Printing Office, 1903. Facsimile edition, Urbana: University of Illinois, 1965.

Hendricks, George D. *The Badmen of the West*. San Antonio: The Naylor Company, 1959.

Jackson, Dora Portworth. "A Pioneer Texas Woman." *Frontier Times* 21, no. 2 (September 1944).

Johnson, Dave. *The Horrell Wars: Feuding in Texas and New Mexico*. Denton: University of North Texas Press, 1986.

Kerr, Homer L. *Fighting With Ross' Texas Cavalry Brigade C.S.A.: The Diary of George L. Griscom, Adjutant 9th Texas Cavalry Regiment*. Hillsboro, TX: Hill College Press, 1976.

Marohn, Richard C. *The Last Gunfighter: John Wesley Hardin*. College Station, TX: Creative Publishing Co., 1995.

Metz, Leon. *John Wesley Hardin: Dark Angel of Texas*. El Paso: Mangan Books, 2000.

Meyer, Willie Lucille. "Moses Sanders Pearce and Mary Alford" in *The History of DeWitt County, Texas*. Dallas: Curtis Media Corporation, DeWitt County Historical Commission, 1911.

Miller, Rick. *Bounty Hunter*. College Station, TX: Creative Publishing Co., 1988.

———. *Bloody Bill Longley: The Mythology of a Gunfighter*. Denton: University of North Texas Press, 2011.

Morgan, Jo Ann. "Vigilante Justice (?) Accounts for two of Rockport's Oldest Graves." Aransas County Historical *Newsletter* 10, no. 1 (March 2013).

Mullins, Marion Gay. *Hopkins County, Texas Marriage Record 1846–1880*. Fort Worth, TX: Privately printed, 1959.

Mundie, James A. Jr. *et al. Texas Burial Sites of Civil War Notables: A Biographical and Pictorial Field Guide*. Hillsboro, TX: Hill College Press, 2002.

Muschalak, Robert. *Davy: Old Salt Creek Community, Its Beginnings, Its Development, Its People*. Privately printed, 2010.

Parsons, Chuck, and Marjorie Parsons. *Bowen and Hardin*. College Station: Creative Publishing Co., 1991.

Parsons, Chuck. *The Sutton-Taylor Feud: The Deadliest Blood Feud in Texas*. Denton: University of North Texas Press, 2009.

Parsons, Chuck. "The Dangerous Career of Bill Taylor: Death in Oklahoma for a Texas Fugitive?" *Journal* of the Oklahoma Outlaws-Lawmen History Association (OKOLHA) 7, no. 4 (Winter 2010).

Parsons, Chuck, and Norman Wayne Brown. *A Lawless Breed: John Wesley Hardin, Texas Reconstruction and Violence in the Wild West*. Denton: University of North Texas Press, 2013.

Pickering, David, and Judy Falls. *Brush Men and Vigilantes: Civil War Dissent in Texas*. College Station: Texas A&M University Press, 2000.

Ripley, Thomas. *They Died With Their Boots On*. Sydney, Australia: Angus & Robertson Limited, 1936.

Rose, Victor M. *The Texas Vendetta: or, The Sutton-Taylor Feud*. New York: J.J. Little & Co., 1880; reprint by Ed Bartholomew, The Frontier Press of Texas, Houston, 1956.

Smallwood, James M. *The Feud that Wasn't: The Taylor Ring, Bill Sutton, John Wesley Hardin, and Violence in Texas*. College Station: Texas A&M University Press, 2008.

Smith, Karon Mac. *On the Watershed of Ecleto and the Clear Fork of Sandies*. Vols 1 and 2. Privately printed, 1983 and 1987.

Sonnichsen, C.L. *I'll Die Before I'll Run: The Story of the Great Feuds of Texas*. New York: Harper & Brothers Publishers, 1951.

———. *The Grave of John Wesley Hardin*. College Station: Texas A&M University Press, 1979.

Tanner, Karen Holliday, and John D. Tanner Jr. "Lon Oden: The Rhymin' Ranger." *Old West*, Summer 1988.

Tise, Sammy. *Texas County Sheriffs*. Albuquerque, NM: Oakwood Printing, 1989.

Truitt, Eddie Day. *The Taylor Party*. Wortham, TX: Privately printed, 1992.

Tuck, James E. *Civil War Shadows in Hopkins County, Texas*. Sulphur Springs, TX: Self-published, 1993.

White, Gifford, editor. *First Settlers of Lamar County, Texas*. NP: NP, 1982.

Texas Marriage Records

Aransas County: Catherine A. Dickey Choate and William W. Wallace

DeWitt County: J.J. Helm and Margaret Virginia Crawford

Fannin County: J.J. Helm and Minerva McCown

Gonzales County: John Wesley Hardin and Jane Bowen

Gonzales County: Thomas Lemuel Patton and Lucy Virella Wells

Refugio County: Catherine A. Dickey and John C. Choate

Interviews Conducted by Author

Ann Rose, February 5, 2015.

The New Handbook of Texas

Alwyn Barr: "John Leal Haynes"

Dovie T. Hall: "Creed Taylor"

Cecil Harper Jr. "Freedmen's Bureau"

J. Marvin Hunter. "John Warren Hunter"

Laurie E. Jasinske. "Mustang Mott, Texas"

Laurie E. Jasinkse. "William Prissick"

John Leffler. "Tilden, Texas"

Vista K. McCroskey. "Charleston, Texas"

Craig H. Roell. "Cuero, Texas"

Craig H. Roell. "Clinton, Texas"

Smyrl, Virginia Elizabeth. "Caldwell County, Texas"

C.L. Sonnichsen. "Jack Helm"

Correspondence

Billie Rhodes Smith to G.D. Albright. December 1, 1972. Letter in Judy Falls Collection, Texas A&M-Commerce.

"Statement of Hans Pattillo" September 1, 1950. Document in Roy Sylvan Dunn Papers, Briscoe Center for American History, Austin.

Letter of C.L. Patterson to Roy Sylvan Dunn January 15, 1950 in Roy Sylvan Dunn Papers, Briscoe Center for American History.

Charles Tipton to Parsons, May 8, 2015.

E-mail

Ken McCracken to Parsons, November 29, 2010; June 27 and June 30, 2014; July 6 and July 17, 2014

Debbie Blalock to Parsons, November 15, 2014

Marc Coker to Parsons, August 15, 2013 and January 3, 2015, February 15, 2015

Roger S. Raney to Parsons, September 22, 2014

Jim Mundie to Parsons, July 9, 2014, March 20, 2015, June 3, 2015

Doug Kubicek to Parsons, August 28, 2014

Judy Falls to Parsons, September 14, 2014

Ron DeLord to Parsons, July 7, 2014

Kate Ruckman to Parsons, May 8, 2015

John Lackey to Parsons, March 19, 2015

Rick Miller to Parsons, April 23, 2013

Linda Wolff to Parsons, February 9, 2015

Paul M. Spellman to Parsons, October 29, 2014

Legal Records

Commissioners Court Minutes, Wilson County, Book A, Floresville, Texas

Court Records. Minutes. Book A., Bee County, Beeville, Texas

Death Certificates: Arden Sommers Crawford, # 35656, Lamar County, Texas; Mrs. Armittie Virginia Helm Crawford, # 27339 Lamar County, Texas; Horace G. French, # 16831 Bexar County, Texas; Sarah Ann Helm, # 26388, Childress County, Texas; John Frederick McCrabb, #15541, DeWitt County, Texas; James O. Murphree, #8825, DeWitt County, Texas.

District Court Records. Minutes Book A. Bee County, Beeville, Texas.

Goliad County Election Returns, 1867. Confederate Pensions: Lorenzo D. King, # 15512; Moses Sanders Pearce, #906

Marks & Brands. Book I, DeWitt County Court House, Cuero, Texas

Adjutant General Papers—Texas State Archives

James Davidson. *Report of the Adjutant General of the State of Texas, from June 24, 1870 to December 31, 1870.* Austin: Tracy, Siemering & Co., 1870.

Frank Britton. *Report of the Adjutant General of the State of Texas for the Year 1873.* Austin: Cardwell & Walker, 1874.

Letters Received, State Police, 1870-1873. Call # 401-985. State Police Correspondence, 401-863; Adjutant General Letters Received, Ledger 401-985; Arrests of State Police, Ledger 401-1001; Muster and Pay Roll State Police, Ledger 401-1058; Police Record Book "No. 1 Police July 1, 1870 to Jany 18, 1871"; Record Book "No 3 Police April 26 '71 to Aug 12, '71"; Police Record Book "No. 2 Police July 1870 to Jany 18 1871."

Letters to Adjutant General, Ledgers 401-701, 401-703

Muster Roll, Company A, Regiment State Guards.

Unpublished Manuscripts & Miscellaneous

Albright, Douglas A. "Criminal Cases of Delta County" in Barry A. Crouch Papers, Victoria College, Victoria Regional History Center, Victoria College/University of Houston.

Hunter, John W[arren]. "Literary Effort" Call # 2-23/993. This paginated and also sections without pagination work written on legal size paper appears to be Hunter's effort to write a biography of Creed Taylor as he is frequently quoted. There are numerous examples of material copied from other sources, such as Rose's book on the Sutton-Taylor Feud.

Pease, E. M. "Communication from Governor E.M. Pease of Texas, Relative to the Troubles in that State." In House Miscellaneous Document, #127, 40th Congress, 2nd Session, May, 1868.

Secretary of State Papers, Executive Record. RG 307.

INDEX

Page numbers in *italics* indicate illustrations

J

K

S

T